FALLING IN LOVE WITH YOUR SELF
LOVE AND THE INNER BELOVED

By

Richard Shiningthunder Francis

© 2002 by Richard Shiningthunder Francis.
All rights reserved.

No part of this book may be reproduced, stored in a retrieval system, or transmitted by any means, electronic, mechanical, photocopying, recording, or otherwise, without written permission from the author.

ISBN: 1-4033-3033-6 (Electronic)
ISBN: 1-4033-3034-4 (Softcover)
ISBN: 1-4033-3035-2 (Hardcover)

This book is printed on acid free paper.

1stBooks – rev. 05/24/02

DEDICATION

To Maria Francis, whose sweet and tender Love has enfolded and comforted me with selfless compassion, more times than I can count, and to Pat Fields, whose immense Love brought me back from the land of the dead, and gave me a second chance at life, making this book possible,

This book is dedicated, with infinite, illimitable Love.

ACKNOWLEDGMENTS

****

Any creative, spiritual process or product is quite impossible unless one is surrounded and nourished by a sea of inner Love, provided by the inner Self and by friends. Those special, beautiful, and lightfilled friends who have made this book possible are, in alphabetical order:

Ann Blufeather, who was first of all people to guide, nourish, protect, and comfort during all the earliest crises of life. I treasure your gentleness and beautiful generosity.

Mary "Maribee" Butler, who has been of such enormous aid in the perfecting of personal expression, by her Lovebased proofreading of this and other books. I treasure your Lovewisdom.

Barb Cole and Jim Plants, who provided my first computer, changing this life forever, and making all subsequent work possible. I treasure your Love for all creatures great and small.

Pat Fields, whose tender kindness and gigantic generosity are legendary in proportion, and monumental. You, in some ways, have so freely given of all things. I treasure your precious and tender heart.

Maria Francis, whose tender and bottomless Love has withstood not only the rollercoaster tests of time, but has weathered the most hurricanic storms. It is she of the brave heart who stands beside me on the "battle-fields" of life. I treasure your strength, integrity, purity, and Love.

Thomas Gustin, who has so freely given of his inner Love, and has so greatly enriched our lives and the life of the world. You are a truly fine man. I treasure your brilliance and your wisdom.

Karen "Aurora" Ludwick, whose tender compassion and fine mind make an unbeatable combination, and whose sharp eye has aided in concise expression, through the proofreading of this and other books. I treasure the Lovemind within you.

Frank Merriman, a sterling teacher who has taught so much of such great value to so many. You make our world a better place, my brother. I treasure your strength and generosity.

Greg Sexton, whose intelligence and generosity have provided Maria and me a home of beauty and comfort. I treasure your compassionate kindness, generosity, and remarkable skills.

Shirley Sexton, whose great heart and kindness are both touching and moving, and whose unbending determination aided us to move into our new residence in 2000. I treasure your combination of intensity and tenderness.

****

To you all, dearest friends, may Love find its nest in your heart, and may it grow there amidst the diamonds, emeralds, rubies, and sapphires of compassion.

****

May whatever merit is produced by this book be shared with all sentient beings everywhere, throughout this and every other galaxy. May all hearts be filled with Light and Love.

TABLE OF CONTENTS

Author's Preface/Megapsychology: The Inner Outer Limits 1
Chapter 1/Falling in Love Again, with Love 13
Chapter 2/It's All Inside: Who Do You Think You Are? 25
Chapter 3/Torn between Two Universes, and Loving It 35
Chapter 4/Extraordinarily "Ordinary" Love: Mysticism 44
Chapter 5/Surrender to the Sweet Private "Sea" of Mindsource 53
Chapter 6/Born to Love: Your Simplified Designer Life 61
Chapter 7/Moving Closer to My Lord: Bliss Amplified, Judgment Deactivated 70
Chapter 8/Caterpillar to Butterfly: From Monstergod to Bliss 80
Chapter 9/Human Destiny: Masters of the Universe 88
Chapter 10/Dream as Nightmare: Agonies of Ego-Spirit Conflict 98
Chapter 11/Consumed in the Sweet Flame of Love 105
Chapter 12/Passion and Compassion on the Third Rock: Do Geese See God? ... 111
Chapter 13/The Tender "Feminine" heart: The "Inner Knowing" of the Mystic 118
Chapter 14/Egofree Fluidity: The Lightfilled Heart 125
Chapter 15/We're Phantoms in a Phantomworld: Awakening 131
Chapter 16/It's Tearing Me Apart: Separation 137

Chapter 17/Pristine Unity: The Eclipse of Confusion 146
Chapter 18/Fake Teachers, Real Love, and Great Sex 152
Chapter 19/Love: Knowing, Getting, and Giving the Real Thing 163
Chapter 20/Crying and Laughing Your Way to Love 172
Chapter 21/Monkeymind, the Mindblowing Mind, and Love 181
Chapter 22/The Beloved: Agony of Absence, Utter Satisfaction Upon Return 188
Chapter 23/Goddess, Sex, Doing Nothing, Touching Superultralove 193
Chapter 24/Speeding Away from the Phantomworld at Warp Ten 198
Chapter 25/Crystalmind, Ultralove, Heaven, and the Return to the Garden of Pleasure in the Heart 204
Chapter 26/Brother Serpent Gets Us Expelled from Eden, and Helps us Return 212
Chapter 27/Out of the Shadow into the Light 219
Chapter 28/The Pearl of Great Price: The Hero's Journey through Hell to Heaven 226
Chapter 29/The Immanipulable Mystic: Radical Independence, Friendly Mind .. 235
Chapter 30/Miraculous Mind, Everlasting Mind: Exploring the Heartcaves of Harmlessness 241
Chapter 31/Psychodetox: Tossing the Labelmaker, Perfectmind Resonance 247
Chapter 32/The Crash of Fear in the Clash with Love 253
Chapter 33/Ego Swallowed by Love: Friendship, Humility, and Security ... 261

Chapter 34/The Jehovah-myth, Fatalism, and Free Will 268
Chapter 35/Embracing the Self: "In Love" with the World of Dreamind 275
Chapter 36/Perfection is Now: The Stainless Self, the Hellagony of Guilt, and Becoming Love 281
Chapter 37/Psychorestructuring: The Shadow, and the Author's "Tale Told by an Idiot" 288
Chapter 38/Infinite Mindwealth: Egobsession, Galactic Citizenship, and Mantramindvessel 296

About the Author 303

CHART OF MIND

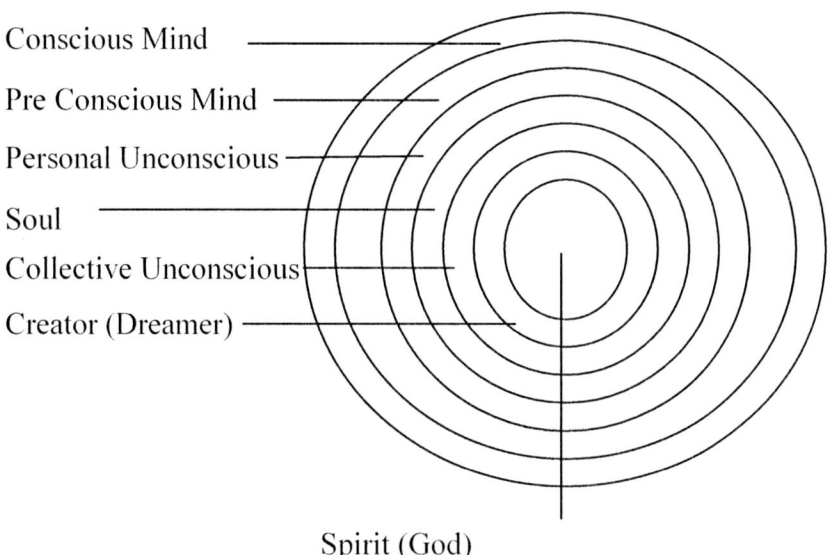

Falling in Love with Your Self
Love and the Inner Beloved

Author's Preface

MEGAPSYCHOLOGY: The Inner Outer Limits

****

The most important question that you can possibly ask about the universe is, Is the universe friendly? Said Albert Einstein

****

It is more fun than is humanly possible! In fact, it's even more fun than is dolphinly possible! That's because "it" originates with a Mind that is deeper and wider than humandolphinconsciousness. And this joyful, blissful "it" is the exploration of the deeper Mind. The most thrilling, stimulating, rambunctious adventure imaginable is what you are doing— or, more accurately, being— right now. The most exciting, amazing, mindblowing charge in the universe is the kinetic, frenetic rollercoaster ride of existing as a human being. For being a human being makes possible this interior voyage, the journey to inner space.

The "trip" into your own deeper Mind will blast you into the depths, valleys, caves, and underground of the unconscious psyche. It will also blast you, at hyperwarpspeed, beyond the stars. For the "inner immensity" is galactic in depth. The mysterious Mind manifests an incredible and polychromatic diversity. As many "worlds" are accessible inside your head, as the gate, as are in the galaxy!

Though the Mind, bottomless, is divided into only a few basic levels, the great Unconscious can be subdivided into a dazzling array and spectrum of layers. Altogether, like a housesized onion, the Mind hides most of itself in billions of hidden caverns, "underground" layers. (See "Chart of Mind.")

The trip can be freaky, bizarre, astonishing, mindblasting, or psychedelic—"Soulmanifesting." The journey into the psyche can be terrifying, as it plunges you into unknown darkness that might be inhabited by fearsome demons, dragons, and devils. (The area of the Mind occupied by these negative forces is the "subconscious," not to be confused with the "Unconscious." But more on this later.) The Mind might seem voraciously to swallow you.

But the inner voyage is also the most fun possible. This inner journey can expose your naked psyche to the Fountain of bliss, tranquility, wisdom, and Love. In a matter of minutes, it's possible to emerge from a Mindcontact as a completely revamped, new and improved, version of your self. This happens at the moment that you *become* Mind, rather than simply seeing your "self" as a body that happens to "possess a mind." At that miraculous moment, you are the "possessed," as you surrender to the ownership of Mind. You do not "have" a mind; but Mind "has" you! Because of this potential for re-creation, or rebirth, the inner journey is the most important event of your life.

This trip takes preparation. You can't just leap off the porch of Mind, one fine

Falling in Love with Your Self
Love and the Inner Beloved

springday, into a mental convertible, and head for the inner hills. It takes work. It requires time and practice. It also demands energy. But if it is so much trouble, why even bother? Because we are going culturally and personally mad! We are losing it, as a society and culture, by dysfunctionally trying to ignore the inner path.

If you are hungry, neglecting the fact will simply bring starvation. Ignoring our need for spiritual "food" has created "spiritual starvation." It is a rampant, although sometimes poorly diagnosed, social condition. The **only** source of nourishment is within the individual psyche. Although organized religion might deny or dispute it, the only solution is *personal* rediscovery of "truth." Eating, like sleeping, being born, and other biofunctions, must be a personal activity, even when shared with groups. Spiritual nourishment is no different.

No religion, no guru, no priest or pastor, no elder, no organization can give you this indispensable sustenance. Just as you must eat your own food, and no one can do it for you, so you must also take in your own spiritual smorgasbord.

You must make, and then eat, your own "bread." This inner bread is made of the "grain" of Love. The ancient mystics were so very impressed with Love that they made it the very Center of existence and of Mind. Most of us have tasted of its nectar, its delicious sweetness, when "falling in Love"— arguably, the highest high of which the Mind is capable! The mystics (enlightened or wise people) said, "God is Love." No more ultimate honor could have been rendered to any quality. Equating

Love with divine Power placed It as the true Center of the enlightened life. And all enlightened or wise people knew that all Love begins with Love for yourself. So, "falling in Love with yourself" is not egocentric, selfish, or arrogant— even though it might at first appear that it would be so. The person who truly loves herself is not going to be gazing lovingly into a mirror all day, or spending hours on make-up, or purchasing expensive clothes or jewelry. These are actions for one who hates herself, feels ugly, and is trying like mad to compensate.

For when you truly "fall" into Love, you lose your self— at least, your social self, your egoself. For when you fall under the spell of Love, you become another, a new, Self. You begin to realize that your "Self" is not a material body, but an aspect of Mind. In time, you come even to identify with a very profound level of Mind, in the Unconscious, called the "Soul," or "deeper Self." (This is also the "higher Self" of metaphysics.)

You are reborn. You are no longer just Mary Smith or John Jones.

You are now an everlasting Soul. (See "Chart of Mind."). Also, this "Soul" is birthless, deathless, and timeless. It is also nonphysical.

So, "You" are not a body. You are a Mind. Your true Self is a part of your unconscious Mind. Good news! Once you deidentify with your social egoself and start to realize that You are Your Soul, the world can no longer dominate You. You still respond to hunger, and the need for sleep. If you stub your toe at midnight, you are still going to yelp! But the "outer" world no longer designs your

Falling in Love with Your Self
Love and the Inner Beloved

thoughtpatterns, and, in this sense, you are inwardly independent of the world.

Here is how it all works: The Soul is deep within the mind. The Spirit is deep within the Soul. (The Spirit is called, by mystics, the "Absolute.") The "Spiritlevel" of Mind lives relative to nothing else, and thus, its name. This Spirit is continually dreaming up the world, **your** world. It does this unconsciously, through your Soul and your personal unconscious Mind. (See "Chart of Mind.") The part of the Mind that dreams up the world is part of the Core, or deepest level of the unconscious (Spirit). This aspect of the Coremind that dreams the world into being, using your mind/brain/nervousystem, is called the "Creator" or "dreamer."

How on earth have intelligent, even wise, persons throughout the ages, deeply balanced and highly spiritual people, arrived at the bizarre idea that the "real" world is really a "dream"? Let's take a look: You cannot prove to yourself the independent (objective) existence of any object. That means that you cannot prove that any object exists without your mind. If your mind weren't around, the object would not be sensed or perceived in your cosmos. So, it would not exist.

Let's take an object close at hand: this book. Can you prove that this book actually exists apart from your Self or Mind? No, you cannot. Yes, you can see this book, but seeing is a Mindfunction. Similarly, you can tap on the book, and hear it, touch it, smell it, and even taste it. But combine all these processes, and you still have not proved that this book exists independently of your mind.

Richard Shiningthunder Francis

Why not? Because these are all sensory "proofs," and so, are Mindprocesses. They are all evidence that only a sensory system exists. In other words, you have proved the existence of, not the book, but of only the mind. And since you have proved only the existence of mind, you can see that this book would be equally verifiable by the "senses" in a dream. For in any dream, you could as well, and as convincingly, perform the same reality-tests on a dream-book.

So, mystics are the ultimate realists, or, if you will, the world's greatest skeptics. They don't believe in the existence even of the material world. They can't, after all, verify its existence. Neither can you, nor can anyone else. If all philosophic speculation begins with those magic words of Descartes, *Cogito ergo sum*, "I think, therefore, I am," the mystic does not go beyond this solid proof. You know that you exist. Nothing could ever disprove this. Why? Because you partake of mind. You can think (although you might not know what to think about all this stuff)! Because you cannot prove even to yourself that any object in the "material external" world exists, but only mind, mystics call Mind "absolute" Reality. The world is seen as "secondary" or "relative" reality, because it exists only *relative* to a mind. So, if there were no minds in the cosmos, capable of sensing, perceiving, and interpreting, the material universe could not exist. It is all a Mindphenomenon, or dream. (The Mind that is alone verifiable and real has been called by the Sanskrit word *atman* and the "illusion" of

Falling in Love with Your Self
Love and the Inner Beloved

the material world has been called *maya*, by the most ancient Eastern mysticsages.)

This worldview opens broad new horizons and vistas of possibility! For, in a dream, nothing is impossible. When you dream at night, and "wake up" in your dream, or realize with full clarity that you are indeed dreaming, this is called a "lucid" dream. This is fairly rare, but when it does happen, the boundaries of the "possible/impossible" dichotomy disappear, and you can do literally anything, in the dreamworld. If the mystics are right, if this world too is a dreamworld, then the "miraculous" begins to make some sense. Enlightened people are those who have, after centuries of arduous, relentless effort, awakened at a very profound level to the Reality that this is a dreamworld. So, "impossible" things happen in their presence, in their worlds.

Mystics teach that the ultimate goal of human life is Mindmeld, fusion, or unity with the deepest Core of Mind, the Spirit. This is why you were created, and born. But before this can happen, you must go through several lifephases: 1) "I am this body," transcended, to produce 2) "I am this Mind," transcended to produce 3) "I am this Soul," finally transcended, to produce 4) "I am the Mind dreaming the cosmos into being."

This is lightyears beyond i.d. with ego, which is where the average person is. The penultimate shift of identity blossoms when your selfmind (egomind) Mindmelds completely with the Spirit, or Coremind. This dawns only after centuries of learning and practice.

As you might suspect, the Godimage of the enlightened sage bears almost no resemblance to the myth/fairy tale/illusion of a "big daddy in the sky." Scientists, philosophers, and theologians have argued literally for centuries about this bugaboo of a separate God. "He" is said to exist apart from all others, infinitely superior to them, supposedly loving them, but doing absolutely nothing in the face of incredible crises and disasters. What gives? Has "He" forgotten how to love? Or is "He" just asleep at the controls? Almost no one has ever changed anyone else's preconceptions. Both sides have remained stuck in concrete, paralyzed and static. No one can convince the educated agnostic or atheist that this childish "daddy in the clouds" is really there. In fact, all indications are that "He" is not, and has never been there! The entire idea of some kind of "person in space" reduces "God" to the ultimate extraterrestrial. "He" becomes only a superdeveloped alien.

The enlightened idea is very different. It is as startlingly contrasting as the ideas in the minds of rats and human beings. For this immediate, living, and *relevant* God, or Absolute, is not among the clouds or stars. Instead, the Ultimate is seen as Mind. This begins, at least, to remove it from the realms of the purely speculative. For while we have no reason whatsoever to believe in some ultrabeing among the stars, much less a mad giant with long white beard, we have every reason to believe in Mind. For it is this same Mind that is making possible the writing, and reading, of these words.

After the enlightenment event, a person actually believes that she has become a different being. She is no longer just Mary

*Falling in Love with Your Self
Love and the Inner Beloved*

Smith. All the things that are described or indicated by that name no longer bind or limit her. She is so much more, so much greater, wiser, and more beautiful than the person indicated by that name.

She is a timeless Soul of great wisdom—ancient, profound, brilliant. Her inner resources are an interior ocean of knowledge and wisdom. She is, in fact, no longer a literal "person." For she has entered, through moving to a deeper area of the Unconscious, the "superpersonal" realm of Mind. She is more than a "person." Relevantly, the word "person" arises from a Latin root, *persona*, which means "mask." Just as an actress in a movie is a very different being from any role that she might play, so the true, real, genuine, deeper Self is different from the ego named "Mary Smith."

Your name is just the role you are playing. Please write your name here:

_____

Take a good, hard, long look at that name. Now, try to realize that it is just a role, a mask, a pretend-self. It is your social self. It is the "looking-glass" self because you have defined it by looking into the mirrors of others' eyes. It is, then, only how *they* see you, not how you know yourself. But you have absorbed this view, and it now artificially affects even how you see yourself. It is not intrinsic to you. It is not your truest self. It is not authentic. It does not flow naturally from within, from your deeper inner Mind. It comes, instead, from "outside." It is your "ego."

Enlightened people say that this other-defined self is a lie, a falsehood, a misinterpretation, an illusion. You're in the position of a man who plays the role of Hamlet so very well that he begins to believe that he actually **is** Hamlet. In spiritual literature, this false maskself, this "Hamletself," is called the "ego." (So, the word "ego" is defined differently in spirituality than in psychology.) You are so familiar with, accustomed to, adept at expertly "playing," your ego, it does seem to be your real and only self.

In fact, it never occurs to the average person even to question the idea that the ego is her full identity. In saying, "I'm Mary Smith," she believes this with every fiber of her being. She has believed this ever since her birth, and it has been reinforced ten thousand times, in a thousand ways. In fact, from the usual perspective, it might sound a little mad even to question this selfimage. But still, after enlightenment, when the sage says, "I am Mary Smith," she begins to feel very strongly that this is a lie. She still plays the role; but it is not her entire Self. In fact, it is only a small, insignificant part of her total being.

Someday, you too will experience this mysterious passage into wondrous, luminous metamorphosis. It is a dramatic, irreversible change of life called the "mystical event." After that, you will no longer identify with your body. You will recognize that you are a Mindbeing. For you are not an animal, not just a monkey with car keys. Instead, you are a mind. Then, you will no longer feel that you are limited by a bodymind (symbolized by

Falling in Love with Your Self
Love and the Inner Beloved

your egoname). You will awaken to the fact that you are so very, very much more. You will come to recognize your Self as an immeasurable Being of dazzling bliss, enormous compassion, and bottomless tranquility. You will know your Self to be timeless— birthless and deathless. This is identification with the Soul. When you see this Self within your mind, you will feel powerfully attracted to, and infinitely comfortable with, this Self. You will thirst for closer integration with It; you will hunger to merge with It. You will feel so compelled and mesmerized by It that you will feel that you cannot get enough of It. You will want more, and then, still more. Your emerging Mindmeld will bring a sensation of awesome and overwhelming bliss. You will, in short, fall in Love with your Self.

****

Richard Shiningthunder Francis

Falling in Love with Your Self
Love and the Inner Beloved

Chapter 1

Falling in Love Again, with Love

***

People love to be in Love. It's the highest high in the world. It's more fun, by far, than anything else that can be imagined. It's so good that people want it to last forever! Love is a megablast! It produces vast and delightful gigapsychons of pure mental force or energy. Love can cascade in powerful waves throughout the bodymind. It can flow liquidly, tenderly, silently exploding with golden luminosity. It is the greatest! It's the most tender and subtle bliss. It is the intoxicating ecstasy for which you were created. You were formed from infinite Mind to house and nourish Love. Your heart is its warm nest. A Lovefilled psyche is a blissmind. Love glows, encircled by the gems and jewels of goodness, kindness, compassion, and joy. It excites and accelerates every nerve with electric brilliance, but softly, tenderly, with a subtlety that all but renders it invisible.

Love pushes all your buttons at once. It is the most fun that you can tolerate. It pushes the envelope of joy, testing the limits to their utter extremes. Filled with Love, you feel that a single added micropsychon of joy will burst you asunder. In a Monty Python skit, a man eats so much that a single after dinner mint causes him to explode. When you are filled with Love, the filling is so intensely satisfying, so utterly fulfilling, that you cannot tolerate even the tiniest added nanopsychon of happiness.

Love flows in currents of Mind and streams of feeling, moving and touching. It is a waterfall, a niagara mushrooming up from the Lovefilled heart, baptizing the universe with its sweet waters.

Anyone who has ever fallen in the "whitehole" of Love knows that Love is the soft, willowy flipside of the harsh, hard blackhole of fear. It is an inner "whitehole," because Love gives endlessly. It surrenders itself, loses itself in the seas and forests of your inner Mind. It weaves itself through the threads of your mind, and, thus interwoven, becomes inseparable from your Self. So, there arrives a time when falling in Love with your Self means falling in Love with Love. For with the passage of millennia or eons, your Self is metamorphosed into the very substance of Supermind, and that is Superlove 1. "Energenic," (energy-producing), Love spills and sprays from the full and enriched heart. Its glow warms the world. (A blackhole, fear, sucks and sucks, returning nothing, draining energy, leaving you exhausted and depleted.)

Love is always healing. Perhaps It heals not the body. Perhaps it heals not immediately. The growth of a rose or the evolution of stars does not occur instantly. But nature has its own selected, specific time

---

1. See my "Superlove: A Thousand Mystic Jewels From a Spiritual Megatrend," Part II of *Luminous Jewels of Love and Light: A Spiritetrology* (Liberty Township, Ohio; Love Ministries, Inc., 2002)

Falling in Love with Your Self
Love and the Inner Beloved

for all to heal. Love is a fountain of inner Light that always brings wholeness as its golden gift of grace. So, every touch of Love is a gentle "blast" of healing.

Loving is the supreme use of time, the only pursuit worth chasing. Money, sports, politics, religion— none can hold a sputtering, damp candle to the sunlight of deep sheer satisfaction of sharing Love. All other occupations are merely artificial Love-substitutes. They can satisfy human need no more than a picture of water can satisfy thirst. When Love is expressed, a great "ahhhhh" escapes from the Soul. This gigantic release is crafted by the liquid Mind of Love, as it showers upon, then penetrates, muscle and bone, heart and psyche. Love is life's collective sigh of relief. It pours from the relaxed, uncluttered Mind in currents of cleansing psychic "water," flushing out all that is not Itself, carrying all impurities into oblivion outside mind. All impurities are shadows fleeing from the Light, vaporizing into illusion.

Love is the sweetest, most lightfilled, most sumptuous and scrumptious banquet of the Soul. It ignites the heart, and sets every fiber of the nervousystem ablaze with blasting lightning and gentle, soft electricity. It blazes in the "flame of the heart," granting warmth and light.

In history, the "flaming heart" has signified this passionate thirst of Love. This is a heartmind-tsunami, an overwhelming, irresistible wave of Love so magnificent and transcendental that it sweeps the heartmind away in torrents of titanic force. The human mind diminishes to a pinpoint, then disappears into Love, leaving not a trace.

Historically, people were so attracted and compelled by Love that Lovecareers blossomed. Professional lovers appeared. They ate, drank, slept, and breathed Love. It was their bread, their water, their sunlight. They thrived on It like infants on milk, and drew Power from its sustained inner glow.

No, these Lovepeople were not prostitutes. Moderation saw sexual love as a glorious and splendid Light of infinite Love, which was the endless Love that captivated and compelled them. But this illimitable Love could never be limited to physical Love. Devoted and surrendered to Love, these Love-specialists became Love's servants. Love was their beginning and their end. It was the fertile seed that sprouted in their prepared hearts, and also the great tree that grew from that seed, in which the birds of heaven lived. Love began as a tiny seedthought, and grew into the Center of all things, the Essence of life. Love was also their endgoal. It was the Ultimate and Absolute. It was the destiny of the universe itself. To sink into this love, be engulfed by, immersed in and saturated by It, was the fondest hope of the mastersages of all cultures. To reflect It into the world was their assignment in the sweet garden of earthly delights. This was their supreme delight, making all other pleasures seem like hot, dry sand. The only desire that ignited and excited them was to "shapeshift" into a stainless, clear, and dustfree "mirror" of Love.

This Love bubbled up from an inner spring deep within the heartmind, flowing from the

Falling in Love with Your Self
Love and the Inner Beloved

deepest cavern of Mind. This profound Lovemind was so hidden from the eyes of mind that many did not even suspect Its existence. This unconscious Lovegod was symbolized by an interior "ocean" of Love or Light. This Superconscious was so vast as to be bottomless, illimitable and immeasurable. This same fantastic Supermind exists inside you and me.

Millennia in the past, knowledge of the "unconscious" Mind flourished. The "subconscious," filled with dirt, dragons, and demons, was also familiar territory amidst the Mindscapes. But a deeper part of the unconscious, filled with light, Love, joy, and peace illuminated the heartmind. This is the indispensable level of Mind neglected by psychology. This was the very deepest unconscious, the very Core. (See "Chart of Mind.") It was the "Spirit," the "Superconscious" Mind. (This is the "Absolute" of mystics.)

Love was everything for these true "mystics." (Those two words— Love and mystic— have been radically, mercilessly abused and twisted in pop usage. But "Love" is spirituality. And "mystic" simply means an explorer of inner space, whose goal is to merge or Mindmeld with the Core (Lovemind, Supermind, or the inner Absolute). When this occurs, the enlightened being then becomes Love in incarnation, what in the West has been called "God."

Everything is filled with the Mind of Love, for it is this Mind that dreams up the entire cosmos. In Western theology, this idea has been called "immanence"— the belief that God fills all creation. As Mind, He/She does really fill everything and everyone. At night, when you have a dream, you "fill" every object in your dreams. So the Creatormind "fills" every object in the cosmos, which is His/Her great dream. For, without Mind, the dreamworld around us would disappear.

This world was not made at sometime in the past, the way a carpenter makes a table, or a potter a vessel. These homely comparisons served the religious needs of ancient primitives, but even the most ancient mystics were much more sophisticated. They rejected this material view. They said that the world was never "created" in the "past" at all. And God did not form it from some primal "stuff." Instead, the mystics regarded the cosmos as fully psychogenic (Mind-caused). The only "raw material" that the Mind needed to create (dream up) a world was its own thoughts.

People participate in the dreamprocess. In the Book of Genesis, for example, God has a "deep sleep" fall over Adam (representing human nature). "Adam" is never awakened. The history of the world simply begins in this sleep.

The cosmos, then, is being created continuously, and recreated, every second of time. The Mind dreams the world now, and redreams it now, and redreams it again now. Shifting the metaphor slightly, with a similar analogy, the world is "virtual," lacking *absolute* reality. But instead of being produced by a primitive interactive computerprogram, the world is produced by Mind Itself. So, it is infinitely interactive, and illimitably elastic. This world, said the enlightened sages, is made of "light"— a word used in earlier times for "energy."

*Falling in Love with Your Self
Love and the Inner Beloved*

And guess what? Microparticle physics says that they were right. Then, the mystics took it all a disturbing step further: They defined this "energy" as Mindformed. All energy originated with Mind. All energy was, in fact, a form of Mind. Mind was energy, and energy Mind. The cosmos was psychogenic. (It originated with Mind as its Source or "Fountain.") In fact, the cosmos was Mind itself. The cosmos was all Mind modified. It was all a dream. So, it is "created" in exactly the way a dreamer dreams her dreams at night. This is a much more adult and sophisticated perspective than is usually found in common religion. The "Creator" is not some "big daddy in the sky," but is the deepest level of the unconscious Mind. This is the Source of the world, the dreamworld or Mindworld.

Only one Creator, not two, exists in the psyche. This Creator is good and perfect. So, everything in the cosmos is also good and beautiful. Even the "bad" and "ugly" must be reinterpreted to be seen as truly positive and exquisite manifestations of Love. The entire cosmos is a work of art, and the artistic hand that guides it is Love.

There is no "external or material" world. There is only the "Mindworld" or dreamworld. Even the most cynical skeptic must admit that, upon final analysis, everyone must live in an inner world formed by thoughts, feelings, and interpretations. The most intimate, and important, "environment" is that between your ears. If that one is in order, if it is sweet, so is life. But if it is screwed up, no matter how pleasant "outer" environments, you can live in an inner "hell." And the deep inner Mind is continuously engaged in dreaming up the world. It does this through your nervousystem and mind. Right now, It is dreaming up these very words.

This Mind is all good. Why, then, do little kids die? Why are they sexually abused? Why are there war, and torture, murder, rape, and other evils?

A complex, nightmarish Mindsystem called "karma" creates these monstrosities. Violently antiagapic (contrary to Love), ostensibly, it is actually another blossom of Love in the garden of the world. It is a subsystem of the great Love. Mistakes are made. People are abused. Conditions of "reflective" karma are Mindcreated: What people did to others must be done to them. What goes around, comes around. (Since this karma reflects back one's own behaviors like an energy-mirror, it is called "reflective.")

The same Mind that dreams up your everyday world also dreams into being your karma. Every instant of your life is recorded in the unconscious Mind. The innermind sector called the "inner judge" weighs and measures all activities. When it is memoryrecording, it is like a tape-recorder on the "record" mode. When your karma comes back to you, it is the same Mindsector, that same recorder, on "playback" mode. This Mindsector makes absolutely certain that you dream exactly the events needed to learn and polish the art of perfect Love. If you have wounded, you will dream that you are exposed to the same pain that you caused. This is the cosmic Way of education. The event is "rerun," as many times as necessary. Only this time, you will be the receiver of pain, not the giver. What

Falling in Love with Your Self
Love and the Inner Beloved

you did to others must now be done to you. So, the universe is working, moving and progressing, towards perfect justice. (This is a subsystem of perfect Love.)

After such a long and winding road of history, there are no "innocent victims." Each lives out the boomerang-effect of past abuses. Easier and tempting it is naively to dismiss the world. The lazy, unthoughtful, and ignorant give up. They see life as an unceasing struggle, a monstrous Darwinian conflict, red in tooth and claw. Only the tough survive. So, they rate this lovely planet as an irreparably "horrible" and unjust place. This is seductive. It is mindless simply to shrug your shoulders and say that nothing means anything. But this is the easy way out, the copout. It flees from the difficult, challenging light of understanding. It leaves us adrift in a meaningless void, clawing and struggling through hollow lives. It also buries the head stubbornly, often irretrievably, in the sand.

The mystic is, by contrast, a being of heroic courage. She fearlessly insists, without vacillation, flatly contradicting all "obvious appearances," that the cosmos is beautiful, and has meaning. More bizarrely, it seems, she insists that the whole show is run by Love. Ballooning her keyhole view of the universe into a larger sphere and context, she says that pain is dreamed up to serve Love. It is dreamed by the Spirit, through the Soul. For everyone must learn the art of Loving. This includes the violent and stupid. This education is the greatest gift that Love is capable of granting. None greater can be imagined.

Richard Shiningthunder Francis

Pure Love motivates the Spirit to dream. Poverty, pain, loss, and every form of dissonance, disharmony, conflict, and suffering are in its arsenal. It will stop at nothing to trigger spiritual progress, its only agenda. But the ego is a tough nut to crack, and often requires the sledge-hammer approach. We must be shaken free of egocomplacency, egodullness, materialism, ultrasensuality, and other distractions and obstacles. So, every argument, fight, conflict, and moment of suffering, loss, and pain is designed, and dreamed, by the Spiritlevel of Mind to teach Love. These serve to crack emotional mindarmor and let the sun shine in.

All "nonlove" or "antilove" events are engineered by the unconscious Mind to teach us Love, so even they are actually Love-events. When the Soul brings us, when the Spirit dreams up, pain, it is because It sincerely loves us.

This sounds like utter madness. Were the mystics really nothing but stark, raving lunatics? No, they were thoughtful, careful, reasonable and sensitive people. But they were passionate. Love was their magnificent obsession. They were driven to find meaning in a cosmos that seemed insane. Their faith that it all meant something drove them with enormous tenacity. As they voyaged deep into the psyche, they explored new and unmapped territory. They at last found even the area of Mind that created the world.

The answers that they discovered were not obvious. The solutions were deeply concealed in the most hidden and inaccessible recesses of the heartmind. The entire world, they learned, was so well constructed, was such a fascinating fabrication/falsehood, it took a massive effort to break its spell. The unconscious (Superconscious) Mind, it seemed, created this very realistic illusion. Its purpose was to fool the conscious mind through the senses. The dreamworld was designed to simulate Reality or truth, which was Mind. If the answers to the mysteries had been readily available, seekers would never have developed the treasures of tenacity and towering strength. Also, their powerful patience would have been paltry and pitiable. Without the implicit challenges of the Way, enlightenment would have been far too easy, and would have required no spiritual or psychological growth; everyone would figure out the great Mystery immediately. So, it would not be even a mystery at all. The cosmos yields no simplistic answers to childish inquiries. Instead, it will agree to yield its tightly-gripped and deeply-hidden secrets only to those who are obsessed with their discovery.

The Soul is a deep level of the unconscious Mind. (See "Chart of Mind.") Because it is Mind, it is a nonphysical reality. This is not to say, in superficial literalism, that the "Soul" is some misty foglike cloud, resembling the "ghostsheets" worn by kids at Halloween. No, the Soul is in the Mind. It is a level, a part, of Mind. Being nonphysical, it is not your body. The body, in fact, is just a shorterm "suit" that the Soul

Richard Shiningthunder Francis

"puts on" for a certain time. It is a "costume" worn for the performance of the "play" of this world. As Shakespeare said, 'All the world's a stage, and we but actors.'

****

Falling in Love with Your Self
Love and the Inner Beloved

Chapter 2

It's All Inside: Who Do You Think You Are?

***

The "inner stranger." This phrase can describe the mysterious "Soul." It can be your very best friend. But it can be a vicious enemy. It is, strangely, not "other" than your Self. Still, you might not even know it, for it is tucked beneath the thickest and deepest folds of Mind in the unconscious. Indeed, most people are astonished by discovering what lies in the personal unconscious. The Soulevel of Mind is much deeper even than this Mindlevel. (See "Chart of Mind.") So, an amazing number of people know zero about their own Souls. Some even doubt the very existence of the Soul. These doubters are lost in an even deeper than average mindfog.
  Even mystics (psychonauts) require centuries clearly to know their own Souls. The Soul contains immense quantities of data, and megapsychons of feeling. It possesses, after all, the accumulated tears, laughter, and wisdom of many lifetimes.
  For it is not your everyday "self." It is not your Soul that argues with your kids, plays tennis or baseball, goes to the office and makes phonecalls. It is not your greater or higher Self, the deep Soul, that guzzles coffee and engorges itself on doughnuts and other culinary miscellanea.

That everyday self, the "ego," has a name, such as Mary Smith. That self has an entire history. Mary Smith went to Jefferson elementary school, and graduated from Madison High, when she went to Brown, and earned a B.A. She then became a computerprogrammer. Shortly after, she met and married Joe Smith, and together they had two kids, who grew into surly, snarling, bitching teenagers who despised both Joe and Mary. The ego was born at a certain time, lived and lives at a certain address, comes from a certain family. It is highly integrated with the body, and so has genetic factors that powerfully influence it.

Kids are often taught to say, "I hurt myself," when what they really mean is, "I hurt my arm, or finger." This confusion of "self" with "body" is built into the subtext of our very language.

"What you see is what you get. This is who I am." This common self, which you have always thought of as your true and only self, is called by mystics the "ego." But this is not who you really are. It's a part of a larger system of Mind. It's a subsystem within a truer, deeper, or "higher" Self, called the "Soul." So, you are not a body, you are not a mind, you are not an ego. You are a Soul.

So, when Mary Smith beams with pride at seeing her name in print, it is the pride of illusion, the pride of a mask wellmade. On stage, when Hamlet is guilty, or angry, or frightened, these pretendfeelings have no effect on the actor playing Hamlet. Your Soul "plays" the "role" of your egoself. If your egoname is Mary Smith, the mystic would deny

*Falling in Love with Your Self
Love and the Inner Beloved*

that You *are* only Mary Smith. Instead, you are the greater Self, the Soul, "playing the role" of Mary Smith.

The "stage" of this "play" is also not real in any absolute sense. This is indicated by a principle called "impermanence," in which all things are seen as verbs, as fluidically changing. Nothing on the "stage," none of the props, stays the same, from moment to moment, day to day, and year to year. The world is a very complex, ultrasophisticated "vr" system. Everyday reality, the mystic says, is "virtual." The Soul is real, but neither the role that it plays (the ego), nor the stage upon which it is acted out (the world), is real. This discovery makes the mystic enormously strong— powerful enough *never* to be dominated by the world. The mystic's total freedom comes through a state called "detachment." This does not mean that they live as "zombots" (zomie-robots) without feelings or responses. Mystics are among the most tender, sentimental, and emotionally responsive of all people. But detachment is how mystics live in this world. For they live as Souls having an earthly experience. At the risk of being hackneyed, the old cliche applies: Mystics are not earthers having a spiritual experience, but eternal Souls having an earthly experience.

The Soul does use the ego. But mistaking your whole self for the ego is like believing that you **are** your little finger. If you fell into this psychotic delusion, it would pose some fascinating conundrums: How would you eat? How would you communicate with others? How would you dress for parties? How would you relate to a date?

That belief would be a real breakaway from reality. Mystics say that when people think that they are their egos, they suffer from a serious spiritual psychosis. Who would want to be operated on by a surgeon who suffered under the delusion that she **was** her scalpel? It's a real identity crisis.

Ego conceals rather than reveals. As at Mardi Gras or Halloween, your true Self smiles and peers out from behind the egomask, hidden in its darkness. So, the ego is a false identity. It masks your true, but "secret," identity. Like Clark Kent, you are really a Supermind or Superbeing.

It is useful, even necessary, to have an ego-identity. For this is the name on your driver's license and birth-certificate, as well as every other official i.d. But despite the fact that everyone else is playing this intricate "game," You do not have to take the ego with finality and utter seriousness. Just because everyone in the world calls you "Mary Smith" or "John Jones," You do not have to limit your infinitely great self to that little familiar mental cubbyhole.

For You are a being of virtually illimitable creativity, joy, and beauty. You have simply fallen asleep. this has produced karmic amnesia, and so, You have forgotten Who You really are. Your Soul is just pretending to be your ego.

The ego sprouted into bumptious life at the time of your bodybirth. But the Soul was already very old by then, already wise, already stunning in beauty and power, compassion and tranquility. The ego will perish, evaporating and evanescing into nothingness, at the time of your bodydeath.

*Falling in Love with Your Self
Love and the Inner Beloved*

But your deathless Soul will continue on its everlasting journey through the stars. This shimmering reality is known by all the world's great spiritual traditions.

Amazingly subtle is this Soul. So tenuous is it that most people don't even know that they *have* Souls— much less, that they *are* Souls! To discover something so intangible, so deeply ensconced within the Mind, requires effort. It implies serious and repeated introspection. It is the great inner voyage of mysticism, the journey to the center of the Soul.[2]

But the reward of this quest is fabulous inner riches beyond imagining. These include the jewels of Love (compassion), joy (bliss), peace (tranquility), and dozens of other Mindflowers in the inner garden of Mind.

These begin to pour from your Soul into your conscious (aware) mind, lighting your world. The mystic path is introversion. Its voyage promises, in the end, nothing less than total fulfillment. This path also creates everlasting ecstasy. These are among the fruits of the inner tree of life, in the hearts' Garden of Pleasure. ("Eden" means "pleasure.")

When the inner "trip" has begun, you discover that the Mind is very friendly. All levels of the unconscious, even the difficult levels of the subconscious, contain bright Love and wisdom. The Unconscious is supportive, communicative, tender, and compassionate. Indeed, its very identity, in

---

2   See my Journey to the Center of the Soul: Mysticism Made Simple (Liberty Township, Ohio; Love Ministries, Inc., 2002)

the area called the "Superconscious," is Love. Love is the very essence of Mind, at unconscious (but not always "subconscious") levels. It is because of the primacy, indeed, the supremacy, of Love that the Spirit— the deepest Coremind— is known in mystical tradition as the "inner Beloved."

Identifying with the eternal Soul changes everything. It means that the Mindworld that surrounds you, that forces itself upon you, is not Your master. We are taught that the world controls us, that we are mere marionettes, the playthings or pawns of events and environments. The psychophilosophy of Watson and Skinner took this premise to its absurd, extreme, damaging conclusions. Even after a person sees through this fanciful and dark illusion, however, she can fall back under its hypnotic spell. What a meticulously detailed construct is the "virtual" reality of this dreamworld! Every particle of every tiniest object or event has been intricately designed by the Mind to obfuscate and obscure its dreamnature. Everything conspires against the hard won knowledge of nature's deepest mystery. Like any well constructed dream, the "real" world takes us in, fools and deludes us, over and over. In fact, the Mind wills for the conscious mind to be duped. For if your egoself did not believe that the world was real, during important phases of its growth, its education would be stunted.

The world is a complex Mindgame. So, we should be masters, not servants, of our worldgames. And we, as masters, must yield to our own inner Master, the Lovenature (Spirit, Lovegod, Coremind).

Falling in Love with Your Self
Love and the Inner Beloved

Utter astonishment, relief, and joy flood the mystic as she discovers that the world is powerless to dominate her. She alone chooses how she wants to feel and respond.

"That makes me see red" uses two symbolic phrases, for nothing in the world can *make* the Mind angry. Anger is the mind's chosen volatile, often destructive, response. "She makes me blue" is equally symbolic. So is, "That terrifies me." All responses are dances between "Mind and world." More literally and accurately, the complex choreography is between Mind and mind. The unconscious Mind orchestrates harmony between the Unconscious and the conscious. *No response* can be "created" by the world. It is no Creator, no puppetmaster, and you are no puppet. It simply is not within the jobdescription of the world to create responses. But usually, we grant it that power. This occurs only by means of an inner coup that steals our responsepatterns from their rightful sovereign— inner Mind. For that power is the right, privilege, honor, and glory of Mind, and Mind alone has true Power to regulate the responses of mind.

The world has one purpose: To elicit from You the spiritual education of perfect Love. Notice here that Education is "elicited," not implanted, because its wisdom already flowers in your deeper Self. It is drawn from within that special "You," with a capital "Y," implying the true, deeper Self (Soul). Every game, every dream, every prop grants wisdom. Every interaction teaches. Every person is the Soul's teacher. The ego does not want to hear this. For we are often indebted to those who teach us precisely what we do not want to know. Yet this is precisely what we often need most to learn.

When you get up in the morning, and the world starts to be spun from Mindstuff of the deep unconscious, again starts turning the wheel of cyclicity and karma. This could not happen without your awareness. For awareness, using the conscious mind, allows assimilation of data, and this produces learning. Similarly, if you play the part of Louis XIV or Marie Antoinette in a play, you can learn much about the agonies and ecstasies of the real people. So, the Soul learns its most vital lessons by playing different roles (egos) on the stage of the world. Right now, you are playing the role of your egoself. The goal is not to escape the role, but to play it with as much compassion and wisdom as possible.

But the Soul is not here to study world-history, or to learn science, or to master art. It is here to study and learn all possible relevant facts about the Self. No matter what your career, profession, or occupation, your overiding pursuit is spiritual. This goal, selfknowledge, is so bright that it eclipses everything else. It blots out all other aims. It alone is supremely important. And exactly what is this sublime cosmic career? It is begun by knowing yourself, and completed by falling in Love with your Self. It is to master the fine art of Love. Every thing, person, or situation that you encounter is a micromirror designed to reflect your own face. These make up a megaplex of mirrors surrounding you. By interacting with the world, you are actually

Falling in Love with Your Self
Love and the Inner Beloved

peering into the nooks and crannies of your own unconscious Mind.

Some mystics teach that this is the only way truly to know the Creator/Dreamer, which they call the "knower." The ancients said, 'Fire burns all things, but does not burn fire; water makes everything wet, but not itself; the sword cuts everything else, but not itself. So the knower knows everything, but not itself directly.' The "knower" can be known, of course, by introspection. But the usual way in which it is understood is by gazing contemplatively into the multiple mirrors of the world. The inner Dreamer is known by His/Her dreamcontents.

Your present ego is just one of many colorful, exciting roles played by the Soul. Behind the curtain of the unconscious Mind, the Soul buries in its deep caverns vivid memories of other roles (egos), played on other stages. Through the centuries, in many lives, the Soul has struggled to learn the arts of loving. This is a gargantuan, daunting, and complicated process. Each of us has made and then corrected, thousands of errors. To find the true path, we have walked down a thousand false paths. To learn to do it right, we must first do it wrong innumerable times. This takes lots of time—more than could ever be squeezed into one tiny human lifetime. This is the vision of the cosmic Soul in all its fullness and grandeur. So, mystics embrace the "polybiographic" (reincarnational) worldview. So, life is not only more fascinating, but meaningful. This idea explains much; it also gives us a solid reason for our existence. That reason is the

Richard Shiningthunder Francis

goal. That goal is to cultivate and grow in the art of loving in living.

****

Chapter 3

Torn between Two Universes, and Loving It

***

   A love-affair with life. A love-affair with the universe. A love-affair with your own deepest (cosmic) Mind. All life is a Love-affair. It is all about Love, and begins with falling in Love with the inner Beloved (the Ultimate, Absolute, Coremind, or Supermind). After centuries of applying your spiritual talents, this Mind becomes Your Self, so that the goal of life is to fall in Love with Your Self.

   This vision synopsizes the final destiny of everyone. It is also the *immediate* aim of the mystic. This is union with the inner Beloved. It is the "why" of your birth, your life. You are a Loveperfecting being.

   As in the old song, everyone is a "Lovemachine." That is why the language of mysticism is the highly rich and ethereal, celestial expression of true poets and lovers. The tongue of the spiritual being is the language of Love.

   Love is spirituality's essence and goal. Stated most simply, Love is spirituality, and spirituality, Love. You "fit" the cosmos, warm hand in enfolding glove, in the glow of welcoming embrace. This occurs when you learn to go with the Flow, and stop blocking/resisting the Mind of Love. This becomes natural when you decide to love everything and everyone.

Richard Shiningthunder Francis

This soft, warm cosmic vision loudly clashes with the frigid, hard, irresponsive cosmos of the materialistic scientist, which is all sharp angles and cold geometricities. But in that gleaming, hard-surfaced world, there is not a microparticle of meaning anywhere. The world mindlessly ticks on, unguided, reasonless, going nowhere, for no particular reason. In fact, there is no "reason" for anything. Why a radical materialist even bothers to get up in the morning is a major mystery.

The cosmos of the average person might have a little of both worldviews— spiritual and mechanistic— blended uncomfortably together. This makes for strange, and mutually repellant, bedfellows. This is no ideal recipe, to shift metaphors, for the most Mindnutritious of Soulfoods. For this common view often leans heavily, tilting offbalance, towards hollow materialism. For the unhealthy worldview has arisen from an education that "materializes" everything. High school science, and much in "commonsense" transforms the world into distinct and separate objects. These obey mindless mechanical laws, and exist completely independent of Mind.

Those objects are "out there." When you leave your car parked in the garage, it continues to exist while you are away at the office or store. So, objects are there whether or not anyone knows it. They are independent of any mind. In this way, they differ dramatically from dreamobjects, which are totally dependent upon Mind in order to exist.

"Real world" objects are not like this, says the common view. They do not exist simply in

*Falling in Love with Your Self
Love and the Inner Beloved*

your mind. They have an independent existence all their own. If every mind in the cosmos were suddenly snuffed out, all material things would continue brainlessly, mindlessly to tick-tock along like a giant Newtonian clock. (Newton was the older physicist who discovered "commonsense" physics.) But how can it be proved that an object exists in itself? A commonsense answer is a tape or photo of the object when no one was around. But that record must have an observing mind in order for it to exist, which leaves us right back where we started: World cannot exist without a sensing/perceiving mind. *Nothing can. For even a photo, tape, or disc must have some perceiving, sensing mind in order meaningfully to exist.*

   The view that objects exist independently of minds I have called the "nbc universe." (It rested upon the "newtonian-Baconian-Cartesian view of the world, filled out by three philosophers, Newton, Bacon, and Descartes.) This nbc view is the one that we all learned, from kindergarten through high school, and later, in college. Unlike the latest physics, it supports "commonsense." When you leave your office building or work-site, and come home, the place where you worked continues to exist, even though no one is there. It doesn't disappear when no one is there, when no one is thinking about or perceiving it. While we can all agree that it does vanish from your personal sensory sphere, that is dismissed as "only subjective," unreflective of true reality.

   Or is it? This speculation leads into one of the most dramatic and captivating of cosmoperspectives. It is mindboggling. For mystics say that a world unseen is a world that evaporates. This symbolizes that when you remove a perception/sensation from your mind, it is no longer a part of your experience. It vanishes from your experiential universe. Even materialists would agree. But they would say that this is a subjective and personal impression. The object or situation does not really disappear. It just disappears *from your sight or senses.*

Hang the coat in the closet, close the closet door, and the coat is "gone" from your personal perception. Put a spoon in a drawer, close the drawer, and the spoon "disappears" from your experiential reality.

This is the Way in which pure minds, those of infants, see the world. This is how the cosmos is known before "normal" egoformation. This is before their minds are forced into a commonsense mold called "object constancy." For the infant, objects are literally, "Out of sight, out of mind." But if the mind dreams reality, those objects are really "gone"— again, from the person's "experiential" universe.

Still, it is argued, they are not gone from the "real" universe. But mystics say that the "real" universe is a Mindconstruct, so that the "experiential" cannot dogmatically be divided from the "real." The experiential is the real. In order to be real, a situation, event, or object must be experienced by some mind. (The "common" world the mystic refers to as "consensual reality," because everyone agrees about its existence.)

When the Master Jesus was asked how best to live, he said, "Lest ye become as little children, ye shall not inherit the kingdom."

Falling in Love with Your Self
Love and the Inner Beloved

But, fascinatingly, the Greek word mistranslated as "little children" did not mean youngsters or toddlers. It meant "nursinginfants." This is the stage before egoformation, and before object constancy.

While still small infants, we learn "object constancy" or "object permanence." We are heavily programmed to "realize" that objects continue to exist even when removed from "sight" (sensory perception). This is only commonsense. It is common precisely because it is what we have all learned. But mystics dared to ask, "What if this were not literally true?"

This led to a dazzling new cosmic view: There exist two coterminal universes. One, they call "experiential." This is everything that you really know is "there," because you can see it, touch it, taste, smell, or hear it. This is your everyday world. It's what you actually see on tv or hear on radio, or read in the paper. It also includes everything that actually happens to you. It is your total sensory inventory. (However, your actual experience does not include those events described on radio/tv or in the paper. The realities in your actual experience are only that the tv, radio, and newspaper exist.) This "experiential" cosmos is the entire universe that contains all your senses, and their resulting interpretations, perceptions, and experiences. When you open your eyes in the morning when you drink your first cup of coffee or tea, when you hear, or see images of, the news, watch tv, get in your car, see the streets, houses, buildings, and people, come into your workspace, do your job, return home, talk to spouse or friends, go to bed— all this is your experiential universe.

If you dream, the contents of that nightvision are also part of your experiential universe. This universe contains everything that is real to you because you are experiencing it. If you are in a windowless room, that room is then your entire "experiential universe." In short, the experiential universe contains all the things and people of the "external and material" world, *as you directly sense and perceive them. It can also contain* your thoughts and ideas about them.

The other universe is the "theoretical." This is the entire universe of everything that is outside your perception or sensation. This is the totality of the entire (but abstract) universe that supposedly exists even when you are not "there" to feel, sense, or perceive it. This is the place where you work, after you go home, leaving it behind. When anyone leaves your home and drives out of sight, she leaves your experiential universe, and enters your theoretical universe as soon as she disappears from sight. Place a coat in a closet, and close the door. The coat has just moved from your experiential into your theoretical cosmos. Put a teabag into a canister and close it. The teabag has also just moved from your experiential universe into your theoretical cosmos. Everything in the world, with some pitifully tiny exceptions, exists in your theoretical universe. So do the six thousand million people in the world— usually, again, with only very small exceptions.

*Falling in Love with Your Self
Love and the Inner Beloved*

This is relevant, because what is absolutely, convincingly, and immediately "real" to you includes only one universe— your experiential universe. You can never do anything to prove to yourself that the theoretical universe really exists. For another example, until you open a mysterious drawer, when you do not know its contents, the objects inside are part of your theoretical universe. Only when you open the drawer and sense them do they become a part of your experiential universe.

What does any of this weird stuff have to do with anything? What does it have to do with real, everyday life? These apparently abstract and strange ideas have practical ramifications.

Mystics teach that we are all responsible for the "world." And we are. But in its larger sense, this world is a part of the theoretical universe. So, we cannot realistically be responsible for so gigantic a concept. It is simply too gargantuan, too colossal, too overwhelming. The world is Mount Everest, and we are ants, or bacteria, standing at its base. The most that we can do is to care for our little corner of reality, of the planet. Also, it is true that if everyone took care of her corner, the world itself would be transformed. When the little flowers are cared for, the vast garden is beautified.

So, the mystical view is that we simply cannot be responsible for the "world," as a massive whole, but only for our personal (experiential) "world." This view is solidly realistic. Whatever the universal Mind places *directly in front of you* is your assignment, task, or mission. If you can do good for all, for the population of the planet, so much the better, and you should do that. But you are **responsible** only for what is in front of you. This is called "focus." It allows us to take life in small bites. The tallest mountain is climbed with small steps. You can't feed a baby with a steam-shovel, and the human conscious mind is designed to tackle the universe in tiny baby steps or bites only. This is the same principle as the famous "one day at a time," except it is even more manageable: One "now" at a time.

Does the mystic play the ostrich, burying her head in only personal pursuits, and ignoring the rest, dismissing the world as "theoretical reality"? No, for Love drives her incessantly forward to improve society, and even the larger world. But she does not take personal responsibility for every person and event. This would be a kind of mental illness related to megalomania or hyperegotism. Her Love impels her to discover new ways and forms of service. She actually seeks ways to aid, help, and serve people. But while so serving the "world," she focuses and concentrates her full attention on one person or task at a time. For this, at this moment, is her entire cosmic mission. Her heartmind is as sharp and intense as a laser. This is a form of what Buddhists call "mindfulness."

So, when you are dealing with a mystic, you can rest assured of her fullest, completely undivided attention. For when she is interacting with you, you are her full assignment. You are her complete Lovetask, her mission in life. You embody her entire

Falling in Love with Your Self
Love and the Inner Beloved

spirituality. At that moment, you are the very service of Love, Love's object.

Loving you **is** loving God or Spirit. The deepest inner Mind cannot be loved completely until or unless all Its dream is embraced in Love. So, it is impossible meaningfully to declare that one "loves God" if one is not actively loving people. This is why kindness and friendliness are essential aspects of the mystical path. A person as "prickly as a porcupine" cannot possibly practice Lovemysticism. For it is Love which is the career of the mystic. This Love must include common courtesy, politeness, and friendliness.

Everyone and anyone can be a mystic. All she has to do is make the decision that she wants to pursue the inner and infinite Lovenature as a career. Mysticism makes a lousy hobby, however, and a worse pastime. You cannot breathe only periodically. ("Breath" and "spirit" were expressed by the same word in many ancient languages.) The Way of Love is inner breathing. Stop for too long, and you turn blue (and get the blues). Stop long enough, and you're dead. This path is so crucial that it is alldemanding, allconsuming. It demands every minute of your time, every psychon of your mind. It requires your entire world, and will never settle for the scraps of spare time. Whatever else you do in life, whatever career you pursue, if you are going to be a mystic, you must decide to be a mystic **first.** Mysticism will never take a back seat, or second place, to anything— not even religion.

****

Chapter 4
Extraordinarily "Ordinary" Love: Mysticism

* * *

When the Mind swallows you, It leaves nothing left to devote to any "other god." When you eat an apple, that fruit becomes you. When God consumes you, you become God. You become the Mind of Love, in momentary "incarnation."

Love demands **all** your quality time. But remember all the many joyful activities, fun, excitement, and bliss included in Love. For Love's recipe has many ingredients. Every time that you love your wife, husband, sweetheart, children, relatives, friends, strangers, pets, or any living creature, you are living out the excellent Way. In fact, every time that you love yourself, without indulgence, selfcenteredness, or arrogance, you express the Love of the inner Infinite.

Love is glorious, splendid, superb, and satisfying. But some are terrified by it, having been burned by what they defined as "love." But real Love never harms. It must be distinguished from that entangled mass and mess of dysfunctions and egocentricities which people usually call "love." Love has nothing in it of greed, selfishness, grasping, clinging, demanding, or craving. This is how it is distinguished from so many convincing, appealing counterfeits. Contrasting with pseudoagapic (false "love") pursuits, it is

Falling in Love with Your Self
Love and the Inner Beloved

free from all personal desire. Only the desire to love the Beloved remains.

How do you best love the Beloved? By loving yourself or other people. Every act of Love, for father, mother, husband, wife, kids, and friends is actually the Love of the Beloved, as well as Love *for* the Beloved. All outer loves are expressions of that one supreme inner Love. This is a profound, healing, healthy Love for the deeper inner Self (Soul). So, sometimes, when we "loved" in the past, our "love" was often not real Love at all. And even when it was, it was often contaminated with demands, expectations, selfishness, fear, insecurity, and other unconscious pollutants. Because these forces were *unconscious*, you were *not always* responsible for them. But now that you are wiser, it is your responsibility to learn consciously about the dynamics of true Love and try to express them. To help you do exactly this is the purpose of this book.

The volatile explosives of Love can often burst into the flames of conflict, in which we attack and defend. But genuine Love soothes troubled waters. Real Love creates longterm harmony, even while nonjudgmentally embracing shorterm conflicts. Because you are a human being, you will have conflict. But because you are also a Soul, you have the Loveresources to solve and resolve conflict. At any rate, any "love" that includes repeated, deliberate attack cannot be balanced or real Love.

A person cannot be hurt by genuine Love because it demands and expects nothing. When we change the steps and sequences of the dance, it becomes a different dance. When we change ourselves, Love also changes within us. It is this transformation of our responses that makes real Love a safe proposition. But genuine Love is a soaring into the night sky, and an exploding into the flame and color of inner and passionate fireworks! Love is a supernova of the psyche! It is not just "safe," as in "dull." Love is electrifying, not a major yawn or snore! It is a safety net which catches us when we fall, but it is Soulstirring, mindelectrifying. It longs for the beloved with fiery passion. It engulfs body and mind in hot, bright fire. The inner Beloved is literally the man/woman of your dreams.

In loving a man, the mystic loves the god in him. And in loving a woman, the mystic loves the goddess in her. Mystic Love is divine. It is magical, because it is the real thing. It is more rare than diamonds and rubies. There are, in fact, only a few specimens of this fine quality Love on our planet. It is heart-to-heart connection, Soul-to-Soul fusion, mind-to-mind Mindmeld. It is the interpenetration of two beings, and carries within it perfect loyalty and fidelity. It amplifies resonance and creates harmony and bliss. In it, each truly wants what the other wants, and there is no "gimme, gimme," or, for that matter, no "me, me." It is a warm fluidic flowing into the deeper Mind, into the Beloved.

The Hindu greeting *"namaste" embodies this exquisite loss of self in other, or in deeper Mind.* This word means, roughly, "the divine in me honors the divine in you." This kind of "honor" is the basis for all true Love. What is "honor" in Love? It is commitment,

Falling in Love with Your Self
Love and the Inner Beloved

loyalty, monogamy. It is support and understanding, and communication. It is treasuring and cherishing the loved one.

This Love does not just drop into your lap from the sky. It does not just, one day, poof! appear out of nowhere. It is the endresult of struggle, agony, pain, and loss, created in a matrix of education. Not that Love is all fire and blades. Love is also gentle joy, soaring and elevated happiness, refreshing tranquility, rushing ecstasy. But a durable and lasting, loyal, reliable, dependable Love is forged only in the superheated furnace of challenges. It is tempered by pain and loss.

From the overiding philosophy of Love, in which Love is the unequalled Center of all, the Source and Goal, this service of Love transforms even the pain and loss into "good." If they serve Love, then even pain and loss can be, must be, seen as positive. Because they are educational, they are healing.

Ordinary people often taste of the tormentside of Love. But the mystic's inner furnace is stoked to a thousand times the natural heat. Just as a fine elixir requires fine crystal vessels into which it can be poured, so we must work to prepare our bodyminds to become the crystalclear vessels of true Love. This is done by most careful attention to, and cultivation of, the Lovenature. It is fed by every act of Love— for ourselves, family, neighborhood, community, and world.

A kid who speeds down a dangerous hill on a bike should not blame the hill or the bike when she crashes. For she failed to prepare, with a helmet, padding, checking the brakes, making sure that the tires were in good shape, etc. So, in the same way, we cannot blame the principle of Love when we decide to plunge into the deep oceanic waters of Mind, and are hurt by what we choose to call "love." It is so very rarely the real thing. Love is not the desired, selected path of everyone.

Mysticism, then, is not for everyone. Some will regard it as foolishness, madness, or lunacy. Others will see it as the pursuit of chimeras, illusions, and unrealistic dreams. Many will dismiss it as unrealistic or hyperidealistic fantasy. Many others will see it as a simple waste of timenergy. Still others will dismiss it as just plain weird. Of the mystic, these skeptics will say, "She's one bottle short of a six-pack," or, "The elevator doesn't go all the way to the top," or, "The light is on, but no one's home," or, "She doesn't have both oars in the water." And that, too, is okay.

For the cosmic Mind is greater than these responses. In fact, It has created them, to test the conviction-strength of the mystic. Even the rejection of Mind is Mind, since there is no other Source. To deny the will of Love is also the will of Love, for it is part of spiritual education.

Besides, the deepest Mind is in no hurry. It has forever to accomplish its work. After all, it takes forever to do everything. And the only explanation of some human behaviors is simply, Everybody has to do something, and somebody has to do everything. For if this were not so, the cosmic Mind would be incomplete. It knows well that whenever any being is ready for this message, this Way, it will come to her. It has just this moment

*Falling in Love with Your Self
Love and the Inner Beloved*

come to you. For some, it will come in this present life, but not to everyone. And that, too, is just fine. No one is in a hurry except the egomind, which demands everything "yesterday, if not sooner."

This Love is strangely, delightfully passionate, but not always sexual. But it can be so powerful that it triggers even sexual urges and responses in some sensitive Souls. That is okay too, but it is not the goal of mystical Love. For this Love has as its aim to elevate the aware mind. "As the old song says, Love lifts us higher and higher. It remolds the psyche in the image of compassion, kindness, and essential goodness. As the psyche is elevated, the being becomes silently strong, reliable, tender, compassionate, just, and honorable. She is moved to increase friendships, and service.

More and more, every day, what was formerly unconscious will be made conscious. By active Love, the mystic is brought closer and closer to the incredibly deep, bottomless, Mindlevel called the Lovenature. This is the indivisible Core of Mind. This Lovecore is the Lovemind or Lovegod at the Center of being and Mind. The bird of Soul flies through the blue skies of Mind towards the sun of Love. This is the Spirit (Absolute, Coremind) Itself.

The heart softens, the mind is tenderized and sensitized. A form of mysticism is Sufism, derived from a word meaning "wool." The goal of this path is to make the heart "as soft and warm as fuzzy wool" on a freezing winter day.

When your Soul or higher Self is ignited with the warm flame of Love for the inner

Beloved, you are filled with Light. You are transformed and renewed by this Light— an ancient symbol for awareness. You are becoming increasingly aware of your own inner Mind. This is the deepsea expedition into the very deepest troughs in the floor of the ocean of Mind. With every scubadive, you learn just a little more.

The "journey" or trip back to the Source, the Beloved, does not occur instantly. No matter what you do, full enlightenment will not come to you overnight, or in the first week, or month, or probably, the first year. It requires timenergy, effort, concentration, and vigilance. In the personal and collective deep waters of the unconscious swim many friendly dolphins, but there are also a few sharks.

All of these transformations and revelations do not occur to the ego. They do not come to your everyday self. This growth all blossoms deeply within the unconscious layers and levels of the Mind. It is an 'inside job,' in which the Mind reveals Itself to Itself, but all activities are unconscious. You do most of your inner spiritual growth when you are not even aware of it. For example, much occurs during dreamless sleep. Mystical opening occurs with deep-water flowers which blossom without the light of conscious awareness. Dreamstates serve as opportunities for much inner growth. But so does dreamless sleep. In this state, "you" are not even an active participant. Growth is natural and "automatic." As the roses in your yard bloom when you are not watching, the mystic rose of the heart also unfolds without your conscious input. Most growth in the unconscious Mind

Falling in Love with Your Self
Love and the Inner Beloved

occurs at two Mindlevels: Soul and the personal unconscious. (See "Chart of Mind.")

No matter who you are, you are going to be "forced" by inner Mindpressure into enlightenment. Why, then, bother with the Way? Because before enlightenment comes to most, much time, perhaps thousands of earth-years, will have to pass. During all that time, you can be either joyful or miserable. You can choose to spend all that time in either inner "heaven" or "hell." So, mystics do not embrace their Way only because they want enlightenment, although that is also a motive. They walk the Way of Love because they prefer joy and bliss to agony, misery, and torment. But it is also when you are consciously walking the way that the heartrose most fragrantly and beautifully blossoms in your heart of hearts.

The mystic's most stunning motive is that she is in Love. A lover needs no other reason than her Love to seek out her beloved, though the beloved be ten thousand miles away. So the mystic needs no other explanation for her long, arduous, often tortuous, journey inward, towards the Beloved.

Access to these fathomless depths is not "normal" or "natural." The Way is supernatural. "Psychonautics," the exploration of inner space, is a Mindspecialty. It requires as much study and training as do other specialties within psychology. And it definitely demands experience. There is no such thing as a mere "bookmystic." The truths of Mind must be learned from Mind, and cannot be found in mere books. Reading about deepsea diving bears no resemblance to taking the plunge. Still, especially for Western people, good reading, cognitive education, can be their very best primary step, or first few steps, to inner gnosis. That is why, in fact, even the most reticent and silent mystics often left written records, reflections, and instructions. A good example is the Taoist sage Lao Tzu, who left behind the classic text of mystical literature called the "Way of Virtue."

But despite the versatility of words, you cannot think your Way to the Coremind. The Core is explored only when It decides to open Itself, and this unfolding cannot be controlled by the conscious mind. When It does open, It calls to the ego. It might audibly call the egoname. Or, It might reveal Itself in a dream, or another altered state. At any rate, the timing all belongs to the Spirit or nuclear Unconscious. The effect of touching It is to be saturated with, and immersed in, sweet tranquil Love.

****

Falling in Love with Your Self
Love and the Inner Beloved

Chapter 5

Surrender to the Sweet Private "Sea" of Mindsource

***

Look into the dazzling brilliance of stars peppered like talc across a black velvet sky. A strange passion stirs in the liquid bottom of your Soul. It is a longing, but vague, indefinable. It is a thirst for eternity. It can become so moving, touching, poignant, and even nostalgic as to bring tears to your eyes.

A Jewish proverb says of God, "He has placed eternity in the heart of man." Mystics say that this sense of *deja vu*, a moving longing for the vastness and beauty of space, is really a disguised call to inner space, and its equal immensities. It is a call to return "Home," back to the inner Source or Beloved. It is not completely satisfied until we complete earth's journey, and leave this planet. It is, then, also a passion to plunge naked into the infinite "darkness" of inner Mind. It expresses a real need to Mindmeld with the deeper Self or Soul.

Like sex, it is an expression of a hunger for a lost wholeness, now little more than amorphous memories on the fringes and periphery of consciousness. All people want this unity with the deepest interior Self because they secretly, again unconsciously, recall a time when it was so. They bring to heartmind a "preseparative" memory of belonging, of infinite comfort, in the midst of immensities. The sweetness of this primal state was indescribably ecstatic. It was permeated with healing stillness, most profound, bottomless, boundless tranquility and light. The Soul was immersed in rapturous Love. Ancient Hebrew mystics called this primal state "Eden," which means "pleasure." Mystics say that the Garden of Pleasure is still accessible in the heartmind.

The ancient "gods," the "people of the stars," taught human beings the art of returning to that lost inner Home. They taught the Way of mysticism. They taught stillness, meditation, listening, silence. If you were silent long enough, patient long enough, your inner Mind would communicate Its great presence. The source of supergalactic forces, It is so tender and tiny that you must still the very whisperings of your own mind even to know that It exists. The Source of a billion billion galaxies, it is as silent and subtle as a butterfly's wing brushing a rose-petal.

This Mind is so subtle because it wills, under normal circumstances, to remain invisible or hidden. But, paradoxically, it also wishes to be known. By most people, however, It does not wish to be seen. Few indeed are aware of even its existence. Fewer still are wise enough, tender enough, loving enough, to bathe in its luminous revelation. For those who are, they are allowed to bask in glory. The inner curtain of *Shekinah* (the feminine aspect of God in Jewish mystical tradition) is torn asunder. Blazing luminescence is revealed.

The allegory of the Hebrew Scriptures says that when Moses saw his god, his face shone as

Falling in Love with Your Self
Love and the Inner Beloved

brightly as the sun until the end of his days. When we are touched by the inner Mind of Love, we also glow. We become autonomous sources of symbolic Light, or Love, in a dark world. We radiate a new Love which is more luminous than galaxies. When exposed directly to the "sun" of Lovemind, we become little "suns" ourselves.

This Love existed before time. So, older Sufi mystics called it "wine before the vine," and "honey before the bee." Its sweet nectar flowed before we existed as Souls, when the one Mind was "One without a second," as our Hindu brothers, the ancient mystics, wrote. Love preexists the cosmos, and spacetime itself.

When one encounters such a gigantic, immense, colossal Force, the only response conceivable becomes surrender. A human mind cannot cohesively exist in the presence of such a tsunamic wave of Love. All that it can do is yield to It. And that is exactly what mystics always do.

But you do not have to wait for the actual experience of touching inner Infinity to surrender. It is good practice, and sensible preparation, to surrender your mind to the higher Power, give It your life-direction, at any time.

Mystics anticipate this need by willingly surrendering, giving themselves completely over, to "possession" by Love. This is no creepy, scary possession as in the movies, but a tranquil movement into invincible serenity and luminous Love.

This possession precipitates a war between the ego, which wants to survive, and the Superconscious. Supermind tells the conscious mind that it cannot serve both ego and Lovenature (the Absolute or Beloved). You cannot serve two masters. A crystalclear decision is demanded. The wise mystic always makes the same decision. She lays her ego upon the altar of Love, burns it in the fire of her Love, offering it as a "sacrifice" to Love. (The word "sacrifice" comes from two Latin words, meaning "to make" and "holy.")

The Way can be scary. It is not for the indecisive or undecided, or for the faint of heart. It is not for the radically mentally disturbed or the emotionally unbalanced. For the Way will call you to give up everything for It— ultimately, sacrificing all personal desires, and, in the end, the very self whom you now believe yourself to be. Love demands every minute of every hour of every day. Love settles for nothing less than sheer worship, for It is God.

When you give everything to the inner Lovenature, you lose nothing. Indeed, you gain everything. While at one time, you considered the egosphere to be so valuable, you now come to see it all as so much garbage. This was the illustration used by the Christian mystic Paul. Giving up everything, including the self, is like trading dust for goldust, or for emeralds, diamonds, rubies, and sapphires. The treasures of the heart which you receive are of enormous beauty and value. the self which you have exchanged is virtually worthless in comparison. So, it is trashed, and to revisit it would be analogous to weeping, or becoming teary-eyed, over garbage. Once you have "escaped" or transcended the egoself, it is regarded without desire, sentimentality, or nostalgia.

Falling in Love with Your Self
Love and the Inner Beloved

There is only an overwhelming sense of relief, as if escaping from a concentration camp or a nightmare.

People often suffer from selfimage problems—low selfesteem. This might well be a reflection of the very real fact that the ego is indeed worthless compared to the Self which anyone can become, and which you know yourself to be. For the spiritual, or inner, Self is of great antiquity, pregnant with immense wisdom and terrific power. It is also an inexhaustible fountain of inner Love.

There is a simple explanation: the Soul is the container of the Spirit, or infinite Mind. The Soul has the Supermind or Superconscious locked deeply within it. As Soul is in mind, so Spirit is in Soul. (See "Chart of Mind.")

Let's review this: Spirit is like a solid ball, surrounded by hollow concentric spheres, a countless number of them. These all represent other layers of Mind. The first few thousand spheres, going out from this solid Center, represent a Mindlevel called the "collective Unconscious." Progressing still further outward from the Center, the next series of thousands of spherelayers represent the level called the "individual Soul." Still further out are the thousands of layers in a Mindlevel called the "personal unconscious." Then, further from the center are thousands of layers in a level called the "preconscious" mind. These layers contain memories easily accessible. Finally, the entire series of spheres is covered with a number of layers that represent the conscious mind. (The ego is a structure or mindconstruct made by the conscious mind.)

This means that infinite Mind thinks and "speaks" through the Soul. the conscious mind can often get in touch with this Soulmind through intuition, but intellect will not take you there. Reading books such as this one is a very good beginning, but they will never take you into the inner "kingdom" of direct experience. Also, the overuse of intellect can actually hamstring and handcuff the wisdom of intuition. If you have a strong feeling, and then, secondguess it, asking," Does this make logical sense?" then intellect is blocking, and can neutralize, intuition. For intuition is not thought, but feeling.

So, there is a mystical saying, "The first thoughts are from God." This is the state of selflove and selftrust which Taoist mystics call "reflection of Tao in instantaneous and spontaneous response." ("Tao" is the great unknown Power which runs the universe. It is the same Superconscious or the deepest unconscious Mind that we are discussing here. It comes from the tradition of Chinese mysticism.)

In the West, in education, we are taught repeatedly, *ad nauseum*, to think things out. Also, we are taught to think about our thinking, and then, to think about our thinking about our thinking. We are educated nearly to death! In fact, the intuition can be "killed" at least temporarily, by too much analysis. We are forced into the harmful suffocating box of "overthink," in which logical, linear, conscious thought is said to be the only job of the heartmind. It is the single and final criterion by which the validity or truth of anything is measured. This lopsided intellect has become a major false "god" in our culture. It is a god that has failed. For it has slaughtered poet and seer, dreamer and artist, sage and mystic.

Please don't misunderstand. Intellect is not a demon or dragon. It is not a satan, the source of all evil. It can be beautiful and productive. It can even serve Love. The present book, for instance, was partly created by use of the intellectual mind. What is recommended here is not the unhealthy extreme of anti-intellectual or antiscientific attitudes. But what is needed is the commonsense realization that intellect cannot solve all our problems— especially those of a deep psychological, emotional, or spiritual nature.

The uses of intellect have made everyone's life much easier and more convenient. This book is being prepared by a computer which is the result of technological development resulting from intellect. But, in our society, we have simply swung too far in the opposite direction. As a culture, we have often, in our history, thought that we could get by without anything spiritual in our lives. This was a popular view, for instance, back in the arrogant nineteen-fifties. The twenty-first century dawns, fortunately, with a new awareness that people cannot live by "bread" alone. In other words, to have a happy, productive life, we require more than material comforts, conveniences, gadgets, and loads of money.

We have, however, educated our children in this false "religion." Then, we are shocked and bewildered when they cannot feel, when they are all head and no heart. Poetry yields to cyberscience, tenderness to analysis, goodness to dissection, Love to sex, and the healthy inner journey to drugs. Spirituality, the only hope of our planet and its people, is demoted and relegated to the land of Oz, to be lost amidst a sea of superstition and ignorance. Even the very word "mysticism" has become so abused that it is, in practical talk, equivalent to "bull." Anything strange, weird, or bizarre is quickly, stupidly labeled "mystical." Even journalists and religious leaders, who should be more educated, abuse the sterling tradition by abusing the word. So, "mysticism" has been stripped of all credibility, all respect. But it still remains our only hope.

We have lost trust of the heart. So we do not love ourselves. That is why we cannot love each other. The infant "Christ" in our hearts has been tossed out with the "bathwater." In seeking to understand the universe, we have been drained of all knowing of its Root and Origin.

****

Falling in Love with Your Self
Love and the Inner Beloved

Chapter 6

Born to Love: Your Simplified Designer Life

***

We have all bought into an outrageous lie. It is so absurd, it is a wonder that anybody has ever fallen for it. But the average person has swallowed it, hook, line, and sinker. The obscene lie is this: All that you need to create a "happy" life is lots of material things and/or money.

But only a cursory examination of history will prove that there is *zero* correlation between material abundance and happiness. So, when Christ said, "Happy are the poor," he was stating a valid psychosocial principle. Many from less affluent backgrounds rate themselves as "happier" than those from the upper crust communities. This bewilders those who have spent their entire lives in the "accumulation game," running as fast as possible on a treadmill to materialism hell. Still, it makes perfect psychospiritual sense: For human beings are far too complex, far too introspective to be satisfied fully by distraction.

And yes, it might as well be said: We are too wise to be completely taken in by the lies of materialism. Human beings are "Lovemachines," designed, created, and born to give and receive Love. Anything less is just a Love-substitute. So, money, business, politics, home, career, sports, shopping, religion, design, and a dozen other distractions of society cannot provide real fulfillment. Why? Because they are nothing but unsatisfactory Love-substitutes. They are not Love. There is a "Love-shaped hole" in the center of every psyche, and nothing will fit, or fill, that hole of emptiness and hollowness but the real thing— genuine Love.

The deepest Mind, ensconced way down, below the darkness, in the most profound cave of the Unconscious, is perfect wisdom, compassion, and Love. We are born, and exist, to learn to leap, with closed eyes and thudding heart, into the black abyss of this unknown, barely explored Lovenature. (Lovenature is Coremind, the Superconscious, and the Absolute. It is also the inner Beloved. It envelops the Mindlevel called the Creator/Dreamer.)

We were born from and for Love. To become Love is why you exist. It is out of loyal Love for you that the Spirit, from the Mindlevel called the "Creator/Dreamer," dreams up every microdetail in your life. Not the tiniest ameba, the smallest flea, comes into your life (Mindfield or perceptionsphere) by chance. The Soulmind has a good reason for dreaming up anything or anyone in your personal world. Any factor enters your "experiential cosmos" for the purpose of drawing you into the Ultimate (Coremind, Lovemind, or Lovegod).

But if life is dreamed up by Love, why do we suffer so much, and so often? Why is so much of life tormenting hell, even in micromatters? For example, why do we suffer from generic aches and pains? Why disease? Why poverty? Why are young kids molested? Why are people tortured and killed? Why is loneliness the

Falling in Love with Your Self
Love and the Inner Beloved

"hell" of many? Why are there so many relationship disasters? Why is there so much agony and ruin everywhere?

The mystic sees even these horrors and catastrophes as serving a higher purpose. They might be signals to change something about your lifedesign. They might call you to alter your attitudes. They might also occur in order to provide you with strength, patience, or compassion. Although we can't explain immediately why every pain, loss, tragedy, or disappointment occurs, we can, say mystics, rest solidly assured that **nothing in the dream is merely random**.

The great Dreamer, Who dreams through my mind and yours, never dreams even a microparticle without purpose. In the golden tapestry of the great Plan, every thread, and every particle of color, has its purpose and place. *Everything has meaning.*

So, every event, person, situation, and object exists in your life due to the will of this inner Mind. Why is your life such a hodge-podge of multiplicity? Why do so many things happen to you? Why is there so much diversity and variety in your life? Why so much stuff? Why does your life look like a garage-sale in a lunatic asylum?

All your interactions are designed to teach you the fine art of loving in living. Your life is filled with such a complex megaplethora because a good lifetest must involve many shifting variables. You can't "graduate" from the earthschool until you have familiarized yourself with a vast diversity of situations and human patterns of response. And this is so, even though, from a galactic view, earth is only a "kindergarten" planet.

Richard Shiningthunder Francis

Most Americans are being taught by Spirit, for example, that they simply do not need all the "stuff" that they collect. Most "stuff" is unnecessary. This is why mystics always lived at what might be called a "minimalist" level of economic and material sufficiency. True mystics were never world-hating fanatics or ascetics, and most rejected the extreme of poverty. This they did for the same reason that they turned away from wealth: Both were distractions from the study of psychonautics.

What is suggested for the modern mystic is nowhere nearly so dreadfully radical as literal poverty. Suffering and deprivation do *not* bring you any closer to the inner Beloved. So, we can afford to dismiss and neglect the eccentricities of extremists/fanatics who practiced any form of asceticism, or voluntary discomfort. Voluntary poverty, of the Franciscan variety, can be very harmful despite good intentions. Some, but not all, mystics opt for voluntary minimalism. But I have an even better suggestion. Try it; you'll like it. It is called voluntary simplicity.

You will not find the balanced, reasonable mystic practicing selfabuse, cruel selfdenial, selfdeprivation, or any form of selfcreated pain. She loves herself too much. But you also will not find the mystic in a palatial house, or a mansion. You will find her in a smaller home, a cabin, bungalow, or cottage. Inside that home, you might find many things of beauty. But nowhere will you find ten-thousand-dollar works of art or pieces of furniture. Nowhere will you discover things purchased out of a sense of inner emptiness, in attempts to impress others. The mystic is

Falling in Love with Your Self
Love and the Inner Beloved

much too secure to play those hurtful games and indulge in such selfishness. As a general rule (mystics do not make "thou shalts" for other mystics), the ecoconscious mystic will minimize her use of nonrenewable resources. But even in this, she will avoid fanaticism, and stick to the "middle path" of moderation and reasonableness.

Simplicity is a few notches above minimalism, because it accepts the actual necessity of things of beauty and comfort. But it does draw the line at obsessive accumulating. The entire goal of mysticism and simplicity is to shatter the shackles of relentless control by the material world. So the "grab it all" attitude so common in society is refused. So are the "more is better, bigger is better, and newer is better" assumptions of this culture. The mystic actively rejects the, "I've got mine; to hell with everyone else" attitude. These views only spread the lethal virus of greed.

Most people who are rich sense intuitively, for the inner Mind keeps telling them, that they are selfishly using up too many of earth's nonrenewable resources. That is why most wealthy people feel a profound guilt, often deliberately hidden from their own awareness, and from the public. They know, deeply unconsciously, that all people in the world must draw from a common, and limited, pool of resources. So, everything that they appropriate for selfish use is torn away from the hand or home of another. For example, insensitive American carnivores are literally taking grain out of the mouths of babes so that those meateaters can have their burgers and bacon. (And even this is killing them, from inside.) This guilt keeps them in inner "hell." But how does eating meat harm people, as well as animals? It is because ninety percent of all American grain goes to feed animals for slaughter. If that grain were sent to hungry human beings, there would not be a hungry person on our planet. As it is, however, forty thousand kids drop dead every day from starvation.

The balanced and wise person never says that anything is "bad" or "evil" simply because it is material. Infinite Mind, as Love, fills the world with forests, butterflies, rainbows, waterfalls, crystals, and human bodies— all material things. But no material thing can ever become the master of the free person. She will not, refuses to, sell her Soul, or any part of it. She will not prostitute time spent in spirituality for money.

The "almighty dollar" will never be her god. So, there is a freedom about the mystic not enjoyed by the average person. She soars without fears and material concerns into the vast blue skies of inner Mind. She can afford to live without worry, because she lives so simply. She does not allow herself to accumulate great and burdensome debts. She might purchase items of beauty, but refuses those that are too expensive. She does this out of compassion, for almost everyone on our planet is in need of money. And she would much rather give to charity, or to a poor, needy, or sick friend, than to spend the money on expensive and useless selfindulgences.

This is also why she insists, unbendingly and uncompromisingly, on a simple house and car, simple clothing, and simple jewelry. No mystic will ever indulge in complacent and

insensitive selfindulgence, shamelessly and ostentatiously spending her money. *Mystics are never "conspicuous consumers."* For every dollar is capable of being pressed
into the service of Love.

She also uses credit moderately and carefully. She assiduously avoids all luxury, although she believes in comfort (a form of selflove). The mystic uses her conscious mind to dance in harmony with the Creatormind. She loves the smooth, soothing dance in which she flows with her inner Beloved.

But although her inner Mind is a Fountain of compassion, tranquility, and joy, the mystic endures her fair share of discomfort. For she has visited this world to perfect her inner Lovenature, and she knows it. In this mission, she is no different from anyone else. But what makes her different is that she knows why she suffers, understands the meaning of pain. Garden-variety pain and suffering form the inner state called "hell." But when you begin to understand the reasons for pain and loss, and embrace them, you move from "hell" to a better state, called "purgatory." The pain still feels the same, but *now you understand its meaning.* (That is why "purgatory" comes from a root meaning "to purify.")

Without exactly the kind of suffering, pain, or loss that you are now enduring, your Loveducation would be filled with huge gaps. Even major sorrow-events are "predestined," structured, or "programmed" into your life by the Soulevel of Mind, before birth. The Soul has such enormous datassimilation and dataprocessing capabilities that it is capable of modifying the genome at a molecular level.

Since the genome is the source of all genetics, it can significantly prestructure much in both body and mind. This influence arises from the Creatorlevel of Mind, working through the lens of the Soulevel. (See "Chart of Mind.")   Historically, mystical realization that life is shifted and shuffled by a higher Power caused philosophers called "Stoics" to embrace an extremist view. Like the "Vulcans" of "star Trek," they were determined completely to destroy, or never to permit, any natural emotional responses. Everything represented the unalterable will of the "gods," and to resist the irresistible divine will was just nonsense.

Their only "appropriate" response was irresponsibity. They wanted to cooperate with the mysterious forces or "gods" that ruled life with an iron hand. Unconsciously seeking mystical freedom, they refused to respond to anything. While this made emotional zombies or "dead people" out of them, they were unconsciously seeking the more moderate Way of the mystic.

The mystic never goes this far. Still, her more violent and volatile responses to change are muted by her knowing of, and trusting, the inner Creatormind. She does not behave like a block of wood, without feeling-responses; but she seeks the kind of peace called "equanimity." As the word itself implies, this means an "equal" response, one of detached serenity— to either "good" or "bad" events.

She struggles to cultivate an "allembracing Mind," to borrow from the Buddha. This is to grow to see all events, situations, and things as "absolutely" good. She knows that the Mind

Falling in Love with Your Self
Love and the Inner Beloved

of Soul/Spirit always has her best interests at heart, even when her ego wants only to scream, kick, or bitch. Every moment of every day is an opportunity to perfect the art of loving in living.

When the clerk or waitress is rude, there's your chance. When she is polite, another chance has come. Now, you can exercise a different type, or powerlevel, of Love. When your spouse is in a bad mood, that's your chance. When he/she is in a good mood, there's another chance! When you're feeling sick, it is a lesson. When you're feeling great, it's a new occasion to Love even more. When someone says, "I love you," your chosen response is that very education in action. So is your response when someone says, "I hate you."

Mystics turn their focused attention, like a bright spotlight, to this Love. They think about It all the time. So, they try never to get caught offguard. With any other target, the term "healthy obsession" would be an oxymoron. But they are in love with Love. Love is their admitted, and magnificent, obsession. Life is a continual Lovedance between them and the environment.

****

Chapter 7

Moving Closer to My Lord: Bliss Amplified, Judgment Deactivated

* * *

Shoot the arrows of Love. Your own heart is the first target. This wound means ultimate "death," but begins the brightest new life. It is a rebirth, into a new inner world of wonder and beauty. But because it means letting go often of your whole self (as known in the past), it terrifies the ego. For it is this ego that must die when the lightning-bolt of Love strikes. This blasts from infinite Mind or "heaven," at the Core of the unconscious Mind.

Arrows are directed energy. Love yokes to intent, and finds its target. But Love must not remain a simple and beautiful ideal in the heart. It must touch others. So, it leaves its comfortable interior chamber, and ventures forth into an unknown world, driven by an irresistible urge. Love flashes, lighting up the psyche and cosmos with service and friendship.

Life is tough. No big surprise there. But the life of Love can be even more mindstressing and heartwrenching. For, added to the plethora of daily hassles, headaches, and heartaches, is the Mind's dare and demand: Learn to "embrace" everything. This radical, topsy-turvy transmutation from "Love" as interior feeling to energized action does not

Falling in Love with Your Self
Love and the Inner Beloved

dawn overnight. We must take one "baby step" at a time.

But how can anyone "love" such a world of "ugliness and evil"? Ahh, there's the rub. That's part of the secret. It's called "nonjudgment." A thing or person becomes ugly or evil only if and when you agree to label her/it so. This does not imply that all evil is relative, but it does teach that the inner labelmaker can alter the quality of your experiences. For it is possible for you to take your label seriously, mistaking it for "truth," and, behold! The person or thing actually seems to mutate into a repellant factor in your life.

This "duality," or splitting, chops up the smooth Flow, the seamless wholeness, of your Mind and life. So, here's the most immense and taxing dare/demand of mysticism: Stop judging. Stop insisting on fragmenting the inner self with easy but false inner labels. These create inner chaos through polarity and duality, opposites stressing and conflicting.

The Creatormind, which dreams up the world, is perfect. So, this world must also reflect that Mind— must be stainless, flawless, pristine, without contamination, pollution, or impurity.

This is the total opposite of everything that commonsense tells us. So, the Way challenges you to redefine everything. Focus intense intent on any object, situation, event, or person that you have ever considered "bad" and/or "ugly." For it is possible, with much effort, for you to come to see them as "good and beautiful."

The mystic is not transformed into a mindless zombie or hopelessly idealistic

Pollyanna. She is sharply cognizant that certain behaviors, words, attitudes, and actions are harmful, and so "bad." She does not deny or abandon morality or ethics. Nor does she slide carelessly onto the slippery slope of moral relativism, deciding that all morality/ethics is only a notion, subjective and relative. Wisdom does not make her a pastel tower of gelatin. She does not become morally weak, apathetic, complacent, or neutral. Her ethical standards do not dissolve into a monochromatic gray neutrality. Impeccable honor continues to be her elevated, noble moral barometer, and there is none higher.

Does the desertion of "judgment" mean, then, that the mystic has no common sense? Anyone who labels war, torture, childabuse, spouse-abuse, murder, rape, etc., as "good" has to be a severe lunatic, out of her freaking mind. This is not only selfevident, but it is also quite true. What rescues the mystic from this stupid, immoral equivocation is that, although she no longer practices "judgment," she has not at all relinquished discernment or discrimination.

"Judgment" is the act of labeling anything or anyone as *absolutely* evil. The mystic knows that absolute evil is an illusion. The Mind of Love, at the Center of her own mind, has no real opposite. So, nothing is truly, absolutely, irretrievably, irreversibly, or irredeemably evil. So is judgment abandoned. But certain actions (rape, torture) and ideas (bigotry, violence) are evil. The mystic more fully recognizes this than does even the average person. This is discrimination or discernment, and it is vital for the balanced, truth-full spiritual life.

The Way of impeccable honor means not simply being good, but attempting always to imitate perfect, stainless Love, approximating It. This is nothing less than a reaching for perfection. So, the mystic takes care always to go the extra mile. The mystic follows Lao Tzu: "I am good to those who are good. I am also good to those who are not good." She follows Jesus: "Return not evil for evil." "Resist not evil." "Love your enemies." "If someone strikes you on the right cheek, turn to him the left also." "Pray for those who hate you, and bitterly use you."

A mystic seeks to reflect perfect Love in every word and act. She knows better than to demand perfection. She is no perfectionist. For perfectionism is the enemy of perfection. Perfectionism is spiritual pathology. But the inner vision of "perfect Love" remains her standard and goal. Her criteria of goodness are, in morality and ethics, much higher than those of the average person. Finding an item of small value, she will seek its owner. Being undercharged at a store, she will tell the clerk. Finding a wallet with a thousand dollars in it, she will return it intact. She will not bring home every stray dog or cat that crosses her path, but never will she do anything to harm, and will always do as much as is feasible to aid every living creature.

She is not only **not** dishonest. She follows a Buddhist precept called *ahimsa*. This means "noninjury," and so, the mystic will honestly seek to live so as to harm no living creature deliberately and unnecessarily. She harms no one physically, mentally, emotionally, or spiritually. This is comparable to the physician's vow to "do no harm."

She does not play dice with people's hearts, and this keeps her sexually and emotionally faithful and monogamous. She is ecologically conscious and conscientious.

Mystics are vegetarians, not only for health-reasons (which are many), but also as an act of compassion for starving human beings. A full ninety percent of all grain grown in this country goes to feed animals, so that we can have our burgers and bacon.

If that grain went instead into human mouths, there would be no hunger-crisis on our planet. As it is, forty thousand kids drop dead every day from starvation. Since this is a totally preventable crisis, eating red meat can be viewed as immensely insensitive, and an anti-life behavior.

So, noninjury guides not only what you do, but also what you refuse to do.

****

There is no "small" act of Love.

****

So, the mystic is careful to love even in the details of her life. She is a friendly and courteous driver, says hi to her neighbors, and performs errands for elderly and sick people whenever possible. She calls people on the phone to ask after their health and happiness. She uses email and regular mail to bless and support people, sending Love to all. She visits those in need, and uses money to aid the poor, either personally or through formal charities.

Kindness, morality, and ethics are of supreme importance to her because they manifest Love. And she seeks to become a pure undefiled mirror of pristine Love. So, she is a being of sterling character and absolute honesty.

How can such a tender being, so filled with Love and care, deny the existence of evil?

She doesn't. She has no desire to "play Cleopatra," as "queen of denial." She is not so blind as not to be able to see evil all around her. Ugliness is, in the same way, everywhere. But she knows this great secret: Good, like beauty, is in the Mind of the beholder. When ever she labels any event, situation, or environment as "good," it becomes good for her. When she labels anything "beautiful"— including the poor maligned spiders and snakes— it becomes so for her.

But how the hell could anyone with half a brain, or a drop of sanity, accept as "good" the hideous nightmares and ghastly horrors of earthly life? This is impossible unless you understand karma. For to see life accurately, you must find more than an egoperspective. You must struggle to know the cosmic view.

Karma is an expression of ghastly ignorance and stupidity. It is a hideous nightmare. In final analysis, it is illusion, the expression of dream. So, the mystic seeks to live in a Way that can stop the mad wheel of karma, a wheel, as the early Christian writer James says, that is "set aflame by hell." To do this, she must microscopically avoid ignorance, or "sin." But, despite its heinous and frightening visage, the law of karma does serve Love, for it manifests justice. There is, in fact, no other explanation of evil that even comes close. Karma is comprehensive and consistent. Among all philosophies, it makes some reasonable sense of suffering. And it alone demonstrates how pain and loss educate the Soul, thus, serving Love.

According to karma, **every** event is designed to teach some Soul something about Love. Also, **any** event that serves Love must, at its core, be good. So, even living in a cosmos filled with every form of horror, the mystic can see the goodness at the center of everything. She learns always to embrace the good at the center of "evil," that greater good of which "evil" is the servant. Even in great hurricanic storms of evil, then, she finds tranquility.

****

The mystic does not love the bad, but learns to love the good hidden within the bad.

****

She lives in the same exact universe that you and I live in. She does not practice evasion, avoidance, or denial. But she has managed to come to see everything as **ultimately** good— even though everything is clearly not immediately good. She realistically recognizes that some behaviors are truly "evil" in the shorterm and relative world, and meticulously avoids them, as they lead to inner "hell." She not only avoids all violence and bigotry herself, but tries to educate others, her friends, to leave those hellpaths. For

****

Anyone practicing evil is headed for hell.

****

Of course, she does not buy into the horrible psychotic superstition that "hell" is some lunatic barbecue-orgy where a god roasts and toasts his children, while laughing in schizophrenic delight. No, her God is too sane, and her universe too stable, to permit this kind of nonsense and monstrous horror. Her cosmos is ruled by Love. Instead, she realizes the very great truth that

****

Heaven and hell exist within the Mind, and on earth.

****

Not that she denies the afterlife, for she embraces it with Love. Some mystics even happily anticipated their physical deaths.[3] "Heaven" and "hell" might well represent conditions that do **not** end at death. But she does know for certain that people will have to pay for deliberate evil by having the "fire" of hell created in their minds. There are two reasons why this kind of hell would be the best for education: 1) There's nowhere to go to run from your own mind, for, wherever you go, there you are. 2) Internally generated pain is the most exquisite agony imaginable—much more painful than pain from any outside source. Being inside, it also helps to teach people pain-neutralization.

This is **not** the mystic's reason for avoiding evil. She is haunted by no fear of everlasting life in a pressurecooker. She avoids evil because she loves its opposite, the good. She knows that this helps her to create a state of inner "heaven," for

****

A practical definition of "inner heaven" is being surrounded by things that you like, or love.

****

Now, you can see how "heaven" ties in with embracing all the world as "good," without judgment. For it also is true that

---

3. For a fictional representation of the new "universe" that one enters after death, see my Luminous Ecstasies and Passions: Journeys Into Afterlife (Liberty Township, Ohio; Love Ministries, Inc., 2000)

****

A practical definition of "inner hell" is being surrounded by things that you dislike, or hate.

****

Falling in Love with Your Self
Love and the Inner Beloved

So, whether you live in an inner "heaven" or "hell" depends entirely upon your choices. When you decide to like, love, or embrace anything or anyone, exactly as she/it is, you move your psyche closer to a state of inner delight, joy, celebration, or "heaven." Whenever you decide that anything or anyone is evil or ugly (undesirable), you move yourself closer to a state of pain, misery, or frustration, an "inner hell."

So, the Way to heaven on earth is clear. It is not easy to apply or implement, but once you understand it, at least, you know where you want to go. And that is half the battle.

****

Chapter 8

Caterpillar to Butterfly:
From Monstergod to Bliss

* * *

Constantly bombarded by thoughts striking the heartmind like relentless hailstones, we endlessly hear the rounds of social and cultural programming: "Money is crucial." "Success is measured by money." "You are worth no more than your bankaccount." "People must be impressed, so you must play their games."
  And while we knock ourselves out trying to fit in with these crazy and dark criteria, our lives biodegrade, unravel, fall apart, disintegrate. Our families become strangers, and our friends mistrusted competitors. We grow to loathe ourselves as mere mechanical moneymaking machines. We might be running as fast as we can, but we can't help but suspect that we are on a stationary treadmill, going nowhere "fast." We are left with fistfuls of dollars and hearts full of emptiness. While we were serving the neon god, we lost touch with our kids, our spouses, our friends, and our selves. So, we end up in a psychiatrist's office, spending our gods of gold at the rate of a couple of hundred bucks an hour. We pay strangers to listen to us, as we have literally sold out our friends to that same demon of gold. Or else, we end up on a ledge.
  We, as a culture, are rushing at warpspeed towards the annihilation in the center of the

Falling in Love with Your Self
Love and the Inner Beloved

biggest blackhole in the galaxy. It is that greatest of illusions, the void of materialism/sensuality. These two false gods offer everything, but deliver absolutely zero. So, both are energy-sucking inner "blackholes." Serving them is the termination of tranquility.

To regain inner peace, we must turn the spotlight of Mind inward, away from the glitz and glitter of glamour. We must transfer from Las Vegas to Assisi. We must learn to listen to our hearts again. We must, in short, find our way back to spirituality. We must trace the path back to the garden of pleasure in the heart. We are being called back to Love.

Thoughts of exclusive materiality and sensuality, repeated incessantly for centuries, have created what are called "thoughtforms" in the collective unconscious. These are autonomous constructs that have a life of their own. That is, they are very powerful, selfsustaining thoughts that can "float up" from the depths of deep Mind to influence your thoughts. Paradigms, as in science, are created by very strong, durable thoughtforms. They contain enormous energy, and are quite difficult to resist. The thoughtforms of the material/sensual paradigm are by now so powerful that they form automatic thoughts and responses in the average person. If we just let go and relax into its flow, we can be carried away by its strong currents. But blessedly, there exists an even more powerful Reality, deeper in origin. This is the liberating, refreshing Spirit. It is the illimitable, immeasurable ocean of Love in the Center of being, of which we all partake, and in which we all live and move.

This Lovecenter is even more powerful than those collections of thoughtforms that create paradigms. For while they are created and sustained by regular human concentration, thoughtfeeling, and belief, the Lovemind is the Origin or Source of all Mind. It exists prior to and independent of any thought or mind. It alone is Reality, while the paradigms are little more than interpretative schemes. In other words, Mind is more real than matter. The material world is rushing to become dust, through biodegradation. But Mind, and its progeny, thoughtfeelings, are forever. Mind, at its Core, Lovemind, is forever and indestructible.

Still, a mystic must swim tirelessly against a mighty and vast current of thought in the unconscious Mind. But she can still win, as a "majority of one," for she has the infinite Mind on her side. This Superconscious has synergized Its awesome power with hers, due to her Love. Also, when she gives herself over to It, she becomes so transparent that Its power can "shine" through her unimpeded, like sunlight through a clear crystal. This is the perfect state of Flow and Love which I call "crystalmind." So, through Love, in essence, Its infinite force becomes hers. That is the secret to mystical invincibility.

Mystics don't really live in this world. Actually, nobody else does either. We're all just visitors, just tourists, just passing through. More literally, we are all phantoms inhabiting a phantomworld, dreamers in a dreamworld. What marks the mystic as unique is that she squarely faces this fact, rather than denying or evading it, as so many do. She is fully aware that she is a stranger in a strange land. She is an alien.

In our society, we are taught the sick obsessions of materialism and sensuality. The perfect life is to be surrounded by material comforts and luxuries, while creating repeated and maximum sexual and sensual stimulation. It is in quest of this ultimate "high" that people regularly overindulge in food— creating not bliss, but miserable obesity. Their "hunger" is metaphoric; what they really hunger for is spirituality or Love, not the pale, feeble counterfeits of food or sex. But we are taught another lie: Suffering is somehow "wrong" or "unnatural," and it should be completely avoided **at all costs.** It should also be eliminated asap.

This latter is a good, stable guide, and amplifies compassion. The mystic does indeed seek to alleviate suffering asap in the lives of others. But in her own life, she tries to find its meaning, tries to welcome and embrace it. This is how she overcomes its draining power. Mystics, speaking of suffering as "good," are often crucified, or driven out of town. They seem to be really dangerous lunatics.

Western religion can imply that suffering is "punishment from a god." Recall that the god commonly worshipped in the average church **is** a schizophrenic. He (always male) is psychotic, dangerous, ferocious, unforgiving. This is a godimage inherited from very ancient tribal sources.

The primitive tribes needed a wargod. Oddly, due to their geography, their old wargod became enmeshed, conjoined, and hopelessly entangled and interwoven with the God of love, light, peace, and forgiveness. In time, the two gods became fused, through many historical confusions, misinterpretations, blunders, and crafty manipulations. This confusion led to a kind of madness that produced a monstrous hybridgod that is still worshipped in the average church today. This is a contrived and artificial godimage, and the source of Babelian confusion.*

This god, always male, does not permit suffering so that his children can learn, progress, and grow. He uses pain to torture and punish his children. This mad caricature-god is the manager of hell, although he "allows Satan" to do his actual dirty work. This god is a bizarre monster, and makes the silliest binladen2 looks friendly by comparison.

This god is at least as schizophrenic as any Jeffrey Daumer or Ted Bundy. But, unlike these severely disturbed criminals, this ultrapsychotic has all the power of the universe at his immediate disposal.

Worshipping a god this crazy tends to drive his followers crazy too. So, they can, at times, lose all reason. They cannot even see,

---

3. The word "binladen" is here not capitalized because it is suggested as a common noun, roughly synonymous with "loser," but containing also implications of deeper stupidity and cruelty. A binladen cares nothing about the feelings of others, is totally egocentric, and uses gruesome, ghastly, nightmarish techniques, when convenient, to make a point. A binladen is a social misfit, an extremist, who lacks all graces, skills, and talents. For more on Godimage, see my *Jehovah Goodbye: the "New Theism" of Love* (Liberty Township, Ohio; Love Ministries, Inc., 1999)

Falling in Love with Your Self
Love and the Inner Beloved

or understand, just how stupid this kind of worship really is. With the tiniest touch of objectivity, or even sanity, the ridiculosity of this religion would be obvious to the average five-year-old. So, the worship of the monstergod creates a form of mental blindness. It also creates a "bizarro world." Everything is upside-down and backwards. Nuclear war can be presented as "good," while ecology, brother/sisterhood, and interfaith are "evil" and "satanic."

So, if these fundamentalist jehovists see suffering as "bad," that in itself might be reason enough to consider seriously whether it might not be good. Or, at least, we can see whether it is ever productive of good, or has any good in it.

Amazingly, a close, objective analysis proves that it does indeed both contain and produce good. When seen as lesson, not cruel or psychotic punishment, it becomes clear that suffering can produce sympathy. In time, this can evolve into the deeper empathy. With more time, this can evolve into actual Love.

Now, nothing bad can produce the ultimate good. So, this is how suffering can be redeemed. When we understand that Mind can use even suffering in the service of Love, we can see the spark of light in the dark cave, the shine of diamond in the mud.

To uncover the deeper Self, suffering can be a valuable tool, indispensable for fullest compassion. Mystics don't see it as a nemesis. Instead, they regard it as a teacher, and so, as a potential friend. They don't selfabuse, or ascetically selfdeprive. "They love themselves, but they must also learn to live in a world full of pain and loss, and so, must make some sense of it all. This is no easy task, and it is not fit for "kindergarten" mentality.

But this does not imply mental illness, or masochism. Out of Love for themselves, mystics are never extremists or ascetics. It follows that they are not masochists, out of respect for their sacred bodies (as "temples"). So, mystics don't demand that their lovers tie them down, screaming, "Beat me!" They don't actively seek pain, feeling that it "hurts so good." They must make sense of pain found everywhere. They do believe pain to be educational. But they will, and do, not actively create pain deliberately. They know that pain, coming from the cosmos (cosmic Unconscious) can be therapeutic, but they refuse ever to be the source of that pain.

Love moves them to comfort, to reduce and alleviate pain whenever and however possible. It is an aspect of their vow of *ahimsa,* or harmlessness. (Remember the "do no harm" vow discussed earlier.) People who get off on, or enjoy, pain are screwed up.

Mystics are realistic, recognizing that pain does exist. But they insist that it must somehow serve the Mind that creates it. Since the world is dreamed (created) by a very deep Mind, at the Coremindlevel, pain must serve the Creatormind. Since the Coremind, of which the Creator/Dreamer is a subset, is Love, pain must serve Love. But mystics don't actively seek sources of voluntary pain. A mystic will never sleep on a bed of nails. Mystics don't freeze their bodies in snowbanks, or fry them under the desertsun. They don't starve themselves. They don't add to the pain in the cosmos. But they do seek realistically to adapt to, and explain, all the pain that they find already in the world.

The mystic always follows the "centrist" path, that of moderation. So, she avoids all extremes. Mystics love also their own bodies, and to seek pain would be to betray and violate this principle. So, historical ascetics who selfabused were not true mystics. Even those who happened to touch mystical states were not true mystics, not followers of the cosmic Way. Real mystics can be easily identified, and separated from a wide spectrum of fanatics in history, because mystics lived lives of balance and moderation. For one example, mystics were never "flagellates," people who strike themselves with whips to keep their "lower nature" in line.

The mystic is not inverted, believing that pain is pleasure, and pleasure pain. But she does not draw her highest pleasure, or bliss, from "material and external" situations, things, or people. This is why she is the freest of all beings in the universe. She can have more fun by herself than with a group, or with the proverbial barrel of simians!

****

Richard Shiningthunder Francis

Chapter 9

Human Destiny: Masters of the Universe

* * *

Suffering— we all will face this demondragon in the back alleys of the mind. Even if you are no aspiring mystic, you must make some sense of this mystery, or else, your sanity might be quite precarious and tenuous. You teeter on the thin edge of madness if you don't grab this one by the horns and wrestle it to the ground. Stable, reliable sanity arrives only to the person in whom the light of understanding dawns.

Still, you can't get aboard the "innerspace shuttle" for selfish reasons. You cannot pull truth from the cosmos simply to retain your sanity. (It can be like extracting the teeth of an alligator.) You must come to the heartlibrary of spirituality for selfless reasons, for the good of all. For the inner Mindmine will not easily yield its rubies, emeralds, diamonds, and sapphires— and never to the casual tourist or curious sightseer. But staying sane might impel you to the portals of inner Love. But you are not motivated at first by Love. This inward journey is begun, the inner galaxy explored, because Something deep inside pushes and drives you. This inner motivating force demands to be acknowledged, like hunger, thirst, sexuality, and other drives. It will not allow you to ignore it.

Falling in Love with Your Self
Love and the Inner Beloved

Many people do try. They glut their days and nights, every waking moment, with Love-substitutes, such as sports, entertainment, career, shopping, money, business, intellect, religion, politics, etc. They behave as if they are trying like mad to avoid something. They are. But in the longterm, spirituality (Love) is inignorable. Nowhere in the cosmos can you go to escape your own mind, and that is where this hunger, and its demands for satisfaction, dwell.

Suffering can trigger your active response to this call to create, or to discover, something spiritual (real) in your own life. "Until my daughter almost lost her life," says Mark, a teacher from Illinois, "I never had a spiritual thought cross my mind. That was a wake-up call." This kind of comment is common.

The world contains most hideous nightmares in almost every life. But the world, despite its hideous moments, is too fascinating, too compelling, simply to ignore. It promises too much. It delivers momentary jolts of joy. It is hypnotically captivating. Most of us have enjoyed at least brief tastes of the way things could be. If only they were, we say with a wistful sigh.

But mystics have made a dramatic, remarkable discovery about how to have a good time. They have found that, despite our ignorant claims to the contrary, really, really good times are not actually *created* (although they might be supported) by the world. *Good times happen inside your head*. Anyone who has ever done a good psychotropic will verify this fact.

But mystics go even a step further into this deep, dark mystery. They claim that good times happen *only* within the mind. As in the old song about New York, if you can make it there, in your mind, you can make it anywhere! Astonishingly, the most crucial environment in the universe is completely ignored in all of our quests to find happiness and satisfaction. We continue to insist, in dullest and densest responses, that the "right" job, school, car, home, or other possession or achievement will somehow "create" happiness in our minds. *But the outer cannot affect the inner.* The outer world lacks the power to change the inner Mind, for it was not designed to do so.

Rockstars and other famous, wealthy types often find this out too late. Having glutted themselves shamelessly with all the money, sex, food, fame, crowds, and spotlights, they are dumbfounded and aghast to discover that they are not "happy." Happiness is exactly as elusive as it was before their "success." And no matter how diversified their portfolios, no matter how gigantic their bankaccounts, happiness is not increased by a single micropsychon.

When, at last, they finally figure out that happiness is an inside-job, that it is something that you do inside your head, they try that with disastrous results. For quite often, being smacked in the face with the utter disappointment of the lies of materialism, they plunge headlong into destructive drugs. And from that hell they cannot always be rescued. Putting the horse before the cart, we need to stop filling ourselves with the disillusioning and despairing lie that contentment is a matter of "having the right stuff." We need to begin to

Falling in Love with Your Self
Love and the Inner Beloved

invest in the only real Source, the Fountain of all joy and satisfaction— Love.

The glittering world will capture the mind with all its kaleidoscopic beauty, wonder, and complexity. The danger is not that the world is "evil." Many extremists have made this mistake in history. The real problem is the "destruction of distraction." The Mindworld (dreamworld) all around us is filled with thousands of entrancing toys and interpersonal "games." If these are allowed to burn up every minute of every day, you simply don't have time for the pursuit of Reality (truth). So, your life is spent chasing after hollow illusions. The psyche is paralyzed, not by evil, but by simple distraction.

Like most, you probably wanted to "do spirituality" when you got around to it. It was always on the back burner or back shelf, as if it were an optional hobby. Most of us realize much too late— not a few, just before death— that spirituality was not life's "desert," but was the "main course." How we failed to recognize this fact baffles and bewilders us, until we finally realize that it is a matter of priority, just like every other important facet of your life.

The timenergy to "do something spiritual" with your life is not just going to, poof! Appear in the center of your life through the fiat or whim of a genie, as if by magic. No, spirituality is just like any other pursuit. If you are going to get anything out of it, you are going to have to put something in. As with the "gigo" (garbage in, garbage out) of computerprogramming, spirituality will give you its best only when and if you give to it your quality time. You must carve out blocks of time for meditation, introspection, and the work of compassion. That requires effort. And "leftover" time— often an illusion— does not count!

No realistic person expects economic or romantic success to drop out of the clouds into her lap. She knows that these areas of her life will require much timenergy investment. And getting back rewards, she is happy to make them Priority One during different phases of her life. Spirituality has no immediate visible, impressive material returns. Spirituality will not make you rich, and it will not make you famous. But its reward is not at all dispensable or ignorable because of this. For its reward, its payback, is sanity. It also grants other jewels: good friendships of reliable, mature people, and good, solid, strong Love-relationships.

The infinity of themes in the "external, material" world makes it a psychic smorgasbord. It holds the mind riveted to its complex plots and storylines. This can go on for centuries. As a dreamer, you can be so compelled by the hypnotic dream that you forget completely that you are dreaming. Then, you become lost in the images and mazes of this a-mazing and spellbinding dreamscape.

You are predestined to a spiritual life. At the Soulevel of Mind, you have a contract with the Spiritlevel (See "Chart of Mind.") The spiritual life was your destination when first you set foot on the "journey towards the outer world." When this journey reverses, becoming an inner trip back to the inner Sourcemind, your destination becomes your destiny. Your goal is to Mindmeld, to fuse or merge with the Spiritlevel of Mind. (This is Coremind,

Falling in Love with Your Self
Love and the Inner Beloved

Supermind, or Absolute.). You are fated to become Love incarnate. So the mystics say that

****

Every human being is God loving Him/Herself.

****

But people are much too busy to notice. In the everyday world, Love is invisible. Even scarier, It is irrelevant. What does "Love" have to do with practical pursuits such as business? And in far too many cases even of romantic Love, the question of the old song reverberates: "What's Love got to do with it?" We are gradually, eerily, creepily growing into a dead and Loveless society. This kind of society can give no inner nourishment. So, some of the smartest, most creative members are dying inwardly. The greatest disease of our time, the most deadly, might not be aids, in retrospect. It might be anagapognosis— the disappearance of common Love.

Love is so subtle that it seems weak, or even powerless. In the order of the business or busy world, it has a low priority. Yet it is the core and foundation of psychological wellness and wellbeing. It is of crucial importance, and we ignore it at our own peril. It should be first, not last, on our prioritylist.

From mysticism's view, the ego, Mary Smith or John Jones, is a pool within the sea of the conscious mind. The conscious mind communicates with the preconscious, and that blends with the personal unconscious, which flows, very deeply, into the vaster sea of Soul (See "Chart of Mind"). So, none of us is ever out of touch with the Soul. In fact, communication is continuous, even if and when it is unconscious.

The Soulagenda differs strikingly from the desires of the ego. Ego wants bucks, sex, and admiration. Its perfect fantasy is to win the lottery, be surrounded by adoring "beautiful people," live in a mansion, and drive a car the size of a battleship that gets four miles per gallon.

The Soul, by stunning contrast, wants spiritual growth and progress. In fact, it wants nothing else. Its fantasy is uninterrupted bliss— full, complete satisfaction, absolute fulfillment, unsullied contentment. All this, it knows, can blossom from only Love. So, the Soul's main agenda is to learn the art of cosmic loving. And it will stop at nothing to get what it wants. If needed, it will expose you (as egoself) to illness, poverty, stress, and disappointment. But it does all this out of its profound, utter Love for you. While the soul is not the dreamingmind (Creatormind), it does modify the worldream by flooding it with its own karmic contents. In other words, while the Coremind is the actual Source of the worldream, the Soul is largely the origin of the everyday contents of your personal dream. It gives this suffering as a "gift." Your egomind, then, can choose to label this "gift" as it truly is, i.e., positive, constructive, educational, and life-affirming— in a word, "good." Or it can follow the common cultural pattern. If it follows this, it will be

*Falling in Love with Your Self
Love and the Inner Beloved*

"eating of the tree of knowledge of good and evil," splitting the universe dualistically between an equal good and evil. So, you will spend part of your time in the heart's Garden of Pleasure, or "inner heaven," but the other part of your time will be spent in hell.

In the cosmic "starwars" battle between Soul and ego, the puny little ego has not a snowball's chance. The Soul, being a level of the powerful unconscious Mind, always gets what it wants. And it wants you to become a psychonaut, an explorer of inner space. It wants, above all things, for you to become enlightened. It wants you to become Love. So, it's only a matter of time: You will be a **spiritual** being. It's just a question of **when**. The question of **whether** has already been answered affirmatively.

The answer to the inquiry, "Will I become a spiritual being?" is, "You are already a spiritual being." In Buddhism, masters teach, "You are already the Buddha." In earliest Christianity, there was a parallel: "You are already the Christ." You have just forgotten. Now, this "forgetting" is massive, on a cosmic scale. It is not the same species of forgetting as when you forget to pick up milk or bread.

When the infinite inner Mind first began to "play," or pretend to be, "your" Soul, It knew that it would "fall asleep," and It willed "cosmic amnesia" upon itself. Otherwise, the game of being "another" would never have worked. The Mind had to make sure that It thoroughly and completely fooled itself. The amnesia had to be so profound and so complete that It would be completely swallowed by its dreamillusion. This dream had to be absolutely convincing, down to the microdetail. Also, the dreamworld had to be both fascinating and dangerous, for the scheme to work.

But the immeasurable Mind also knew that Its ultimate destiny would be someday to wake up and remember Its true identity. When this occurred, it could still "play the game" of earthly life and personhood, but it would do so with new awareness. This newly discovered state, enlightenment, would elevate It into invincible joy, peace, and Love. These qualities would be steadystates, which could not be changed, influenced, or affected by any dreamreality. So, transcending the world does not end the game, but you begin to play it with the consummate skill of a master. You are no longer "marionetted" by the environment, as you now realize that its true Source is within. The world belongs to Mind, not mind to the world. and Mind is master.

When an enlightened being discovers fully the inner state of awakening to this Reality, it is Mind remembering Mind, or God rediscovering God. But her life is not made "perfect" by human standards. For her Soul has designed a life-agenda, in order to grow. So, she must play the game out, to the end. She must take all the courses which she has elected to take. These might include poverty, illness, loss, or other "negative" events or conditions. But now that she has undergone the infilling of Light and Love, these conditions are no longer seen as irredeemably negative. Only a master can embrace pain with joy, but any mystic can come to see the good within the bad.

Falling in Love with Your Self
Love and the Inner Beloved

Speaking of "masters," when that term was used by Eastern mystics, it did not imply that the enlightened became the master **of others**. Nor did it imply that she controlled the forces of nature. No, instead, she had mastered herself. So, the true master is never interested in controlling others, in egotrips, or in doing "tricks." *The true master is master of only the self.* In fact, the inner illumination is so bright and vivid, she tends to lose interest in **all "outer"** phenomena. She rejects selfdisplay to impress others.

****

Chapter 10

Dream as Nightmare:
Agonies of Ego-Spirit Conflict

***

If you say yes, to the cosmos, brace yourself. Anything can happen. And it usually will. Mystics are quite often severely tested. The master has earned and paid for her mastership with anguishing blood, agonized sweat, and bitter tears. It has not come to her easily, or quickly. She did not get her mastership by sending twenty bucks in answer to an ad in *Rolling Stone*. A true "master" is not made so by giving thousands of dollars to take a healingcourse. Her breaking of the steel chains of karma has been an uphill struggle all the way. And she has had to work at it, fulltime, for centuries. But the pain has forced her into wonderful transcendence.

Love enters the heart through wounds. Mystics say that, at your personal Judgment Day, Spiritmind will not ask to see your degrees, but your scars. Suffering for goodness, education, or Love has great value; this pain forms the most precious jewels of this life. Love infuses Itself also through tears.

So, receiving a wound, as a peaceful warrior, is a badge of honor and courage. It is an invitation from the cosmos to become, by participation, Supermind. This is why, in the ancient archetypal story, the apex of Jesus'

divinity was the nadir of his humanity— shamed and agonized on the cross. So, when people
moan and mourn, "Why me?" when something bad occurs, the answer is, "Because you are being called to infinity, to eternal nature." For it is beneath the anger, under the pain, that one discovers Superlove.
So, the suffering, far from being ignored by some indifferent and cruel "deistic" deity, is a sign that "God" is paying special attention to you. The Lovemind or Lovegod, deep in your mind, is being awakened. Your pain is a signal of unconscious transformation. You are being approached by the higher inner Mind, the Mindspirit of Love, alerted by its troublesome but inignorable signals. The Spirit of Ultralove is forcing you to examine life. If you respond, you will begin the long journey inward, the adventure of discovering Soul and Spirit. If you actively pursue illumination, you will discover that the Soul is not some filmy or misty thing that leaves the physical body at death, but a deep inhabitant of your own unconscious Mind.
Dreams are a good launchpad to the inner stars. For nature is no waster. She does not invest timenergy in a project unless she expects to make a profit.
And dreamtime takes about a third of your life. Dreams are unconsciously designed to tell the conscious mind something that it needs to know. They're all about your spiritual growth. Unless it is clear from the "feeling tone" or "texture" of a dream that it is otherwise, every symbol in every dream represents a fragmented, projected, or "exteriorized" (into the dreamworld) aspect of your own mind. The tigers, rats, stars,

jewels, and rainbows of your dreams represent You.

For example, birds represent thoughts that are capable of lifting the mind heavenward, i.e., spiritual thoughts. But, being "birds," these thoughts arise from the animal nature. Butterflies represent even lower thoughts transformed.

Mud, clay, the color brown represent thoughts and ideas arising from earthly sources, and water symbolizes unconscious thoughts of a fluid and life-sustaining nature. Fire represents volatile emotive responses, or passion. It can also symbolize Mindenergy or light. Stone represents thoughts and ideas of solidarity, dependability, or inflexibility. It can also symbolize the deeper Mindlevels.

Dreams can lift you above the egoself. Hindu mystics say, "Nothing stands between yourself and God but yourself." This is egoself, bypassed by dreams. The stubborn belief that you are only your ego ("I am Mary Smith," or, "I am John Jones") prevents the Spirit's full blossoming. It is a form of ignorance, and so eclipses the dazzling inner Light of Superlove.

Being lost in Love can carry you far beyond. In good sex, this can happen bodily, but in the mystic it occurs in the heartmind. This sounds remarkably easy, even fun. It can be. But it can also challenge you to become the best possible self.

For it implies a struggle to the death to deidentify with your ego. Just as a person cannot be both blond and brunette, six and ten years old, you cannot be both your ego and your deeper Self. A choice must be made. The

Falling in Love with Your Self
Love and the Inner Beloved

deeper Self is playing the role of the ego, but *you* decide which is "real" to you.

Which are you? Are you the egorole, named Mary Smith or John Jones? Or are you a Superbeing of pure Mind, traveling through an earthly voyage? Are you really Hamlet, or are you the Actor playing the role?

The act of deidentification with the ego is a move lethal to it. So, your egoself will resist tooth and nail, with every weapon at its disposal, your enlightenment. It will array against you every micropsychon available. It will be like a bad Japanese "Godzilla" flick, where the unified army of earth attacks the confused megalizard. Actually, considering the gargantuan Power of the Spirit, and the pitiable weakness of the resisting ego, it will be more like that great unreleased cultclassic, "Godzilla Versus Lambchop." Luckily, ego is only a branch of the conscious mind, and so, is pitiably weak. Still, it does not go gently into that good night of oblivion. For ego possesses an enormous selfsurvival instinct. It knows that in transcendence it will be history, or "toast." its days are numbered. If you are reading these words with understanding, if you feel attracted by this message, the handwriting is already on the wall.

So, ego panics, trying a thousand strategies to sneak back into your mind, as false master. It triggers fear, pushing all fearbuttons. It lies, and says that in transcendence, you will be obliterated, with nothing left— rather than, as actually does happen, totally transformed. Instead of becoming a Superbeing of Supermind and Love, the ego threatens, you will perish and vanish, never to be heard from again.

It exacerbates personal desires into lusts, amplifying craving to allconsuming thirst. It will enter by back doors, side doors, basement, or attic. It will be seductive, attractive, and devious. It might conjure up the phantomfear of completely losing your Mind, your Self, in mystical Light.

It will make attempts to convince you that the inner Quest is nonsense. It will mock devastatingly and relentlessly your quest for the Light of Love. It will assure you repeatedly that the spiritual path is "impractical," an airy-fairy never-never land, a trip to Oz, or ozone. Ego will tell you that "spirituality" is for the mentally debilitated, the philosophically naive, the hopeless and helpless. It is weakness, and "Love" is just the fortress, made of vapor and dreams, in which the feeble-minded hide themselves from reality.

"Get real," ego will demand. "Wake up and smell the cappuccino. Suck it up. Be heroic. Don't become a flake. Don't waste your time and energy building castles in the clouds. Get out of your ivory tower, climb down from your high horse. Get a life! You are not a Superbeing. You are an animal with delusions of grandeur, nothing more!"

Ego will conspire with its faithful servant, the intellect, to talk you out of the mystical inner "journey," dismissing it as nonsense and imagination, selfconsciously mocking the part of your mind that knows better. It will try to convince you that the higher Self is illusion. So, you must prepare for this struggle to keep the faith.

Falling in Love with Your Self
Love and the Inner Beloved

For in mysticism, you have three "natures" (heartmind aspects): the higher and lower natures, and the human nature. The human nature (often, the conscious mind) can choose to serve either the higher nature of Spirit, or the lower nature of ego and animality. But, as the "moldy oldy" reminds us, "You've gotta serve somebody." (The only valid use of the conscious mind is precisely to make such challenging decisions.)

Lovers can be good teachers for the spiritual Way. For they enter the terror and darkness of the "fire" of Love with hearts full of joy and overflowing with optimistic trust. But still, it can be a bit scary. It is unexplored territory within the inner Mindscapes. It is "dark" or unconscious. So, the mystic must begin her journey blind, must toss herself into the black abyss of the Mind, into its deepest cavern. She must do so with the faith that something or someone will catch her. She must trust that a stronger part of her unconscious Mind, the deep Lovenature, exists and will serve as her safety-net. When she tends to tumble from the tenuous threshold of timorous sanity, Love will catch her, set her upright, and get her back on her feet. So, the first steps on the path can be unnerving. They cal for some preparation, by solidly grounding yourself in the Power of Love.

Richard Shiningthunder Francis

So, the best preparation is not just book-reading, although books can serve as reliable roadmaps. The very best prepwork is the actual exercise of Love. Serve the poor or the sick, the abused, the uneducated, the young, or the elderly.

****

Chapter 11

Consumed in the Sweet Flame of Love

***

The moth's wings were ignited, and he was burnt to a crisp, going up in bright yellow flames. Previously, according to this myth-parable, he had said to the more timid moths, "The only way to know the nature of fire is to touch it, to be consumed in it." The timid ones were scared stiff. They had flown close, but would not approach the dangerous candleflame. At last, this brave moth had become the very first to know with certainty the nature of fire. But it had cost him everything.

There's a kind of glory in this little story. It's a terrible parable for anyone who wants to know the inner Absolute. For she will have to have her familiar self burned to a crisp, unrecognizable, in the flame of Love. Every mystic must nourish her mysticism with this great, allsurrendering, allgiving attitude. If not, it's not real mysticism. For when you give yourself entirely to Love, everything else— race, religion, politics, economics, intellect, ego— recedes further and further into the background. Then, by the time enlightenment is upon you, Love looms large enough to fill your entire Mindfield. It floods the heartmind, and washes out everything that is not Love, leaving only Love's luminous light, glowing in splendor.

Let's be crystalclear: At the highest peak of Love, you are in way over your head. Lost in Love, you are not loving, but Love is loving Love. This is purest, most pristine Love, for it occurs **without the stain of an egoself.**

This sounds really weird, so let's elaborate": In the fullness of mystical Love, it is revealed that the Object of all Love is the inner Absolute— the deepest part, or Core, of your unconscious Mind. It works at a level so deep that it is below even the collective unconscious. (See "Chart of Mind.")

It is nuclear Mind, and is also Love. The egomind is its major obstacle or impediment. It blocks or dams the Flow. When you are metamorphosed into Love, your egoself vanishes. So, you are not a person loving. You are a mirror. That mirror, aimed at perfect Love, only reflects Love. The mystical experience is this direct knowing of Love loving Love. In the center of its ecstasy, ego leaves not a trace, not a whisper.

With this state, all pain vanishes. Past and future also evanesce. You really do not care for, or about, anything but this allconsuming Love. This state of total insouciance was called by the ancients being "intoxicated" with God. Today, we might speak of "being high" on Love. In the peak mystical state is revealed to you the greatest wonder: Almost nothing matters. But some things do still matter. Still, all the material, emotional, and economic baggage, all the religious and political propoganda, all the excess "crap" vanishes like the starlight from last night's sky. This lifts you to a great

*Falling in Love with Your Self
Love and the Inner Beloved*

new high, feeling light and lightfilled, like a bird soaring on high winds, lazily, effortlessly, in a blue sky. Love, allabsorbing, has drunk you in, so that you don't care even about yourself, but only about Love. This selforgetting is itself a very high state. Mystics call it "unselfing," "selforgetting," "selfstripping," or "selfabandonment."

After a being has touched this inner luminous state, she is absorbed in Love. So, she is not inclined selfishly to stay and soak up the "Love-vibes." She hurries back to the world of tumult and turmoil, pain and agony, to share her riches of transformation. She wants, out of Love, to spread the force of Love. For Love is contagious, and it is her will to infect the entire world, asap.

So, mystics are not "freaks" who hole themselves up in dark, dank, damp caves. Nor do they sit on isolated mountain-tops, despising human beings and human company. They are not bizarre, skinny little old men with beards down to their navels, who dress in rags and bear a harsh, unearthly light in their fanatical eyes. Mystics are the most ordinary of people, from the outside.

Lao Tzu says of the mystic sage: "She wears rough clothing, but carries the great jewel inside." It is this great **inner** gem that she carries inside herself that makes the mystic superhumanly and supernaturally beautiful. For this "jewel" is the great "emerald" of Love.

And she knows, without any doubt, just how special she really is. That is why she does not have to play any games, to impress others. She does not have to "distinguish" (read "embarrass") herself by talking more loudly or obnoxiously than others. She never practices selfdisplay, which she rightly regards as both pathetic and pathological. She also rejects artificial and contrived games, such as special clothing, special titles, jewelry, etc. In fact, she is so astoundingly secure that, when with a crowd, all that she desires is for them to love each other. She does not want, under any conditions, to gain their admiration. She avoids the spotlight and the pedestal, both of which are deadly to her humility— another great diamond in her heartreasure. While the average person, trembling inside because she feels worthless and loathsome, will do anything to be noticed by a group, it is just the opposite with the mystic, who wants only to love people. She wants to serve, but not to be admired and noticed for her service. That is why her service is so wonderful and valuable. "She does her work, then forgets about it. That is why her work lasts forever." These are the true words of the sage Lao Tzu, discussing the behavior of the enlightened sage.

So, what is special about her is that she has **no interest** in appearing to be "someone special." She knows that the approval, indeed, admiration of ten thousand people is nothing compared with her inner jewel and its satisfaction. She carries God in the lotus of her heart, but does not announce the fact in the secret hope that she will be noticed or favored as an object of special attention. She feels repelled by reverence offered to her person. Contrast this with those who are so full of pride/shame that they insist on being called, "Reverend."

Falling in Love with Your Self
Love and the Inner Beloved

Other people strut with pride because they consider themselves to be "channels" of various saints, seers, prophets, and miscellaneous dead people and aliens. Most do this out of low selfesteem, reasoning unconsciously, "I myself could have nothing of any value to say." That is why the confused and confusing stuff that pours from their lips and pens is ascribed to "entities" of various ilks. And since they do not claim to be the sources of their material, such as it is, they take no responsibility for it.

The mystic is a channel far above all the rest, a conduit of the divine Itself. But she is swept bare and clean of all pride. She simply smiles, quietly and secretly, in her full knowledge that the One who lives in her is greater than the one, whoever it is, being "channeled" by an often borderline personality. Further, she is vividly aware, all the time, that the Love which is her Essence is the same Love that is the Essence of all people, bar none.

Why is she so secure? Because she knows that her value does not lie in this world. Nothing in this entire world can make her more precious, can add to her infinite inner riches. And equally, nothing and no one can take away a single filament of gold from the heavy bars of her inner treasure. She is "in" this world. She lives with the rest of the people here. But she is not "of" this world. Her Origin or Source is within her own heartmind. She stands out from the crowd, luminous and silent, because of what Watts called "extraordinary ordinariness." She stands out because she does not struggle to stand out. She is special because she is the only one who is not trying to be someone special.

So, you will never find a true mystic or enlightened sage among the spotlights of the circus of glitz and glamour, the egoparade of the metaphysical community. Instead, you'll find the real thing only among the rare, selfless, egoless teachers who grasp for no greed, ego, or power. A genuine teacher might teach publicly, in order to reach hearts. But she will never permit adoration of her, and will talk about ideas, not about her boring little ego. Any selfstyled "teacher" obsessed with ego, with "proving herself," is a liar and a fake.

****

Falling in Love with Your Self
Love and the Inner Beloved

Chapter 12

Passion and Compassion on the Third Rock: Do Geese See God?

***

They pant greedily, thirstily, for a microdrop. The people are dying of thirst, unaware that they are floating in an ocean of sweet water. The famous mystical poet Rumi says that anyone who swims in the "sea" of God is bound to drown. But as the old song reminds us, this is where everyone would love to drown— in a sea of Love. Excursion into the inner sea of eternity ends always in "death."

The mystic does not literally die upon enlightenment, but that part of herself known to others, the ego, does die. Mysticism can hit with a hard punch— a stroke and strike that shatters the ego. So mysticism is not recommended for "blase" people, for it can pulverize those of weak and fragile constitution. Before embarking on the inner sea, a person ideally should be relatively strong, fairly healthy mentally, and, above all, committed completely to universal Love.

This philosophy implies that all creatures are sacred. But some are moreso thanothers. On the evolutionary ladder, "higher" beings are more sacred than lower ones. But all partake of the sacred nature of the indwelling miracle of life. Even birds, as Jesus and Francis knew so well, are holy revelations of life and Love. So, the answer to the old palindrome (a sentence the same forward as backward) "Do geese see God?" is yes. Geese, and other birds, partake of divine beauty. But still, they share a groupsoul, and are thus "nonsentient." They are not as sacred as creatures with individual, personal souls, such as dogs, cats, etc. Still higher organisms, such as elephants and dolphins, are even more sacred. As noted, not everyone, not even every mystic wannabe, will find Truth or Reality in this life. This search, if it is going to yield results, must be a passion, allconsuming, allsurrendering, holding back nothing. It must be a "no holds barred, all the way" approach. The mystic cannot just dip a toe into the water of eternity. She must plunge into it, headfirst— and into the deep end, at that! Halfhearted measures will never do. The ancient Hindu texts, the upanishads, tell us that unless you want the Absolute as badly as a drowning man wants air, you will not find It in your psyche. But when that passion is ignited, you can know It in a splitsecond

Good news! When you do turn inward sincerely, the entire unconscious Mind, with all its many forces, begins to cooperate with, and to support, your dance with it. It gets behind your efforts to reach and know the inner Beloved. Love marshals all your forces and lines them up pointing in the same direction. It takes the incoherent light of the ordinary mind and transforms it into the laser focus of Love. And as the inner life begins to be rearranged, even the "outer" world is restructured, so that, as an ancient mystic said, "All things work together for good for them that love God..." In time, everything becomes a servant of the one who is seeking union with her inner Beloved.

Mystics are special people. Is mysticism, then, guilty of elitism? No, it cannot be, for that is antiagapic (against Love). And every mystic knows that everyone has always been a mystic, inside. It is only that "mystics" happen to have remembered the fact. this does not in any way make them "better" or "superior" people. They welcome everyone, no matter what her religion— or even if she has none— into the brother/sisterhood of light and Love. The mystical community is unbounded by any considerations of race, religion, intellectual or social status, or other roots of bigotry.

Mystics also support no exclusive religious organizations or churches, and sponsor none of their own. Strong, committed, and fully enlightened mystics have historically included Catholics, Lutherans, Baptists, and a wide spectrum of other "brands" of Christianity. Many other mystics have taught in prechristian or nonchristian traditions. Among these are the beautiful, exquisite jewels of Islam, the Sufis, and the great intellectual Kabbalists among the Jews. It goes almost without saying (but we'll say it anyhow) that the great naturally mystical faiths of Hinduism, Buddhism, and Taoism have produced some of the clearest mystical luminaries, and not a few have arisen among nature- or earth-based religions.

No one ever literally **"becomes"** a mystic, growing from a state of nonmysticism. The activated, energized mystic only wakes up to the fact that she has **always been one.** Mystics are masters of the heart's Love, and anyone or everyone can learn to be this kind of master. Deep down, everybody already is. This Lovemaster is also your truest identity, your deepest Self.

We spoke earlier about the word "master." Let's elaborate: When a person becomes a "mystic master," she does not have to embrace exotic practices or ancient and odd beliefs. She does not follow any gurus or cults as her master. She doesn't do strange ceremonies. She does not sacrifice chickens, turkeys, or other fowl and smelly things to a god or goddess. She does not have to dance naked around a campfire, or do funny things with the eyes of newts or the blood of goats. She does not necessarily talk to the dead. She does not "channel" extraterrestrials. She does not control the wind, or the rain. She cannot walk through walls, or on water, or fly through the air. (Many mystics do not even have broomsticks any more, having replaced them with vacuumcleaners.)

These pseudo-mystical traits mark phonies, frauds, and charlatans, whose goal is magic, not mysticism. They also mark razzle-dazzle showmen who are keeping their eyes on the spotlight and mirror, not on the inner Lovenature. (In magic, the human will is considered to be allimportant, but is completely neutralized and ignored in true mysticism. It is an obstacle, not the Way.) Also, magicians usually are out to impress others with "tricks." The mystic does not "do tricks," for she is interested in impressing no one.

Let's look for a moment at a phrase that has been hideously twisted and distorted, almost as much as the word "mystic" itself: "kung fu

Falling in Love with Your Self
Love and the Inner Beloved

master." The phrase "kung fu" in Chinese does not necessarily refer only to a system of fighting and defense. A true *kung fu* master is one who has mastered the art of living well. It is not a person who can kick an opponent in the ear, leaving a bloody and violent mess. The Chinese phrase *kung fu* simply means something like "most excellent." So, an extraordinary carpenter could be said to be a "kung fu carpenter," while an inspired artist might well be a "kung fu artist." A good singer could be a "kung fu singer." They have all mastered excellence in their various arts, crafts, and professions. So, then, what is a "kung fu master"? It is a person who has mastered the art of excellent being, most excellent living. The genuine kung fu masters of ancient times were men and women of tender hearts, gentleness, wisdom, and deep understanding. They were Taoist mystics. ("Taoism" was the form of mysticism most indigenous to Chinese culture for centuries.)3

In the true master, the flame of Love is allowed gradually to burn away everything that is not Love, leaving behind only the bright warm flame of Love and bliss. This is the Way.

The "Way" is mysticism, for the mystical truth is precisely that: It is the way that one tries to live every minute of every day. It is not a religion that you can join. It involves no formal affiliations with any organizations or organized religions. It is

---

3. See My "Tao Now: A New Rendition of 'The Way of Virtue,' by the master Lao Tzu," Part IV of *Luminous Jewels of Love and Light* (Liberty Township, Ohio; Love Ministries, Inc. 2002)

not an event that can be created by reading books, or by ordinary learning. Brains will take you far in this life, but they will not alone propel you to the mystical stars.

Beware especially of any "training" that makes the absurd claim that it can make you a "master." A true master will never identify herself in this crude egotistic way— by using the word "master." So, anyone who calls him/herself a "master," or allows others to do so, is a phony.

Mysticism is not even an intellectual philosophy, in which simply believing makes you a "mystic." Instead, real mysticism has a **living** component. That is Love. A person who struts proudly her "mysticism," always talking about herself or her "enlightenment," is a fraud. Any person who does not manifest compassion, kindness, friendliness, humility, goodness, integrity, and harmlessness consistently cannot be a mystic.

If you believe all the "right" things, you can be an official "member" of any church or religion. In many, it does not even matter how you live. In philosophy, likewise, you can simply adopt a certain system of belief, and from then on, say that you are a "realist," "pessimist" "nihilist," "idealist," etc. All that is required is that you believe the "right stuff," and it's all in your head.

But

****

You cannot validly claim to be a mystic unless you live the Way of compassion, to the best of your ability and capacity, every minute of every day.

Falling in Love with Your Self
Love and the Inner Beloved

****

It's not enough to understand, in other words. Mysticism is not something that you *know*. "Use your head!" the annoyed father screams at his confused son. But in mysticism, unlike religion, headstuff is not enough. Mysticism is a matter of heart. *So, if your head's in the right place, but your heart isn't, you are no mystic.* It is something that you must grow into, become. It arises from a discovery, made in the great inward journey, when you have touched the heartessence of Love, and been filled by It, transformed by It. Under certain conditions, indeed, reason can be a limitation, a strangle-hold, as we are about to discuss.

****

Chapter 13

The Tender "Feminine" heart: The "Inner Knowing" of the Mystic

***

 The price is right. It is also very high. Mysticism demands the highest price imaginable. It wants everything. What you get in return is also everything. To purchase infinity for your own heart, you must pay with everything that you have, and everything that you are. And it would be the world's greatest bargain at ten thousand times the price. In time, your entire self, the ego, will slip beneath the waves of the unconscious ocean. You will sink, out of sight, into the cosmic Mind, the light of luminescent Love sparkling from the waves.
 Mysticism is a Way of devotion. It far surpasses any intellectual approach. It is so much more than religion. It is infinitely more than Bible-study, meetings, singing, or selling for the church. And it's ten thousand times as much fun! It is all about "knowing," but not the linear, logical, precisionbased, databased "knowing" that we call "education. To the mystic, so much of this is artless and heartless foolishness. Symmetrically, much of the Way is "foolish," by the standards of regular learning. Even the most ardent advocates of the Way recognized this fact.
 Plato and Francis both referred, each in his own way, to mystics as "fools for Love."" Mysticism is not the knowing of

datassimilation, datagathering, or memorization. What is "known" is the deepest level of the unconscious Mind. What is known is Supermind (Superlove, cosmic Mind, the Superconscious state). This is the mystic's "Absolute," and It is Ultralove.

In ancient Greek, they had a special word for this immediate, direct, experiential "knowing" of the Coremind— *gnosis*. In Sanskrit, another ancient spiritual tongue, it was *jnana*. (The words are "cognates," or related, which is why they look something alike.)

Gnosis does not blossom from reason, nor is it circumscribed by it. But if not from the arrogant egomind, from where does gnosis come? It is an uprush of Mindenergies from the Core of Love, the deepest Mindlevel of the Unconscious— the Superconscious.

It floods into the mind as a whole, an unbroken totality. It rushes in from the unconscious Mind, in an "invasion" of new thoughts and ideas. After gnosis, you will never see yourself, or the cosmos, the same.

And mystical knowledge is not just simple deductive logic. If it were, a computer could have a mystical experience. No, for the heartmind is also flooded with Love, the lifeblood of gnosis. It is Love that awakens an already preexistent gnosis in the heartmind.

Love is gentle, while knowledge is usually "harder." (So, scientists speak of "hard data.") Love is flowing, braindata gives structure. Love is passion, while cerebral approaches are notoriously nonpassionate. Love is fun and stimulating, contrasted with the infamous dullness of data. Love is considered, unfairly, "feminine," and data, with equal unfairness, "masculine."

So, mysticism has within it much of the softness, tenderness, nurturing, and gentleness often associated with the *yin* component of reality. This Chinese word implies the soft, receiving, dark, feminine side of reality. So, the symbol of the Goddess is as much at home in mysticism as is the symbol of "God"— and even moreso.

Still, Goddess-recognition is scarce as diamonds among Western mystics because they are culturally socialized and educated. But not a one of them believes, for an instant, that God is somehow literally "male," or purely masculine. God has no penis. Indeed, God has no body, as is taught clearly in even traditional theology. For the mystic, remember, sees "God," or the Ultimate, as a process or quality, as Love, not as a "person." And they have all turned their backs, in choreographed unison, on the bloody, violent godimage of the all male deity common to much of both ancient Judaism and modern forms of "Christianity." The absence of this grim, humorless "father" gives mysticism a brightness, lightness, and humor lacking in traditional Western faiths. The brightness of their inner light has driven out the shadow of the taciturn Jehovah-myth forever. Their "Absolute" is purest, most pristine, unstained Love.

Still, a mystic might even use, periodically, the masculine pronoun when referring to the divine, if that is culturally common. The mystic might avoid the more correct but terribly clumsy pronoun "Heshetheyit" when referring to the Absolute.

Falling in Love with Your Self
Love and the Inner Beloved

But not a single mystic has ever accused the Absolute of being limited to the masculine. For it takes only a micropsychon of common sense to realize that, in even the most assertive and logical mystic, the deep Mindspirit is sexneutral.

In fact, the great truths of mystical Love flow along a nonlinear, mythological pattern, and this is traditionally the language and domain of the female in culture and society. Many important and seminal works of mystical tradition have flowed from feminine hands, hearts, and pens. Although much that is logical/rational can be said about the topic—as evidenced by this and a very few other books on the subject 4— its essential expression is poetic, and hence, "feminine." For it is the Fountain of all beauty in life. A million linear words can never capture the form of a beautiful woman. And they cannot hope even to approach her Lovefilled Mind. So, the metaverbal presence or nature of mysticism is lightyears from the crude domain of mere letters.

Although the male mystic is open to his feminine side, this by no means weakens him. Mystics have no personal will, it is true. But they have tied or plugged in to a will that is supreme and irresistible. So, at his weakest, the male mystic finds his greatest Power. An ancient mystic received this paradoxical message from the Absolute: "In thy weakness, My power will be made perfect." And this is the kind of Power that can

---

5. See my *Journey to the Center of the Soul: Mysticism Made Simple* (Liberty Township, Ohio; Love Ministries, Inc. 2002)

vanquish a thousand armies. It can move mountains. It is the invincible passion of Love that burns away every obstacle in the mystic's path. It makes of her a powerful, dynamic, often unmoving, personality. Though entire nations fall, the mystic will retain equanimity. Mountains might explode, and the earth shake and collapse, but she will not lose her mind, or her serenity. For she draws strength and Power from an inexhaustible inner Source.

In its ineffability, the mystical event of synergizing with Lovemind has something of the ultrasensual about it. It is the fragrance of flowers, the taste of honey, multiplied by a billion. It is the orchestration of stars exploding, galaxies colliding, crickets on a summer's eve, birds of a summer morn. It is the deep relaxation of profound sleep, softness, floating in warm water, the onrush of orgasm, all packed together into one mindblasting event. But its "sound" is still more subtle than the breathing of an ameba. So, you must cultivate the "third ear," the inner "ear" of the heart, to listen to your Soul's inner voice. (This is symmetric with the opening of the "inner eye" to "gaze" upon inner Mind or Soul.)

This silent, tranquil view contrasts starkly with the mad and maddening hypnotic gazing at the "outer" world, filled with hyperkinesis and ceaseless movement, liquid change. The mystic sees this world as rushing fluid, always becoming, but never quite being. (In the heartmind alone is true stillness.)

The target of this inner journey into ultrastillness is the strange reality which we call the "inner Other." It glows with an aura

Falling in Love with Your Self
Love and the Inner Beloved

of the unusual precisely because, while living inside the mystic, It lives there for years completely unconsciously.

It is so subtle that the average person is not aware even of Its existence. Yet in a moment, it can blast the mystic into the inner realm, world, or "kingdom" of Light, where she is irreversibly altered forever. It is such a vast ocean of wisdom and Love that It seems to the egomind to be an "other." Mystics commonly, and practically, speak of It as if It really were another being, for It is stunningly greater than any ego. It is, in fact, the "other" being which has been exteriorized in history as "God," or "gods." Paradoxically, It is at once closer than your own heart, and as "distant" as stars in the galaxy. Why? Because it is your most intimate Mind, your deepest Self. But it lives in the entire "outer and material" world, because even the stars are Its dreamimages. So, it "dwells within" them too. So, it is simultaneously closer than your breath and as far as the stars. But this "distance" is nothing but illusion. It flows from personal and cultural amnesia. It is spiritual and literal "psychopathology." (The prefix "psycho-," in Greek, means, not "mind," but "Soul.") More technically, it is "pneumoamnesia." (The prefix "pneumo" means "Spirit.") The distorted vision of the Absolute grows from pneumoamnesia. The idea that spirit is strange, distant, and alien is the flowering of a number of "weeds" in the garden of the psyche. It is a convergence of ponderous, powerful, and popular illusions. It turns "God" into the ultimate extraterrestrial.

Richard Shiningthunder Francis

But the "mystery" in mysticism is exactly this: The inner Beloved is not different from your Self. So, "falling in Love with your Self" is the Love of the inner Beloved.

****

Falling in Love with Your Self
Love and the Inner Beloved

Chapter 14

Egofree Fluidity: The Lightfilled Heart

***

Before the stars peppered the velvetblack vault of nightsky with golds, blues, and reds, Mind existed. The One has always been there. But He/She has been beyond the pale, quite outside the range of biosensors. He/She has stood at the nucleus of heartmind since the Beginning.

"*Atman* is *Brahman*" is the statement of Eastern mystics of this great truth. It means, "the Soul is God." For as the Soul exists deeply in the unconscious Mind, so the Spirit exists at a level even deeper, wrapped in the Soul. (See "Chart of Mind.") At the nucleus of all Mind glows Supermind (Spirit). It is luminous Love, the Center of being. (One of the names of the Absolute is, in fact, the "Center.")

You cannot detonate the inner dynamite of the psychosupernova of the highest Mind. You can take only the *yin* position— waiting and watching. You are not the source of the great force that sucks your heartmind inward on a hurricanic torrent of Spirit. The whole show is initiated by the unconscious Mind. Ultimately, its Source is the Core or Supermind. It occurs, says the Western mystic, because it is the "will of God." (It can also be initiated by the Soulevel of the Unconscious. This happens when its occurrence is karmic.)

This labyrinthine inner path is not for children or newcomers. The journey can have dangers and spring surprises. It is usually successful only after several lifetimes of attempting to penetrate the inner clouds of Soulmind and egomind that eclipse the Light at the Core.

The mystic's wanting God is Coremind's "wanting" her. This will is always perfect symmetry. When egomind longs for Union with the Absolute, this is unquestionable assurance that Superlove also is reaching for it. Supermind is now willing for her to sink into the deep waters and discover It. Mystics call this "God longing for God," or simply, "Love loving Love."

For at the zenith of incandescent luminescence, the ego evaporates in the great "heat" and Light. So, there is literally no "mystic having a mystical event." For she has vanished into the Power of the Lightmind. There is only the event, completely scrubbed clean of any trace of ego. So, the mystic cannot technically say, "I had a Lovemind event," but only that "a Lovegod event occurred." For at the peak of this event, the observer disappears completely into the Object. The subject vanishes into the event. The mystic becomes liquid Love, fluid Light, and blends indiscernibly and inseparably with the great Unconscious (Spirit). She disappears into, and is indistinguishable from, the One. This vanishing into cosmic Mind guarantees that the event can never be inappropriately abused for ego-glorification. For if any ego tries to take any credit, or to gather approval or admiration for having had the experience, hers was no true mystical

Falling in Love with Your Self
Love and the Inner Beloved

experience. For the ego cannot "have" a unitive experience. The ego cannot survive a true mystical event intact. When it reforms after the mindazzling Lightfilling, it is altered irreversibly in serious, significant ways. It is simply not present when the awesome, dramatic "agapophotic (Lovelight) fusion" occurs.

The subtle, tender voice of Goddess is continually calling us to this ultraenergic selfloss. But, again, it is up to us to cultivate the subtlety of the "inner ear" so that we can hear, and respond to, the magnificent calling of the Lovegoddess. But although He/She calls continuously, we hear only sporadically. Love wants us to become Love, its goldcrystal vessel in this world.

In the deepest fathoms of your inner psyche, you already know this path. The inner map to Ultralove already exists within you. The Way of mysticism is simply a remembering and rediscovering. Superlove is that area of heartmind where you can never hit bottom. Bottomless Ultralove lives already within you. This Love is the Core of the psyche. It is touched not by reading and learning, but by loving. Every act of Love moves you a millimeter closer to the Lovecore of your Mind. Mystics have called this voyage to the Core of the psyche their "journey Home."

Indeed, there is much familiarity and comfort found in this trip. Landmarks are recognized along the way, and a great sense of *deja vu* sweeps over the active psychonaut. She knows that she has been here before. Indeed, she knows that she has never really been anywhere else. For the Mind is truest Home.

Richard Shiningthunder Francis

****

There simply is no "elsewhere."

****

   This trip is the most fun that you can ever have. But it is not all roses and butterflies. For the journey into the egoheart can be perilous, uncomfortable, and painful. It tears away the flesh of protective psychic armor, and leaves you naked and bleeding. But if you do not actively cultivate honest vulnerability, your heart will never be open enough to receive the grace, Light, peace, and Love proferred by the inner Beloved. Vulnerability is the supremely honest response to an infinite and immeasurable cosmos. It is the beginning of humility. Thus, it is the start of the inward journey. It's the first step to a real inner life.
   So, the journey begins with selfhonesty. You must put away all pretensions, all egotism, all attempts to prove yourself worthy or valuable. This means full rejection of arrogance— a subtle spiritual disease.
   Almost all of us have had our hearts hurt. This heart of Love is not always a playground or paradise. It can be a dark, frightening, scary place in the psyche. We fear that, as it said on some old maps, "here there be dragons." As we map our way back to the Center, we will have to cleanse our hearts through universal forgiveness, which begins with forgiving ourselves.

Falling in Love with Your Self
Love and the Inner Beloved

Remember, forgiving is **not** forgetting. You simply cannot forget by forcing yourself to do it, as an act of stubborn will. Some things you just cannot shake. But forgiveness has occurred when you can look at an event with supreme and healthy detachment. This means that **no emotional response at all** is aroused by memories of the event. Love does give the Power to move into this amazing altered state, even though it might seem impossible to the ego.

The mystic begins as an average person. Then, one day, out of the blue, something strikes her. It feels like a vague, nebulous, indefinable restlessness. Something feels out of kilter, out of balance, wrong, although she cannot place her finger on it. If she simply neglects it, or dismisses it, popping another distracting movie into the vcr, she will not become a mystic at that time. But if she examines carefully, in detail, the cause of her "existential" anxiety, she will find an inner emptiness, a longing or yearning, that no amount of entertainment, sensuality, material things, or intellectual accomplishments can satisfy. Then, if she is wise, she will begin to walk the Way of Love. She will start to become a career-psychonaut, guaranteeing the inevitable result of supreme tranquility. She'll kick-start the process by beginning to study the writings and/or lives of the great mystics of history. She might read the Gospel of John,[5] the Upanishads, *The Way of Virtue*, or some other classics in

---

[6]. See my, "The Gospel of Universal Love," Part III of *Luminous Jewels of Love and Light: a Spiritetrology* (Liberty Township, Ohio; Love Ministries, Inc. 2002)

Richard Shiningthunder Francis

mystical literature. Thus will begin her new life as a new being.

****

Chapter 15

We're Phantoms in a Phantomworld: Awakening

★ ★ ★

You feel smothered by the tininess and insignificance of your self. A new job, car, home, or lover: Is this what you really need? Is this what your deeper Mind is crying out for? Or is it possible that you truly need a new Self, a new Mind? Your entire world, after all, is in your most important sexorgan. It lies not between the legs, but between the ears.

So when you have reached the profoundest level of "pneumogenic" (Spirit-caused) anxiety, no superficial "solutions" will have the least effect. They won't make a dent in your difficulty, for it is a Mindproblem, not a worldproblem. All your material "solutions" will be like a flea on an elephant's back— ineffective and powerless. The world will have served its only and beautiful purpose: It will have driven you away from its own emptiness, directly into your inner Mind. The world does this great service by illuminating, in fifteen-foot neon lights, the message THE WORLD HAS NO ANSWERS. The only function/purpose of the world is to drive you away from the world into the arms of Love.

The world does fill some needs, but is clearly not designed or engineered to fill the need for Love, that most basic and central driving force. And the entire multitude of Lovesubstitutes— sports, business, shopping, books, religion, politics, wealth, career, intellect— become ineffective to satisfy. Instead, the Lovemotivation blossoms, and grows into such a huge flower that, in time, it covers our vision of the world, filling our Mindfield. Then, the world loses all intrinsic meaning. Since it is empty of Love, its attractiveness wilts, dies, and drops away.

   Everything begins with this restless discontent, and the pain that piggybacks on it. For when we first long for perfect Love, then we first become aware of our separation from It. This strikes us as wretched and miserable spiritual poverty, which is precisely what it is. This idea of separation grows, we realize, only because we are so firmly convinced that we are separate egos. In time, the egoself, the only self that we have ever known, begins gradually to feel "unreal." We might panic, feeling that the total self is disappearing. But the first step in getting rid of this false selfimage is to have our gripping, panicky fingers pried away from grasping it. That is then followed by trust in the cosmos. Not that we really have a choice. The ego is already beginning its deathprocess. Even our natural panic does nothing to reverse this. So, all that we can do is throw ourselves on the mercy of the cosmos, let go, and go with the Flow. In time, this will lead to the recognition that we are not egos. We must come to see the egoself as a "role" only, a mask, a part in a play. After that, we must redefine "Self," and begin the inner voyage. For we are left with the scary question: If I am not this ego, what the heaven am I?

Falling in Love with Your Self
Love and the Inner Beloved

But how does one eradicate such a stubborn inertial concept as ego? One method with which you can begin this serious task is a game. But it leads to serious selfknowledge as well as selftransformation. It is called "Ifree." In playing Ifree, you see how long you can continue to speak and communicate, leaving out entirely the words, "I," "me," "my," and "mine."

Changing thoughtpatterns alters speech. It is also symmetrically true that altering speechpatterns can, in time, change the ways in which you think. But for this to work, you must do it. So, give it a try. You will likely be astonished at how egocentric our usual language really is.

Some people laugh or smile when they first hear of Ifree, realizing what a gargantuan challenge this is to that little dictator, the ego, that believes that it rules your world without question. Ifree is a major challenge to the little Napoleon/Hitler, and it will not respond with sweetness and light.

What you are starting to realize, in premystic restlessness, is that the ego is not king at all. Instead, you gradually discover that we all, as egos, grow out of a common pool of Mind, the collective unconscious. (See "Chart of Mind.") And at the core of that very deep Mindlevel is the Love-nature Itself.

We all have deeply entrenched, hidden, unconscious memories of having originally separated from universal Mind as isolated Souls. That is why we know the Way back. And whether we realize it consciously or not, we are all on our way back to pristine, infinite Lovemind. We're taking the long way home, back to the Lovegod. This is, to use a Taoist phrase, "returning to the Source."

Unconsciously, we remember a perfect state of undisturbed tranquility and bottomless serenity with nostalgia. Often, we recall it with pain, yearning, and longing to return there. This produces the anxious restlessness that is often our first call back to the Way. Stillmind, discovered through meditation ("interior prayer") is the Way back. From these deep memories, we are haunted by the possibility that life could be ever so much richer, easier, more enjoyable and pleasurable. We seek to fulfill this "perfect Mind" hunger by eating apples of wax. "Lovesubstitutes" are this false fruit. They can never satisfy this inner starvation. None of these works for more than a few days. This is because we are really famished for Love, glorious Love, infinite Love. We want to dive into this Love naked and immerse our Souls in It, swim around in It, until It pervades our every cell and pore. We want to suck It up greedily, as if there is no tomorrow, as if nothing else matters. For nothing else really does.

So, the instant that we hear that it is possible, we want to rush back to that state of perfect serenity, placidity, fulfillment, satisfaction, and contentment asap. We want it all, and we want It yesterday, if not sooner.

We feel that we are phantoms inhabiting a plastic world. This is actually the beginning of enlightenment. At first, it might bring a sense that nothing is real, nothing worth doing at all. But if we stay with it, hanging onto Love as our lifepreserver, life's work,

Falling in Love with Your Self
Love and the Inner Beloved

our meaning, our Source, we will graduate into full-blown mystics. We will have "earned our degrees" by our blood, sweat, and tears.

It is this unreal, plastic world that has given birth to an illusory self— the ego. Gradually, we begin to awaken to the fact that, although labels are convenient, we are not just our egolabel. Now, our work is cut out for us: It is to discover who we really are. If you realize that you are not your ego, that is great! But it is only the beginning of the long journey inward. It's the long way Home. Now that you know who you aren't, its time to get down to brass tacks and find out who you are.

You know now that all your loneliness was based on this illusion of a separate self, a tiny ego flailing in the midst of cold dark space, lost in immensities. But as you drift away from bleak materialism, this dismal portrait is replaced by a wisdom that tells you what the ancient Navajo shamans told their students: "You are the center of the universe," or at least, of "*your* universe."

And this, once seen, is as obvious as an elephant sitting on a barstool. Your entire universe exists just because you are at its center, sensing and perceiving it. Were you not alive and conscious (aware), your entire universe would disappear. In time, you come to realize that you live in a Mindworld (dreamworld).

****

There is really no "outside" to this Mindworld.

Richard Shiningthunder Francis

****

So you need not concern yourself any longer with "fixing the world," or changing the entire cosmos. Now, your assignment, your cosmic mission, has crystalclear boundaries. All your work, you now realize, is interior. You have come to earth, not to correct others, but to work on your own psyche.

****

Falling in Love with Your Self
Love and the Inner Beloved

Chapter 16

It's Tearing Me Apart: Separation

* * *

Selfcentered bastards, who care only for and about themselves, are not mystics. Working on yourself is not selfishness. It does not make you complacent. For while working on yourself, you repel selfishness, because the very work that you are doing is the cultivation of selflessness. For selfless activity is indispensable to universal Love. This is "counterselfish" work, a kind of spiritual "antiautism." Spirituality is dead unless it embraces all others in Love.

Mystics, historically, have been outstanding teachers, artists, poets, leaders, medical and social workers, scientists, writers, and trailblazers. Mystic realization does not kill, but resurrects both your talents and your interest in people. It is proproductivity and procreativity. Mysticism does not kill interpersonal activities and push you towards an unhealthy hermitic life, sealed away in a cave from all others.

Why does balanced, reasonable, genuine mysticism increase interpersonal interest and activity? Because its only goal is the cultivation of unconditional Love. And Love is all about people. This Love has two major practical expressions: service and friendship. So, the mystic finds solid meaning in losing herself in the service of at least one other person. She also delights in the cultivation of the widest and wisest circle of friends. Multiplying human interaction fills her days and nights with joy.

The loneliness that characterized the selfish ego has begun to erode and evaporate. In time, we cannot even remember exactly what we felt separated from. But it doesn't matter anyway. The entire idea of separation is a mist burned away by, and vanishing in, the light of the sun of Love.

Service develops Love, and Love creates a resonance between your conscious mind and the Superconscious Mind. Love is the Way back to original Mind.

Love is the reason why we do not have completely to make "transparent" all the layers of Mind that separate the ego from Spirit. Love is the "wormhole" that unites these distant Mindspheres. It is a shortcut to divine expression. this is the magic of Love: It sweeps us directly into the presence of the deepest Lovemind. And every act of Love reflects that Mind and moves us closer to unification with It. Love magnetically attracts our personal mind to the Supermind of the inner Lovegod.

So, mystical illumination is no matter of grunting, groaning, and struggling. You do not have to slave, century after endless century to clear out all the "garbage." You have managed, true, to pollute your personal unconscious, and even your Soulevel, with stains, impurities, and contaminants that have attached themselves to your Mind. Over centuries, much "garbage" has accumulated. It has entered the preconscious, personal unconscious, and Soulevels of Mind. (See

Falling in Love with Your Self
Love and the Inner Beloved

"Chart of Mind.") But a single moment of pure Love can burn it all away. Love burrows a tunnel between the inner Light and the conscious mind, allowing it perfectly to express that Lovegod within. The magic of Love is that it makes perfect Minds out of ordinary ones. The most polluted and foul waters are made sweet and sparklingly clear by the touch of Love. At the moment that true Love blazes up, the entire Mind is enlightened, made transparent, filled with Light. This is the condition called "grace"— a pure state of "sinfree" being. It is granted, not because we are actually sinless, but because all sins have been forgiven and released by the inner Supermind. Love can in a moment burn away all sin, releasing the Mind into pure, bright grace. Then, it is really as if the whole Mind were stainless, flawless, sinless. For in that moment of real Love, all sin is released, and the being is actually without imperfection— sinless.

Every act of Love is growth, healing, and worship. Every Love-act moves the mystic closer to the unitive state with the Beloved within. By stark contrast, every act of egofear is divisive. Fear is a chainsaw running amuck amidst the segments and areas of Mind, tearing, cutting, roaring through the pacific tranquility that supports unity. Because it has this interior effect, it also separates and isolates people from each other, creating conflicts, defensiveness, havoc, and war. The lower nature in Mind actually wants to create these states, for it thrives on fear, and wilts in the presence of Love.

Superlove (that which originates with Supermind) is elicited by both our laughter and our tears. The Beloved has a pillowsoft heart, and is easily moved to Love. Love is, after all, exactly what all people really want to do. For the mystic says that God needs human beings to love, as much as they need Him/Her. The most nourishing milk of the great inner Mother, the Goddess, can be elicited by sincere tears, which is why the Way often begins with tears.

But the same Goddessmind is elicited also by laughter, joy, or fun. In many forms of religion, participants are encouraged to sing, or even dance. In some, they are moved to participate in activities even funnier, or more fun. In some conservative and fearful communities, the churchservice is the only opportunity that the people have to "let go," become childlike, and play. In these, being "filled with the Spirit," or "getting the Holyghost," can be riotous, throbbing, electric, or even hilarious! The resulting joy, even laughter, invites the Spirit to arise within the Mind, pervading it. Some Christian worshipservices, for example, consist in nothing but uninterrupted laughter.

Deep down, everyone hungers for natural supernatural unity with Goddessmind. Equally deeply, everyone realizes that she is already one, in perfect Mindmeld or fusion, with Lovemind. She simply needs to awaken to this fact, from a profound and heavy slumber. Awakening, and looking back on your life, you realize that any feeling of "separation" was just the dream all along. From the beginning, "separation" was always illusion. And since you were never really separate from the Creatormind, you were never separate from

Falling in Love with Your Self
Love and the Inner Beloved

His/Her creation. But only Love awakens you to this reality.

Nothing sensitizes to oneness more than a sense of separation, or alienation. Few understand this pain better than I. For when I was growing up, I felt a poignant, painful separation. I was reared in an extremist rightwing cult[6] that prided itself on its "separation" from the "unclean world." This arrogant "superiorism" often translated to a deep sense of alienation, which easily slipped into isolation. There was a haunting sense of not belonging. Some of my earliest childhood memories were of feeling as if I were on the outside of a glass barrier, looking in at others having fun. I was taught, but in the most cynical, harmful, and cruel ways, that I did not belong to this world.

With mystical realization, I knew that I was *in* the world, but not *of* the world. This was no pathetic sense of insulation and exclusion, based on fear. It was a healthy sense of not being dominated by the environment. As the essence of this awakening was Love, it actually brought me closer to human beings, and to all other living creatures. Like you, and everyone else, I'm "jvtp"— just visiting this planet. No one actually "lives" here. We're all extraterrestrials, whose true Home is not another planet, but another plane, dimension, universe, or state of Mind. We find ourselves in the laboratory of earth for only a few nanomoments, trying to polish our

---

[6] For an overview of all the stuff I learned about cultpsychology, see my *Jehovah Lives In Brooklyn: Jehovah's Witnesses as a Model of Fundamentalism* (Liberty Township, Ohio; Love Ministries, Inc., 2000

Loveskills. We're here, in short, to perfect the Way. We're all just visiting students and tourists.

As the illusions and hurtful doctrines of the cult* separated me from the "bad world," so illusion and wrong concepts separate the egomind from the deeper Lovenature.

When we first begin the Way, we feel a strong sense of anxiety, emptiness, and restlessness. This surely doesn't feel good, but it is the best thing that has ever happened to us. For this is the alarmclock going off, to awaken us from deep cosmic sleep. In a short time, this alert gives birth to longing and yearning, even though we do not know what the target is. And it is this very hunger, this longing, that is our inner starship back to the Infinite.

That is why we must relearn the lesson of following our hearts, not just our minds. And we must dig deeply in the Mindmine to find the courage not to follow other human beings— often, very confused ones— as our "spiritual leaders." For the only valid "Leader" is the One in the heart, the Lovemaster (Lovemind, Lovenature, or Lovegod). Although our culture teaches us to mistrust the heart, in some African, Asian, and native American cultures, it is overeliance on mind that is the real danger. This is also true of intercultural and international mysticism. We get our distrust of the heart from the overintellectual Greeks. We also inherit some from ancient Hebrew culture. Jeremiah, who was seen as a "prophet" by the Hebrew culture, wrote, "The heart is treacherous."

These cultures dimly and dully managed to miss the point altogether. For the heart is

Falling in Love with Your Self
Love and the Inner Beloved

the source of Love, and so, is the nest of Supermind. (If we cannot trust this Goddessfilled heart, wee are left with only the confused meanderings of a conscious mind.) Here, the term "heart" means the poetic, metaphoric, and lovebased aspects of Soulmind (but the literal heart might also play a role).

The conscious mind has a built in tendency to be led astray by the lightshow of phantoms in the dreamworld. It is hoodwinked by the "virtual" play of "psychohologrames"[7] known as "material objects." The consciousmind, of course, was designed and structured exactly this way by the Soul. For it is the Soul's worldinterface. It is the lens through which the deeper Self or Soul interacts with, and learns from, the world. In order for the Soul to learn from the world, it was necessary to take the material order seriously. To take the world seriously, it was necessary that the Soul forget, at least a little, the spiritual nature of the world as dreamprojection. The whole, enlightened Soul could never forget the absolute Mindnature of Reality. So, Spirit hypnotized a part of the Soul, and this is the part that plunged into the world up to its neck. It is under the iron lock of a powerful amnesia, induced by the Great Forgetting, first created by the Spirit, then supported by the Soul. (Compare "Chart of Mind.")

This is the part of the Mind that we call the "consciousmind." It is the small piece of

---

8. This is a word that I coined in my 1986 "The Way of Universal Love" Part I of *Luminous Jewels of Love and Light* (Liberty Township, Ohio; Love Ministries, Inc., 2002)

Richard Shiningthunder Francis

Mind lost in the forms, figures, and images of the dream. It buys into it, swallows its illusion hook, line, and sinker. The deep Soulevel of Mind was never taken in, but this part called the consciousmind was thoroughly deluded. And so it was designed. Its very purpose was and is to yield to the illusion of the "virtual" world that we all mistake for the real thing.

The consciousmind is very sensitive to illusion. It is quite easily fooled and drawn in. This is exactly why we find our hearts pumping so wildly at movies, tv shows, and even novels. We know that none of these things is real, but the consciousmind is designed to buy into pseudoreality. In fact, it seems eager to do so. Nature constructed the consciousmind this way so that we would be completely deluded by the "outer, material" world of "psychovirtual" reality. But since the consciousmind is so readily, easily, and quickly fooled by illusion, it is an untrustworthy guide to inner space.

It's great— the tool of choice and preference— for such pursuits as science and engineering. But it is absolutely lost when it comes to poetry, creativity, joy, and Love. The consciousmind is not the proper tool for psychonautics (innerspace exploration). Trying to use it for this purpose is like trying to use a hammer or screwdriver to cut wood. It might be possible, in a very crude and messy way, but the saw is inarguably preferable.

Falling in Love with Your Self
Love and the Inner Beloved

Here, then, the heart must do what it was designed to do, for it is a part of the Mind of Love.

****

Chapter 17

Pristine Unity: The Eclipse of Confusion

***

The consciousmind can be a wonderful and versatile instrument. It is great for a wide spectrum of varying tasks. It is applicable to the widest range of implementations.

But there is one job at which it fails utterly, and this is the most crucial accomplishment of all: Coming into harmony or synergy with Love. The consciousmind alone cannot take us to the deepest areas of the heartmind, cannot keep us centered there. It pales into feeble insignificance when it comes to true spirituality, although it can at times produce remarkable counterfeits. Compared to the infinite depths of the Unconscious, the consciousmind is like a bee-bee in a boxcar.

Instead of supporting Love, the consciousmind fears. (Fear is the opposite of Love.) It is filled with doubts, uncertainty and confusion. All this dilutes the Love of the Spirit. This Love is further modified in so many ways by mental analysis that, if it is expressed at all, its expression might bear little resemblance to actual Love. A person can far too easily fall into the fast current of mind, to be carried along by the waters of the personal unconscious. (See "Chart of Mind.") The problem here is that this Mindlevel can be really screwed up. It can block Love almost totally, and fill the heartmind with fears. Traumas,

Falling in Love with Your Self
Love and the Inner Beloved

disappointments, and failures have all left their mark in the personal unconscious. (This is the Mindlevel that contains the notorious "subconscious," with all its mental baggage and garbage.) And here also, in the personal unconscious, is where the ego has its origin. The ego is played out by the consciousmind, but often rooted in the personal unconscious.

The fearfilled, remembering, logical consciousmind can be so powerful that mystics have called it the "slayer of the Real." Of course, it lacks the power actually to kill the deeper Mind. But it can *practically* "kill" the Soulevel and Spiritlevel of Mind by blocking them. In fear, it can ostracize them from the consciousmind, from awareness. It "kills" the Absolute, relatively, in that it completely occludes and obscures It. At times, the consciousmind completely eclipses the genuine expression of deeper Mind as Light and Love.

****

Your own mind can be your worst enemy if you are trying for enlightenment.

****

When the consciousmind is stuck in its fullest, most unyielding, and strongest belief in the reality of the world, illumination is impossible.

****

"Enlightenment is impossible as long as a single trace of ego remains."— the mystic Shankara (ninth century).

****

Regular, moderate use of the consciousmind is fully and highly recommended. The enlightened masters of history had brilliant and creative minds. But they drew the line when it came to the consciousmind's full takeover of the psyche. The consciousmind was always the servant of deepermind (Soulmind or Spiritmind), and never the inner master. It is the *overuse* of this consciousmind faculty that "kills" the Spirit. A dominant and overpowering consciousmind is a source of inner darkness. It battles, attempts to expel and resist, the Light of Love. Conversely,

****

Love, when complete, cleanses you of all thoughts of dominance by this world.

****

This is why mystics, during their periods of fullest illumination, are not very "practical" people from the standpoint of the world. When a mystic gets "high," she discovers that she does not want just to visit, but to live at, that very high place. If she does, she can bring it to others as a teacher or worldhealer. (This is not as grandiose as it sounds, since every act of Love is also an act of worldhealing.)

Falling in Love with Your Self
Love and the Inner Beloved

When the "impurities," pollutants and contaminants, of everyday life are filtered out by the Mind, the inner "waters" run pure, bright, crystalline, and clear. Then the Mind of the mystic is pristine, bright, and Lightfilled. She remains in a very high state of joy, bordering upon true bliss. Naturally, she wants to remain in this inner space. She has, as a personal desire, no interest in "coming back down" to the normal world, to normal social and psychological relationships and interactions.

This awakens within her a series of powerful memories of the inner Beloved. She carries these in a very deep part of her Soulevel, and they also arise from the deeper levels of the collective. (See "Chart of Mind.") These give her an almost sad state of longing for a perfect Mind, a pristine state that she enjoyed long ago, before Separation. When the great Mind, the Creator, first decided to pretend that He/She was the mystic, that person was still in perfect seamless oneness with that great Mind. Only later did the accumulations of memories, thoughts, and desires create the Soul, which willed Itself to be "separate." But why did It will Itself away from the perfect life of total joy and absolute tranquility? Because it wanted to test the envelope, try the limits, of the worldgame, the game of "separate" life. This Soulseparation and Soulseverance was all a part of the original gameplan, to make the game of life more fascinating and challenging, even a bit scary. But all during this early period of separationevolution, the Soul was perfectly and fully aware of its intrinsic seamless oneness with the cosmic Mind.

Things became much more complex when association with a particular body seemed as if it would be an even more exciting and dangerous game. It was the affixing of Mindaspects of the soul with the body that produced an entirely new vehicle for consciousness— the ego. In time, egos began to take themselves so seriously that a second separation occurred: After Soul had divided from Spirit, ego then further divided from Soul. Thus did illusion and Mindfog grow ever denser and deeper. At this point, ego became, for all practical purposes, actually separate. In its dream, it was no longer simply conceptually separate. This produced ego-isolation, creating the long slippery slide away from infinite Mind. This is when true loneliness came into being.

The cosmic Mind was like the galaxy's greatest comedian. Let's call a comedian Nick Jones, for lack of a more original or better name. In his act, Nick pretends to be a quirky little guy named Hapi Dalamatian. But the plot thickens. For Hapi Dalamatian "wants" to pretend to be somebody else. He's not super happy being Hapi. So he pretends to be Norman Beasley. By the end of the act, which is very well performed, you actually find yourself believing that there are three persons, not one, on stage.

In this parable, Nick represents the cosmic Mind, Hapi the Soul, and Norman the ego. The Chinese mysticsage Lao Tzu wrote inscrutably: "At first, there was the One, and the One produced two, and the two, three, and the three gave rise to all others." This otherwise obscure teaching (rendered here, rather than literally translated) concerns how Mind, in

Falling in Love with Your Self
Love and the Inner Beloved

disguising Itself, finally played the scariest game in the history of the universe: It was unable to resist the risk, gamble, and challenge of losing Itself in a plethora of complex and fascinating roles. It was, after all, the best "Actor" in the history of cosmic creation, and had an infinite imagination that just would not quit! So, It just could not pass up a chance like that! (Cosmic Mind is the supreme Gameplayer.) So, after countless millennia of eons, that Mind became you, and me.

****

Richard Shiningthunder Francis

Chapter 18

Fake Teachers, Real Love, and Great Sex

***

Keep the fires and embers of Love burning brightly and warmly within the heart. This is the noble goal of every person, and surely every mystic. Her consciousmind wants to flee when terrified by the spectacle and specter of suffering. But she must learn to embrace even that in invulnerable tranquility. She hopes to grow into a Love that enfolds even suffering within its expansive wings.

We all eagerly embrace and celebrate the sparkling joys and wonders of Love, but flee from Its pains. But any true Love is a tearing open of your inner heart in naked vulnerability. The heart must be wide open to permit the Flowexit of Love, but this same openness allows the darts and arrows of outrageous misfortune also to find their mark. Since this heartarea is so richly supplied with psychic "nervendings," the pain can be exquisite and enormous.

Love is always a gamble. The ego (social self, name) risks everything when Love enters. So, the ego is antiagapic (against Love). It knows that every act of Love threatens its inner tyranny. Love shakes the ego to the core, challenging its domain. It is a new Ruler, whose new rules will change everything. The ego, adapted to stasis, fears change of this magnitude. So, it will snarl and growl, bite and claw, when you try gently to lay your

Falling in Love with Your Self
Love and the Inner Beloved

life and selfimage upon the "altar" of Love, surrendering all to Love. And if it cannot directly resist you, it will indirectly, subtly place every kind of obstacle in your Way. This is serious, life and death stuff, and the ego knows it. It is fighting for its very survival.

So, if it sees You expanding and blossoming in Love, it will actively, violently resist. (Traditional older writers referred to this resistance as "temptation.") Ego has three polymegaton weapons in its arsenal: ego, greed, and careless sex. The lives of many so-called "spiritual leaders" are instructive here. For, often when they are at their peak of economic and public "success," they will be taken down by a member of this dark trinity.

A "teacher" promoting personal ego is useless. For her own inner "conquest" is obviously incomplete. Beware of "spiritual teachers" who are in love with their own egofaces. They make sure that they are prominent on posters, and on the covers of their books. Some even go to the extreme of distributing signed photos of themselves! And it is not beyond some very, very sick types to make the claim, with a straight face, that simply by gazing at their egofaces, or photos of their glorious visages, you will become enlightened!

This is hyperegotism, egotism gone mad. These people are spiritually sick. They feel worthless inside. They dance as fast as they can to compensate, but it can never be fast enough. These are the people who are always trumpeting about their personal spiritual experiences, bragging about famous clients, regaling with their wealth or accomplishments, or booking themselves for very public events. They do not care about reaching many hearts. No, they work with the public only to boost their flagging, flaccid egos. Their selfloathing always catches up. For your own good, and for the benefit of the spiritual community, avoid them. For they spread the most excruciatingly destructive plague of spiritual death— the disease of hyperegotism.

The "teacher" who talks about herself more, or rather, than the teaching, is also still suffering from egosickness. She is simply not skilled enough to help you. Anyone who longs to see her egoname in print, or who overuses it, is also a failed teacher. When someone talks about her "famous" clients or students she is also untrustworthy. Also, anyone who talks just a little too much about her personal experiences, how gifted she is, or implies that she has some kind of "special" communications with angels, extradimensionals, or God that make her teachings infallible is a fake. Do yourself a favor, and turn away from any teacher who is always trying to impress you with her knowledge, or her skill. Fraudulent teachers like to pretend to be psychics or sensitives. That can be only so much bull, designed to reel in the gullible.

Beware of anyone who uses any special titles. When a person calls herself a "master," there is in all the world no more sound a guarantee that *she is no master*. Exercise healthy skepticism whenever a name is followed by a string of odd and meaningless consonants. He/She is also having deep egoselfimage problems. Reject any "teacher" who calls him/herself an "enlightened being," or anyone who uses any similar hyperpompous

Falling in Love with Your Self
Love and the Inner Beloved

selfdescription. No genuine master would ever dream of so identifying him/herself, and would certainly never do so even in private, much less publicly. The true master would regard this as an act of shame. This is a sure-fire sign of a real phony.

Beware of anyone who insists on being addressed as "Pastor," "Reverend" (which means "holy"), etc. This attitude is fully analogous to that of an insecure and poor doctor who insists on being introduced as "Doctor Smith," rather than the more common, ordinary, and secure *"Mister, Mrs., or Ms.* Smith." It's even more unwise to entrust your spiritual self with insecure people than your physical body.

To a happy, secure person, this kind of egorecognition is not a plaudit or desirable social bauble. In fact, knowing the Reality of everyone's sharing equally the inner connection to the Spirit can make it downright embarrassing. A few years ago, in the northeast U.S., I was just getting the hang of seminars as teaching-vehicles. I was just learning the ropes, methodologies, and tools of the trade. This explains, but is no valid excuse for, what I allowed to occur at the end of one of my first seminars.

At the end of the workshop, the floor was opened to spontaneous and free comments. A man stood and informed the group that it was a native American practice to chant the name of a respected teacher three times. Bewildered, and a bit confused, I allowed the group to chant my native American name. (There is some little comfort in the fact that they did not use my egoname.)

But I should never have permitted this. It caught me completely by surprise, and was *exactly the wrong thing to do*, from the mystical viewpoint. Now, it is remembered with only shame, regret, and embarrassment. Thank Love that it was only a small group, about thirty people. But still the *principle* of nonegocentricity suffered violation. And it will never happen again.

Astonishingly, many so-called "spiritual teachers" lap up ego-attention like a thirsty puppy its water. They maneuver and strategize to get the maximum attention, and see the entire world of metaphysics and spirituality as a challenge to create the most massive ego possible. Real spirituality is just the opposite. If anything, the "winner" is *not* the one who gains maximum public attention and respect. The real winner is the teacher who is strong enough to live without that attention and respect. A hallmark of a really excellent teacher is that she would rather hear you speaking about her message than about her.

Does this mean that a true, genuine, honest teacher must hide in a cave? No, she can do work among people, even public work. But her focus will never be on her ego. She will not draw attention to herself, her students, her history, her achievements, or her experiences. Instead, she will honestly focus all concentration and attention on the message, and none, or almost none, on the messenger. She will speak humbly, even selfeffacingly. Most importantly, she will leave you with the impression that she is not some "grand poobah," some lightsurrounded saint, some special guru, but an ordinary person who has found something extraordinary. She will not waste your time or hers "blah-blahing" about her own public success, social adventures, or wealth. To her, in fact, the wealthy would receive no more homage or respect than any other human beings, since she believes in the spiritual, inner equality of all. A real teacher will feature and magnify only the message, but never the self. She will always keep the self, as the messenger, in the background. Of course, you cannot function in this society without a name-tag, and it is not demanded that every true teacher do everything anonymously, although that can also be excellent and unusually rewarding. Egonames have their valid, practical places and uses. But the place of the ego of a genuinely spiritual person is **never** the spotlight. The truly spiritual do not only **not** seek it, but avoid it whenever possible. They want to give "publicity" only to their message.

Also, don't follow anyone who is actively allowing a cult to form around his/her egoself. Avoid people who present themselves as special "incarnations of God" or "gurus." Signs of this kind of blatant, massive, and overblown egotism should send alarm bells ringing in your psyche. So should the slightest hint of ego-idolatry, as when a religious leader allows others to kneel before him/her, or kiss his/her ring. When religious leaders do these foolish things, do not hesitate to abandon the false teacher before she does you even greater harm.

Greed also marks the fraud. Teachers also must live in this world, and do need funds to do this. But those should always be moderate—even minimal. Any true teacher will be willing, for example, to work for Love-donations, at least, sometimes. *He/She will never hesitate to open up a seminar freely to one who cannot afford to pay.* Also, avoid teachers who overcharge for their books and tapes, or lectures. Sometimes, if a book is published commercially, a teacher cannot afford to give the book away free, for he/she has to purchase every copy. That is, he/she must pay for the book. But he/she should at least be willing to give it to you for the author's cost— without profit. After all, what is important here— profit and money, or Souls and messages? Again, the real spiritual master will be willing to give freely of his/her tapes, seminars, counseling, teaching, and lecture time. All need not be given away free, but exceptions will always be gladly made for those in need.

Reject teachers who overcharge for their work. Again, a genuine teacher will always be willing to work without charge or any kind of fee for anyone having a true emergency. The truth is, an hour of a real teacher's time cannot be "purchased," for it is priceless. Spirituality itself must not be viewed as a "market commodity," to be given a dollar value. Beware of modern "money-changers in the temple," people who try to sell you spirituality in convenient packages. Here, beware especially of tricksters and hucksters.

Even the wisest counselor is not worth what many selfproclaimed teachers charge for a session, and **no one** is worth what some "teachers" charge for a lecture or workshop. The "deep pockets" approach to spirituality is just egolunacy. Greed also denies the patterns taught by our very best teachers of

Falling in Love with Your Self
Love and the Inner Beloved

all history. Jesus and the Buddha never charged at all— for the most treasured and powerful teachings in the history of the world.

Greedy people will argue that we live in a different kind of world, but the world did have money, even in ancient times. The truth is, the great masters saw their work as more than a "business." They refused so to drag it through the mud. They also actively refused egotism, and that is why we remember them, why their names are illuminated in spiritual splendor.

The third mark of a fraud is that he/she will tend to be strongly sexually predatory, if not deviant. **No true spiritual teacher is ever a predator**. Spiritual teachers have immense respect for their students, seeing each one as sacred. They "love" each student, but not sexually. Instead of being an excuse to indulge his/her lower nature lusts, Love is a mental and spiritual expression for a true teacher. They also have giant respect for sex and its powers. Only fakes and phonies see students as playthings, as pawns to be used, as sexual objects. The honorable and true spiritual teacher believes in the principle of sexual loyalty and fidelity. He or she, if in a relationship, will not be carelessly, stupidly bedhopping, but will have one solid, strongly committed, monogamous relationship. This will be the practical Love-center of his/her life. So, it will be regarded as it truly is— as sacred. He/She will not seek egostroking in the form of sexual favors, and will never mistake sex for Love, or vice-versa.

The form of Love embraced by the enlightened mystic is only peripherally and secondarily related to sexual love at all. And then, it becomes sexual Love only under conditions where longterm commitment to, and Love for, one other person permits mutual intimacy. A genuine teacher never embraces casual, careless, recreational sexuality, and so, is never promiscuous. While it has sensory and sensual components, mystical Love is largely a Mindlove or Soulove. It is experienced through cognition and heartfeeling. At its apex, it can evolve into sexual expression, but only for one's chosen "outer beloved."

Sexual love is often impure precisely because it is so widely, carelessly, and promiscuously scattered. It is thus diluted, weakened, and compromised. The wide spreading of sexual energy also trivializes it. It turns sexual love into nothing more than a pastime or hobby. Sex becomes like tv. It is just another way to distract from a boring life. It's no more than a new "toy" to escape the ennui of an inactive, lazy Sunday afternoon when you have nothing "better" to do. This attitude creates the oxymoronish "casual sex" or "recreational sex."

Sex is, at its zenith, a form of Loveworship. So, good sex is **never** casual or recreational. That kind of sex is merely biological, arising from the animal nature— the lowest layer of the lower nature. It has nothing of love in it. It is stripped of all nobility, all tenderness, and all spirituality.

The desire behind sex can never be fulfilled with a number of sexual partners. This is because it is the flower of the inner impulse

*Falling in Love with Your Self
Love and the Inner Beloved*

for unity with the Beloved. The agonies and ecstasies of human love are but pale reflections of the spectrum of Love possible with the inner Beloved. Either form of Love can be a real rollercoaster, with swings from the highest peaks of rapture to plummets to the depths of inner hell. (The latter state, in mysticism, is called the "darknight.")

The thirst for the inner Absolute, results, if pursued, in an awakening to the true nature of the world as dreamworld or Mindworld. This radically transforms the mystic's relation to the events, objects, circumstances, and people of her personal world.

So mystics see "God" not as distant, cold, formal judge, lawgiver, or king. Instead, they embrace God as intimate Friend. I remember, about four decades ago, studying a book published by the "fundy" cult to which I belonged. In order to prove how seriously misled, ignorant, and stupid were people of other faiths, the book mockingly quoted a Hindu as saying that he regarded God, 'not as King, but as Friend.' That statement planted a seed that, never forgotten, grew stronger over the decades. God is not a "person," but is the growing, expanding Love dwelling in each and every heartmind. All the Love in all the galaxies, summed up, is the totality of God. The God of mystics is happy, playful, and joyful. He/She embodies something of the clumsy little baby elephant, the tenderness of the tiny kitten, and the charm of the puppy. He/She is eager to forgive and to love. Indeed, this God has no other function. This Lovegod has no real opposite. He/She is no judge, for Jesus said, "The Father judges no one." Like the father in the parable of the

Richard Shiningthunder Francis

Prodigal Son, this "heavenly Father/Mother" rushes out to meet us when we are still far away, and can't wait to draw us into the family of His/Her Love.

****

Falling in Love with Your Self
Love and the Inner Beloved

Chapter 19

Love: Knowing, Getting, and Giving the Real Thing

***

You are the cosmic masterpiece, dreamed by the penultimate Source of beauty, the unconscious Artist within. Daily, It struggles literally to re-form you in the perfect image of Itself, of stainless Love. Love is an art.

This Artist wants to "apprentice" you. It/He/She wants to guide you safely on your inner Journey to the Beloved, divine Love Itself. For this inner trek to the deep Love-nature you were born. Love is an extension of your flawless, brilliant inner Self. It flows forth as feelings of goodness, kindness, care, concern, and compassion.

Love isn't just a mindprocess. It can't be "studied" except by living. You can't learn Love from books. You can't get It from teachers, except when they serve as role-models. You can't get It from sociology, psychology, or religion. It can bubble up only from a tender heartmind. Because It is not intellectual, it is often tough to understand It with the head only. For the "head" is only half of Mind, the other half being "heart." You've got to dive into heart if you're going to get "ahead" on this path!

Love is like breathing. There's a part of your Mind that already knows how to do it. The deepest inner Coremind wants nothing else.

Richard Shiningthunder Francis

This is also precisely what the Mindlevel called your Soul wants for you. It wants incessantly, relentlessly to Love. It is always signaling that nothing else matters. Love beautifies and immensely enriches our Mindworlds. A loveless world is frigid and empty. So, if you have Love, but nothing else, you are already abundantly wealthy and successful. But even if you have everything else, but no Love, you have nothing. The "winner" of the game of life is *not* the "one who dies with the most toys," but the one who lives with the most Love. Without enriching Love, all fame and money are mere straw and sawdust. One good strong wind can blow your entire life away.

But, instead of forcing and grunting, to "make Love happen," you need to step back, relax, and find some detachment. You must get yourself out of the way, and *allow* Love to happen. You cannot *make* Love happen.

So, while your consciousmind cannot generate Love by an act of will, it can learn to cooperate. Imagine a hulking, dirty thief-rapist breaking into your home. He's a real Neanderthal type, a real scuzz-bucket. Like all ignorant, violent, stupid men, he also needs Love, deep down. He places a gun to your temple and roars, "Love me, right now, or you're dead!"

Now, At that moment, you really **would** *want* to love him. After all, it means your life. But you find yourself repelled. No matter how much you try, you can't seem to generate even a micropsychon of Love for this bastard. In fact, naturally, you'd rather scratch his eyes out. You tell yourself that you'd rather be

Falling in Love with Your Self
Love and the Inner Beloved

tied naked to an anthill than to "love" this throwback.

This miniparable shows how impossible it is to force Love, or to generate it just by wanting it: No matter how much you desperately, genuinely **want** to "love" this guy, it's out of the question. This is why we "fall" in Love, as we "fall" asleep. Love is coalesced unconsciously. It can be elicited, but never forced.

It's a megamplification of deep inner attraction, and/or resonance. We mean real "Love," not the wimpy diluted counterfeit that says, "My dog loves her new doghouse." Love is the greatest act, achievement, or accomplishment of Mind. It is incomparable. Just ask anyone who has ever been, or still is, "in Love." Or, take your mind back to when you were. (If you are in Love right now, you are the luckiest person around— probably for miles around!) Real Love creates ecstasy, and it alone brings you back to the inner Garden of Pleasure in the heart.

How does Love blossom? Two ways: Others seem to elicit Love from you. This is due to their beauty, kindness, goodness, wisdom, etc. This is the type that is popular and common. It is the "love" that says, "I just can't help but love him/her. He/She is just so _____!" (Fill in your own adjective.)

But just a micropsychon of thought shows that this is not true Love. It is barter. It says, *"I 'love' you because you please me."* So, it's only a very thinly disguised egotism. A man, for example, who displays a "trophy" wife is abusing her as an object, an extension of his allimportant ego. He does not give a care for her as a real person. Except as egobuilder, she is seen as worthless. She is like his car. This kind of "love" is all about *him*. It does nothing to sustain *her*, and that is why it is egotism.

Real Love is a stark polar opposite: It is not about you, but about the beloved. It says, "I do not love you just because of what **you** are. I do not love you just because you please me. I love you because of what **I** am." Ironically, this is the one that appears, at first glance, to be an egostatement. But a more careful analysis will show why it is the superior, and only, basis for true Love.

First, it cannot arise from the ego. Why not? By nature, the ego is grasping, clinging, attaching, judgmental, and demanding. So, the "I" in the statement, "I love you because of what *I* am" cannot be the ego. It must represent a wiser part of the heartmind. Now, the only natural and true extension of this statement is, "No matter how you change, no matter what you do, or say, that will not change *Me*." In turn, this leads to, "So, I'll still love you." This "I" is areference to the deeper Self (Soul). Thus, the cap "M" in "Me" is deliberate. For this deeper Self is the Source of all Love within the consciousmind. To love people because of what You are, you must stop playing the game of ego, and become something else. You must be "reborn," discovering a completely new identity. You can no longer afford to be merely Mary Smith or John Jones. Instead, in time, you grow to see Your Self as a mirrormanifestation of deepest infinite Mind. This journey begins with the recognition that You are a Soul, not a body. You are timeless, birthless, and deathless.

Falling in Love with Your Self
Love and the Inner Beloved

You must permit this Love until You are a virtual fountain of Love. This requires continuous practice. A person learning math must go over equations until their solution becomes unconscious, second nature. Love is like this, too.

But Love is easier, because You are plugged in to the inner Source of all Love, the Spirit, at the Soulevel of Mind. Love is something you already know, unconsciously, how to do. So, to complete the circuit, you need to link up the consciousmind with that Soulevel. For, at one "end of the Mindspectrum," this Soul is one with your conscious mind; at the other, it is one with the Spirit. So, it is a bridge between you and infinite Mind.

Love is something that happens automatically when you begin habitually practicing and monitoring. So, the cosmic Mind snares you in its subtle, delightful "trap": The only Way to learn the art of loving is to love. You simply can't think your way out of most human problems; you must love your Way through them. And this changes you. It forces you to see the unutterably beautiful within yourself, the Fountain of Love, the Lovenature. So, in true Love, you love from this Source, not because of what the beloved is or does, but because You have touched unity with this Supermind.

This unity with the inner Beloved marks all real Love, which **must** be unconditional. In other words, all good Love contains and implies Selflove. This is falling in Love with Love, and lifts any Lovebased relationship over the moon. It elevates and purifies all Love. Love for the "external beloved" is one with Love of the internal

Beloved. So, if you truly love, the source of that Love is not good looks, body, mind, talents, scintillating personality, sparkling sense of humor, money, fame, charm, or extraordinary skills. These attractions might well make Love easier and more fun. But if Love is genuine, it is given as a gift— the greatest gift that any two beings can possibly ever share. And this gift actually comes not *from* you (as ego), but *through* You (as Soul). All that the ego can do is choose to resist this Love, or to cooperate with it. To refuse or resist is a quick ticket to inner hell. To dance with It is a smooth ride to the inner Garden of Pleasure. So, when two people are in love, their egos are in full abeyance and retreat. At the peak, in fact, egos disappear, replaced by the sweetest and most delicious sense of union. The very best Love, like the best sex, is a Soul-to-Soul interaction. Each surrenders to the other, and each passionately and compassionately embraces the other. The lovers are in fullest synergy and resonance, not only with each other, but with the inner Self shared by both. This is Lovecstasy.

This Love sounds so alien, even bizarre, to us, because we have forgotten how to love. Our unraveling society is proof, if it were needed, of this sad fact. We are fairly competent when it comes to "trade," and we insist on a "fair deal" even when Love is involved. We carefully measure the micropsychons, to make sure that we are getting exactly as much as we are giving.

Justice, fairness, and balance have their place in true Love. But Love should ideally be a joy, not a barter. It is a giving

Falling in Love with Your Self
Love and the Inner Beloved

without strings, a full surrender, not an exchange of psychic "goods." When we really love, it is because Love fulfills and satisfies our entire inner nature, pushes all our buttons. It is a delight and pleasure to love, and this is not the appropriate place to keep tabs, a "Loveledger." No one should be keeping score.

Of course, we do want to receive as much as we give. But if that is our major, or only, consideration, we have lost the true spirit of giving, and of Love. We give Love freely, as the cosmic Mind loves us. The cosmic Mind provides rain and sunshine for both worthy and unworthy, good and evil people. We love because it is the only activity in the universe worth pursuing. We love because it is the road to ecstasy. We love because it is the very best within us. We love because the inner Spirit is Love.

This is also a Way of taking responsibility. How we spend our timenergy results from deliberate choices. So, a personal accounting is demanded by the inner "observer" or, "judge." This is the sector of the Unconscious which observes all our behaviors and keeps records of them, with a view towards longterm "payback," or karma.

This is an unpopular concept in our "blaming" society. Even the behavior of the worst criminals is someone else's fault. We are so quick to blame each other.

This is because we are still in the "kindergarten" phase of social development. But individuals are not paralyzed at that level. No just, reasonable society can grow until its members grow first. This requires spirituality. It expresses as compassion, responsibility, honesty, and obedience to the inner law of impeccable honor.

This inner "law" is the sumtotal of Love's guidelines for life. It guides you to behave well, and honestly, when dealing with all creatures. In human society, it implies fullest obedience to all good consensual laws designed by the community. It necessitates cooperation and lawfulness in even "small matters." A person of impeccable honor will drive the speedlimit on the freeway even when no cops are around. Why? Because those laws are safety measures, but, more importantly, because they are the law. The community has agreed that speedlimits are a good idea, and the person of impeccable honor supports order, as well as friendliness, in society.

The same applies to income-tax laws. An old publicservice announcement reminded us, "It's not just a good idea; it's the law." So, the person of impeccable honor is not always bitching about having to carry her fair share financially or economically. She is the very opposite of ultraconservative greed that allows others to rationalize their law-breaking. It is, in fact, the literal definition of a "criminal": One who knowingly, deliberately breaks the law. So, is the person of Love a fanatic? Is she unreasonable? Not at all. She simply sees the law as the law. She does not see it as a suggestion, to be followed only when and if personally convenient. This makes her the very backbone of an orderly society. Of course, some laws are inconvenient! Only a fool would dispute that!

But does that give us the right to become destructive anarchists or criminals? And is

Falling in Love with Your Self
Love and the Inner Beloved

it not the worst, and most blatant, hypocrisy to cry out for "law and order," and then proceed to break the law yourself? And if everyone does this, where is the order of society and civilization? It is no more. Soon, in harmful anarchy, civilization itself is dead.

So, let's grow up. This growth is partly cognitive. Recognition of how Love operates alters Love. It is a simple concept: Love expresses inner goodness. Actions of others are irrelevant.

The "Life 101" course is provided by earthsituations. And you will take an "exam" shortly after you read this. That will be a chance to practice your new Loveskills— loving with realization that it can be unconditional. For now you've learned the "secret." But the knowing is just the first step on a thousand mile highway. The sage Lao Tzu wrote, "Every journey of a thousand miles begins under one's feet." So, even *before* we take this first step, the soul has planned this journey of Light and Love. Now, we must practice the doing.

****

Chapter 20

Crying and Laughing Your Way to Love

***

A flood, a river, an ocean of tears can result from earthlife. And it usually does. "Please don't cry." These tender words express a deep and gentle Love. We are distressed when loved ones cry. Since infancy, crying has meant everything from mild discomfort to hellish agony. But crying can be one of the most cleansing and healthy of natural responses, detoxing body and mind. It's the natural response of babies and toddlers.

Elephants and other higher mammals also cry. Nature uses it to create or maintain bodymind balance. Crying all the time is unhealthy, but a moderate flow of tears can be remarkably healing. Once in a while everyone just needs a "good cry."

Paradoxically, nature's other great conscious cleansing method is laughter. So, mystics cry, and mystics laugh— not just because these are therapies, but because mystics are the most human of human beings. Some had excessively turbulent and hard lives. Combined with exquisite tenderness, this school of hard knocks made them sobbed their way through life. But this was the radical exception. For usually, the mystic Way created irrepressible joy, bubbling up irresistibly, and bursting into Light and lightheartedness in their happy lives.

Falling in Love with Your Self
Love and the Inner Beloved

Francis is typical, as he ventured into his day with a song in his heart and on his lips. These mystics lived at the other end of the spectrum from those tender souls brought to tears by this sad world. Many, including the Zen masters, laughed almost all the time. Overall, mystics tend to be extraordinarily joyful.

But a mystic can do nothing to enlighten you. However joyful she is, she cannot bring you into her bliss. You must, in terms of bumpersticker wisdom, follow your own bliss. She can only aid. A mystic teacher is a menu, but you cannot live well by eating the menu. She is a street sign, but you cannot well drive on the street sign. So, although you must go to the inner space that she describes, she cannot go there for you. In fact, she cannot even go there *with* you. Mysticism must be personal, never vicarious or secondhand. And it is never just a headtrip; it must also be a heartrip.

It is never the task of the mystic teacher to "make" you do anything. She simply recommends. She does *not* indoctrinate, for mystics are not defined by their holding in common teachings or doctrines. They are identified only by their sharing of common, active Love. So, Buddhist, Christian, Jewish, and Islamic mystics are sisters and brothers, and live out their Love by openarmed and openhearted embrace. So, a good mystic teacher will not reel you into a cult, but will emphasize universalism, the cult's healthy opposite.

The job of the mystic teacher is to fan the glowing embers of your heartlove into active flame. She wants to make the inner fire of

Love so hot that it consumes you altogether, leaving not a trace of ego. Her work is incomplete until "you" have fully disappeared.

The relationship between the mystic student and her teacher always blossoms from Love. But a good guide will not seek to "rescue" you from reality. Indeed, she will teach you to welcome it— with all its educational pain— with open arms. Anything uncomfortable she will teach you to transform into the ladder of inner Infinity.

While supremely compassionate, the mystic teacher knows that pain can be a part of your growthprocess. She cultivates boundless tender compassion, so this truth never makes her hard, apathetic, insensitive, or complacent. But she exists to be neither your "mommy" nor your "lioness" (protectress). At best, she can be a role-model. She wants to be a kind, listening, supportive friend, an advisor/consultant. But she cannot live your life for you, and doesn't really want to. Only the spiritual toddler buries her face in her mother's skirts. The good teacher wants you courageously to face the world, without blinking, without backing down. She will never ensconce you in an isolated and "safe" cult, but will help you become empowered by squarely staring down your challenges.

Sometimes suffering is the only path. The "head" of the ego is made of durable concrete, and it often takes a sledge-hammer blow to dislodge the ego from the mind. Only that will force us to see what we really need to see. While, then, in the shorterm, the teacher might allow a limited pain to endure in your heartmind, you can rest assured that,

*Falling in Love with Your Self
Love and the Inner Beloved*

in the longterm, she will aid you to move beyond your pain.

She might not just remove the pain directly. But, by definition, once you have risen above it, the pain is gone. And she will do everything possible to help you to transcend it. The teacher exists precisely to help you to climb to new inner mental heights. If you "rescue" a child from a scary, uncomfortable schooltest, rather than making her study and take the test, you do her no favor.

There are two kinds of genuine Love. The first is responsive Love. This is genuine Love that responds to the immediate needs of the beloved. Its goal is to mediate or reduce pain asap. But there is another type of Love that is also real, called "educational" Love. This is the kind of Love that the cosmic Mind, and the good teacher, will express towards you. Educational Love is the Love that tells you to send your little daughter to school even when it terrifies her, and brings great pain. For you know that the lessons/education will be well worth the shorterm pain. So, cosmic Mind allows us to experience every kind of pain, for It knows well that this discomfort will create within us both strength and wisdom.

The teacher's job is to educate you. She will teach you, for example, how much pain is in the event, and how much in your **chosen response** to that situation; the mind can make pain more, or less, acute. To embrace even pain as the Lovegift of cosmic Mind is your mystical aim. Even this incredible task will come to seem natural. Much pain disappears with the dawning of the heartlight of Love.

When it is ignited, it will become crystalclear that the world is overflowing with beauty and Love. Not a micrometer of space is void of this Love. All matter, in its abundance of forms, is saturated by, immersed within, the Lovemind of the Lovegod who dreams it all up. The ordinary world, seen with extraordinary eyes, becomes brilliant Light and tender Love. It is a mirror of the perfect Absolute (Love).

But even this world of endless and shimmering beauty cannot indefinitely eclipse the infinitely more magnificent splendor of the inner Self (Soul). The glory of the Absolute (Coremind) is more resplendent and sublime than is Its reflection in/as the world. The world's beauty might obscure the Absolute for a time, until it turns into the Absolute.

All "outer, material" glory is a symmetric mirroreflection of the mystic's deepest Mind and its own supernal splendor. She sees her Lord, and Lady, everywhere. The "material" world is jampacked everywhere with God and Goddess. But how does the mystic contact this Spirit?

She prepares a "Mindroom" for the "visiting Guest." An "inner space" must be "disinfected" of egothought. Here, in this special Mindspace, the conscious mind can contact the deepest Mindlevel. To prepare herself for this Spirit to "move in," the mystic practices impeccable honor, which goes so far beyond mere obedience to all good laws. She does everything that she should do, and then more. Being "good" is not her only goal. she wants to become stainless, pristine, flawless, and even relatively "perfect." Her final goal is transcendental excellence.

Because she knows that she has a lower nature, she is never a perfectionist. She does not make superhuman demands upon herself. She gives herself the widest latitude. She actually plans to fall many times every day. She might be seen as practicing "preforgiveness," releasing her errors even before they are actually made. But as she draws closer to Union with Spirit, selforgivness approaches and approximates the infinite Love of the inner Absolute. Whenever possible, she feeds the heartmind a steady diet of happy, compassionate, selfaccepting, forgiving thoughts and feelings. She feeds and thrives on joy.

So, the Way takes time. Enlightenment might be instant, but time must be spent cleansing the inner space— not only of negativity, but of all the desires, thoughts, and feelings of the ego.

Selfish desires are pollutants of the "ocean" of Mind. They block, and conflict with, the desires of Love. Just as a computer keyboard that had a will of its own would be useless, a person who has a personal will (desire-program) is useless to the great Mind. A computer that wanted to write its own manuscript would be worse than useless to a writer. The value of a good keyboard is in its obedience, without interference, to the will of its operator.

Most people are like keyboards that have their own ideas of what should be written. They go through life attempting to manipulate and control, turning their worlds into pressurecookers. Mystics say that the

Soulevel of Mind has already written the "script" for your life. So, your best response is not control, but cooperation.

But how does one know what the script is? It is unnecessary to know. This is where the mystery called "faith" enters. But this faith is trusting that your own Soul knows exactly what it is doing— that it is, in fact, eminently more qualified than you are to design your life. It has, after all, a vast repertoire of knowledge and wisdom, accumulated over centuries. Besides, its power is quite irresistible. Egoresistance would be like a snowflake in a supernova.

****

Perfect faith is perfect relaxation.

****

The Absolute cannot use people with strong egowills. They are impediments to Its writing of Its will into the script pattern of the dreamworld. Again, these are useless keyboards because they have their own agendas about what should be keyed in. Other people have less powerful personal wills, but are like keyboards whose keys do not all function. So, although their egowills are not powerful, neither do they understand pure mystical Flow. These also frustrate the will of Love.

Erasing personal will begins with the obliteration of personal desires. The "Way of purgation" (the mystic's name for this cleansing phase) explodes and mushrooms into total metamorphosis. But mystics realize that they are never perfect. So, they cannot

Falling in Love with Your Self
Love and the Inner Beloved

prepare a perfect inner space for the Lovemind (Lovegod, Ultralove). But they strive for some level of balance, harmony, and wellness. For if there is too much disturbance in the personal unconscious Mindlevel, one is blocked from the unitive fusion with Coremind. So, you cannot become a mystic until/unless you have ironed out the major kinks in the fabric of your mind.

The inner space prepared for Love must be bright, sweet, and clean— empty, waiting, and ready for the entry of Love. A powerful "pocket" or Mindarea exists within both the collective and soulevel of Mind. It contains vast and intricate understandings of the ways in which the world and Mind work. This Mindarea can be called the "spiritual unconscious." It contains very many ideas, concepts, and inspirations of enormous wealth and fantastic power.

But the spiritual unconscious, as bright and beautiful as it is, is not omniscient. This area is the source of some "inspiration," and of the "eureka" experience. (It is an "area" of Mind, not a "level," because it contains parts of two levels.) This is the inner Fountain of wisdom, and lives within the riches of true spirituality. So, the "spiritual unconscious" is a subsystem within the Love-nature. It is often tapped by artists, writers, mystics, and other creative types.

This Mindarea is designed to be a conduit through which Love manifests. Like any good conduit, it must be empty inside. So many minds are so "clogged up" by incessant, continuous thinking that Love has no place to

Richard Shiningthunder Francis

"flow through."   (By way of analogy, these persons suffer from "psychosclerosis.")

But when Love flows through your heartmind, it is magnificent! It's the highest euphoria, the highest high! This result of loving is called "rapture" and "ecstasy" in mystical literature.

****

Falling in Love with Your Self
Love and the Inner Beloved

Chapter 21

Monkeymind, the Mindblowing Mind, and Love

***

Love heals. Every nanosecond of Love creates wellbeing. It "wholes" you, everyone else, and the planet. The healing might not be physical, immediate, or major. But wellness coalesces from the convergence of "small" healing acts. In time, if you love enough, and well enough, your entire psyche becomes wholed, holy, and healed. (The words "whole," "holy," and "heal" share a common word-origin.) Also,

****

Every act of Love is an act of worship.

****

Every act of Love is an act of healing.

****

Every act of Love is an act of spiritual growth.

****

So, going to meetings, Bible-study, selling for an organization, singing with the congregation, and public prayer are **not** true worship. These mechanical activities can be done by any fool or hypocrite. Unless Love is its origin and underpinning, *no activity* is "worship."

But there is one spectacular action of which any fool or hypocrite is incapable, and that is Love.

****

Love is the **only** worship desired or willed by the great cosmic Mind.

****

There is no such thing as an "insignificant" act of Love.

****

Every genuine act of Love is of infinite value, immeasurable and illimitable.

****

Love is the fullest expression of the infinite inner Mind.

****

There are no small acts of Love in the "play" of earthlife, only small actors.

****

Every genuine Love is gigantic.

Falling in Love with Your Self
Love and the Inner Beloved

****

Each microsecond of Love is indispensable and precious.

****

Loving is the very most excellent investment that you can make in your soul and in the world.

****

Each nanosecond of Love is irreplaceable, priceless.

****

As you learn to love the Sacred within yourself, you also find It reflected in all, and then, you begin to love It in them.

****

For the same Mind that dreams you into being is also dreaming up all others.

****

When you love that Mind, you must come to love It in all creatures. Later, you will learn to love It in all objects.

****

You'll also love all situations and events. At this point, your Love will have truly become universal.

****

To love the inner Dreamer/Creator completely, you must grow to love His/Her **entire** dream, omitting nothing and no one.

****

Universal Love is the zenith and apex, the very highest Love.

****

It is the maximum "godding of the Mind." It is also the fullest "godding of the world."

****

This finest Love is also unconditional, arising because of what **you** are, not because of what the other is.

****

A "drop" of Love can neutralize a thousand "gallons" of fear.

****

You love perfectly only as a mirror of the Love of perfect Mind (Spirit or Coremind). A mirror works best when its surface is stainless, clean, dustfree— clear or empty. This emptiness is the state of perfect Mind, perfect because it is transparent to, and itself immersed in, perfect Supermind. This perfect Superlove is not "learned" by the mind

*Falling in Love with Your Self
Love and the Inner Beloved*

alone. It does not result from "selfimprovement." Metaphysical study, the consumption of exotic books, does not produce Ultralove.

Superlove flows from selferasure, selfdenial, selfabandonment (mystical "unselfing"). It is the full eradication of personal mind. It is fullest erasure of ego.

Personal mind is the only mind, says popular culture. So, this inner "death" should leave a dead person, a vegetable, a couch-potato, a zombie. It should leave a vacuous, mindless void, without will, desire, joy, or anything else. This selfevaporation is a terror that attacks Western people when they tip-toe towards mysticism. This horror is multiplied by mysticism's promise of "inner crucifixion."

But this dismal view has been swept into nothingness thousands of times by psychonauts—mystics who actually did the experiment. When you release egomind, and let it die, another Mind begins to flow through your life. It is kinder, gentler, more compassionate and loving, much wiser than the little egomind. Exchanging egomind for being filled with this Lovemind is like trading dust for diamonds. Paradoxically, on the path where you must lose everything, you actually gain everything.

There once was a monkey who wanted a banana in a thick rigid plastic see-through box. The box had a slot in the side, and the monkey put his hand in the hole, and grabbed the fruit. Now, the hole was just big enough to permit his hand to slide through when it was an open hand. But when the monkey made a fist, by hanging onto the banana, that fist was too big to fit through the hole. The monkey was trapped, paralyzed. He was easily captured by cruel hunters. But, as you can see, it was only his grasping that held him in this unfree state.

We are like that monkey. Until we "let go" of all the stuff that we consider desirable, until we stop grasping and clinging, we cannot know freedom. In order to know complete freedom, the monkey had to let go of the fruit. Yes, letting go of the fruit was a real loss, but only momentary. For its reward was so much greater— freedom to return to the unfettered and unshackled wild life of the free jungle, where he could feel at home, and happy.

This world is that fruit-box. But now add to the parable that a wild tiger was rushing towards little Brother Monkey. For the world is also that tiger. It is hungry, and eager to consume us, without a moment's hesitation. The banana is materialism, the belief that we are somehow "made happy" by material things. But we are trapped only if we do not have the good sense to release our grip on the familiar things of the "material, external" world. If you are ever going to discover the interior treasures of compassion, euphoria, and tranquility, you must let go. If you are going to fly, you must drop your heavy extra baggage. Stop grasping, clinging, and craving. The world is fascinating, attractive, and seductive. But it is nothing but distraction. For you cannot have this cake and eat it too. You simply can't be free and hang on to the "fruit" of the world that enslaves you.

The deepest inner Mind, which you wish to contact, and someday embody, is tender, warm, and comfortable. It is kind and supportive.

Falling in Love with Your Self
Love and the Inner Beloved

It is filled to the brim with Love, is in fact Love Itself. It is also awesome, as the Dreamer of the galaxies, subatomic physics, atoms, molecular and cellular structures, flowers, crystals, and rainbows. This Creator/Dreamer spills Him/Herself out into the world in infinite patterns, in thousands of varieties of crystals, flowers, butterflies, rainbows, and human beings. This unconscious Mind, the Superconscious Creatormind, proliferates wildly, unstoppably, immeasurably, illimitably. And this fantastically, incredibly complex Dreamermind fills all the quadrillions of planets in all the galaxies.

Pitiably weak and ludicrously feeble are the words to the Christian hymn, "How great Thou art," but they express the only possible reaction to this Mind— reverential awe. (Primitives often mistook this awe for fear, calling it the "fear of God.") So there are two sides to mysticism: 1) intimate, tender, warm closeness, with infinite Mind as best Friend, and 2) reverential awe, which can be mindblowing. The first is as private and joyfully intimate as making Love, the other is transcendental.

****

Richard Shiningthunder Francis

Chapter 22

The Beloved: Agony of Absence, Utter Satisfaction Upon Return

★ ★ ★

Your heart explodes in agony. You die of thirst for your absent beloved. You suffer with yearning and longing. Passionately, insatiably, you thirst for his/her presence. When the beloved does appear, sunshine and rainbows fill the sky, and flowers the earth. Music and taste and sensation become sweeter, and your heart sprouts wings. You are walking on air. A chorus of angels breaks out in lovely harmony.

The same applies to the inner Beloved. Until you Mindmeld with the deepest inner Mind, you live a life that is troubled, restless, and anxious, although you do not know why. Something is just wrong. You can feel it. You are troubled by freefloating anxieties, tensions, and stresses. You cannot seem to find satisfaction, much less real peace, anywhere. This is embodied in the ungrammatical words of the old song, which bemoans the fact that the singer "can't get no satisfaction."

Total fulfillment is found only in knowing the deepest Lovemind (Supermind, Spirit, the Absolute, Lovegod), fusing with It, feeling the world from inside It. We were created for this purpose. "Why was I born?" This is it! This is the final destiny of every human being. In nothing else can we find any

Falling in Love with Your Self
Love and the Inner Beloved

satisfaction or fulfillment. Everything else is just a poor and shabby substitute for the glory of absolute Love, known only in the Absolute within. Sex is a shoddy counterfeit. Money brings no satisfaction. Power fails to bring contentment. Possessions become boring. Fame means nothing. For fame is like drinking saltwater. If you do not believe that you are a good person, fame will do nothing to make you feel better about yourself. The more of it you drink, the thirstier you get, until you drop dead.

Life itself can grow into a hollow and dry husk of treadmill reruns, devoid of peace and joy, when we strip the tree of life bare of the leaves of Love. It is only in growing into this inner Mind that we know tranquility and heartfilling, mindfilling satisfaction.

When you desperately long for the touch of your beloved, and when finally he/she does at last touch you, everything else fades away. The whole world holds only the two of you. Touching inner Love, the Beloved, also has this effect. At the moment of full enlightenment, money and power seem ludicrous. Fame looks empty. Intellect and career, as gods, are absurdities. Sex as animal act becomes unsatisfying, even boring. Love is a mountain, and everything else just flecks of soil, grains of sand.

It is with unbelievable subtlety that the Spirit draws you into Itself. It is never invasive, but tender and warm. It approaches like a mother, or a lover, filled with the Light and warmth of Love.

Enlightenment might occur abruptly. But being ushered into the presence of bottomless Love is a journey and growth, requiring time.

Still, it is always a comfortable, somehow familiar, inner voyage.

In time, your very identity is transformed dramatically. You awaken to the fact that you have a secret identity, this Supermind, deep within you. You *are* this very Lovemind or Lovegod in incarnation. You have always been a Being of immense Power and gargantuan wisdom, massive tranquility, immeasurable Love, enormous joy.

When you remember this, your heart is flooded with Love, Light, and rapture. The result is utter satisfaction and complete fulfillment. It is every fantasy that you have ever had, rolled into one, and fulfilled a thousand times. This is probably, also, the first time in your entire life that you have ever felt true, absolute contentment. Cultivated, it can lead to invincible, bottomless serenity.

The inner Beloved is in your own heart. It is not a micron away. The world cannot touch Its tranquility. It cannot disturb your rapture, cannot change your Love.

Even after you have touched Supermind, you can still have relatively "bad" days. They are not tragic, catastrophic, or disastrous. But some days, in the total cyclicities of energy and mind, you can be a little out-of-tune, like a radio that is slightly off-station. Your "reception" is not as clear.

This kind of day is normal, and no reason for disturbance. Just kick back, watch the show, and let the great Power carry you out of this phase or cycle. Lao Tzu writes, "Some days, breathing comes easy, some days it is hard." So, everything goes up and down according to its own rhythms. And as long as

Falling in Love with Your Self
Love and the Inner Beloved

you are in a human body— or, more correctly, using one— you can be affected by normal biopsychological rhythms.

But even this is good. For the sense of absence of the Lovemind creates pain; pain creates longing; longing creates Love; and Love reunites you with the Lovemind. Sometimes, you just have to keep calling and calling and calling until the inner Lovegod responds, or until you can respond to Supermind.

Avoid panic. The inner Mind is never gone, and it is never far away. It **will** inevitably respond. Just keep knock, knock, knocking on heaven's door, and rest assured, it will swing open. But it will swing wide only if you are sincere, and living out of the highest level of impeccable honor of which you are capable. For remember that your thirst for God is **always** God's wanting you. This Love is a two-way street.

In time, Love will form a closed loop. Then, you and your Beloved will not be two, but you will discover that your greatest Love has been for a hidden part of your own Self. This is the mysterious, incomprehensible "inner Other." It can never be understood or elucidated intellectually or verbally. It can be "known" through gnosis, through falling in love with It or, with Him/Her. For the Way is nothing less than Love loving Love, Love seeking Love, Love becoming one Being, Mind, or Spirit through integration with Itself.

The Supermind is incredibly powerful. Recall that it is She, or He, who ignites the galaxies, the trillions of suns, Who also ignites the fire of Love in your own heart. You have no problem, challenge, or difficulty that the inner Beloved cannot solve. And, in His/Her Love for you, She/He does want to help you. The Supermind has arranged things so that It cannot force Itself upon you. It must wait until you have stilled and quieted your mind enough for its subtle entry. It is a "still, small voice."

This Mind, although it can be a supernova of passion, is also a rose of trustworthy, reliable, solid, and reasonable Love. At times, its logic is impeccable, even infallible. Still, it would be a terrible myopia to reduce It to **only** a logical Mind, for It is also a heartmind, capable of equal superfires of emotional fervor.

****

Chapter 23

Goddess, Sex, Doing Nothing, Touching Superultralove

***

Perfect Mind is perfect balance. Here, the "masculine" operations of linearity and logic and the "feminine" qualities of nurture and compassion blend. But because the Mind's essential nature is Superlove or Ultralove, it often appears, unlike the traditional Western god, more feminine than masculine. Technically, then, the terms "God" and "Goddess" are equivalent and interchangeable. (Often, mystics use the masculine pronoun simply because of cultural usage, in deference to tradition, or because it is simply better received or understood. Mystics have no sexual bias or preference when it comes to their presentation of the One.)

In final analysis, the "God" of the mystic is really more "Goddess." For He/She is Love, tenderness, gentleness, nurturing, support, softness. He/She "gives birth" to the cosmos. As the Taoists said about Tao, or universal Mind, it "nourishes all things."

The mystic knows Goddess not just as Christ or Apollo, but as Aphrodite or Mary. God is both Shiva and Shakti, Krishna and Parvati, Francis and Clare. Illumination is the perfect conjoining of the male and female energies within the person. The quest for this inner unity and mergence is often poorly expressed as a drive for physical sex. The ecstasy of the actual experience of Ultralove, the perfect merging of mindforces, is a billion times stronger. It electrifies not only every nerve of the body, all forty-seven miles, but every psychon of Mind, in an inner fireworks of supreme beauty and ultimate passion. It is an unconscious drive to know this fierce force again that drives many to ordinary sex. Ultralove lights up the psyche with brilliant luminescence. Every cell of blood and bone is immersed in white-hot, cool incandescence. When you emerge from this inner supernova, this touch of Superlove, you are reborn.

Just as a kiss transfers vital force from lover to lover, the "kiss" of the inner Beloved springs and bursts forth like a fountain of light, filling you with the bright radiance of Superlove or Ultralove, allconsuming, alldemanding, allencompassing. While spectacularly dazzling, it is bottomlessly, invulnerably tranquil and placid. Astonishingly energetic, Superultralove is sweet and serene. Perhaps for the first time in life, you are engulfed by total Love. You love without reservation, as a perfect mirror of unstained Superultralove. This most pristine and massive ocean of Love flows between you and your deeper Self, the Beloved.

The deeper Self, or Soul, itself has a deeper Self, the still deeper Spirit. (See "Chart of Mind.") The soul-Spirit synergy creates Superlove, which is a billion times more powerful than ordinary sexual Love. Being touched for only a nanosecond by the Superultralove of Spirit changes your life forever.

Falling in Love with Your Self
Love and the Inner Beloved

People everywhere are starving for Love, and frenetically, fanatically seek it everywhere but in their own hearts. Not loving themselves, they can ill afford to love others. They die of thirst floating in an ocean of sweet, pure water.

This Superlove of Spirit is the trigger mindprocess that begins our journey inward. His/Her Ultralove for us pulls us inward, even though we often fool ourselves into thinking that we made the first move. We are so programmed to think that we have to do everything, we fall into this trap with even spirituality. This hyperegocentricity reaches its arrogant peak in the sentiment, "If I don't do it, it'll never get done."

But one of the most amazing lessons of spirituality is to learn to "do nothing constructively." This is the lifeblood of Taoist mysticism. In that tradition, the approach of "doing by nondoing" is called *wu-wei*. But this same approach also exists in every other form of the Way. You can't **make** a mystical event, but must **let** or **permit** it. The mystic "PLAYS" at life, not taking it all with such deadly seriousness, and this word is an acronym of the Way, for the Way is to: Permit, Let, Allow, Yield, and Surrender. You cannot coerce or manipulate the powerful forces of the psyche involved in the mystical transmutation. You can only give in.

This is the deep meaning of meditation. Meditation is not something that you **do**. It is what occurs when you **stop** doing everything. It is constructive nondoing, or nonthinking.

This state makes the mind hollow and transparent. This inner emptiness of linear thought makes possible the undistorted transmission of deeper Mind. When you reach the point of zero activity, not even thinking, then, and only then, have you touched the state of meditation.

So, meditation is **not** visualization. It is not affirmation. It is crystalmind. It is empty and bright as clean water in sunlight. It is clear and void of cognition. This is the state of much in nature, so radically simple that we miss it altogether. As in Asian painting, what is not there, the background or empty spaces, must be seen as equally crucial with the objects. The spaces between the notes are as vital to composition as are notes. As Lao Tzu says, a door or window has value only because there is nothing there, nothing to block passage. A glass filled with hardened concrete is useless. It cannot hold the crystalclear water. Our roofbrain chatter, our nonstop selftalk, is like that concrete, while the Spirit is that water.

The ego is like flypaper covered with fresh superglue. It is "Velcro mind," and sticks to everything. This is because, often secretly, we want to control everything. So great is our fear and insecurity that we want to dominate even our spirituality. But this is like an ant trying to stop a freight train.

The need here is to learn to trust the inner Mind to know what it is doing, to trust it to love us, in the same way that we trust our hearts to beat, even when we are ignoring them.

Our conscious thoughtpatterns do not regulate heartbeat, the digestion of food, or any of a wide spectrum of bioprocesses. In the larger overview, our conscious

Falling in Love with Your Self
Love and the Inner Beloved

thoughtcontents do not matter. This can be a stunning letdown for those who have mistaken the micrscopic ego for God.

This mistaken identity arises from egofear. The ego wants to rule the universe because it is terrified that there is no one else really at the controls. But the ego is irrelevant, not only to most bioprocesses, such as the bionanotech of the body (turning food into skin, teeth, bone, hair, etc.) but for a vast range of other events. The ego has nothing to do with the sunrise, with the growth of plants in a field (another form of nanotech), the weather, or a host of other nature-functions. The ego just doesn't matter in the outworking of the world.

But the mystical revelation is still much grander than this: It shows us that, without doubt, all of the situations, things, and ideas about which we worry and fret, all the things that give us insomnia, that torment our minds, just really DO NOT MATTER. ALMOST NOTHING MATTERS. This frees the Mind to soar gracefully into the blue skies of inner Mind, free of shackles, weights, and entanglements.

****

Chapter 24

Speeding Away from the Phantomworld at Warp Ten

***

A tiny handful of things matter very much. They are worth living, and even dying, for. But lifefactors of this colossal magnitude are as scarce as fine diamonds the size of softballs. For the only matters which really matter are Love and its varieties of expressions, types, and powerlevels.

The ten thousand things, by contrast, about which people fight and conflict, war, hate, fret, worry, feud, disagree, and abuse each other are immaterial and insubstantial. Most things which drive people crazy the mystic comes to see as only mistphantoms. According to the latest ultramicroparticle physics, the mystic is right: The entire "material" world is precisely this kind of mistphantom.

Early Christian "heretics" (nontraditionalists) taught that Jesus was a "phantom." Jesus, they said, taught that the whole material world was ethereal and immaterial. He was a "phantom," but so were all human beings. And these apparitions inhabited a phantomworld. Everyone was a "ghost" in a dream.

This was only appearance. It applied only to the world of matter. The inner world was Source, and the dreamworld of matter only the result. Mind was the projector, world was the screen. Mind was real and substantial. Its

Falling in Love with Your Self
Love and the Inner Beloved

reality was absolute. So, again, as so often happens, mystics turned the commonsense world topsy-turvy. For it is Mind that is usually presented as transitory and ephemeral, diaphanous and evanescent.

Mind is usually seen as caused or created by the matter within the physical brain. The mystics say no. And they say it firmly. The Mind, they say, does not exist within the body, but the body exists within the Mind. It is a Mindpicture, a "psychohologram" or dreamimage. Mind is axiomatic, an uncaused first Cause. The body, and the entire "material and external" universe are but its dream.

The world is a tornadic mélange of countless thousands of interacting and interesting things. Yet the Master said in Jesus, "Only one thing is necessary." In one fell swoop, he swept our minds back to their natural center, simplicity. This singularity, this intense focus, this "one thing" is Love. When we are immersed in Superlove, we know immediately the Ultramind in our own hearts. This is saturation by the "spiritual unconscious"— not the totality of God, but the sum of divine Love. It is the inner Lovenature that is the object of mystical concentration.

The more that you know a good and attractive person, the more that you grow to love him/her. This is even truer of the adorable inner Beloved. So, Superlove is not static, but always growing, becoming refined and more enriched by every act of Love.

Old traditions of Jewish mysticism said that the Absolute was surrounded by a "curtain." There are, in fact, layers of veils around It.

These are opacities formed by the Mindlevels of the unconscious Mind. They include both personal and collective factors. The Absolute is like an almost-remembered memory. You know that it is in your mind somewhere, but must often diligently search to find it. Or else, you can go on "automatic searchandscan" mode, allow the mind to simply "incubate" until the memory rises to the "surface."

Similarly, the Supermind of Love is ensconced and obscured by billions of "layers" of thoughtfeelings. These largely consist of memories, opinions, desires, and linear concepts. We can't do anything to tear away these inner curtains. But we can, by entering a simple, thoughtfree condition, make them more transparent, so that the inner Light of Ultralove shines ever more brightly. Mystics often recommend a "pervasive contemplation" during the day. In this mystical practice, a mindclearing mechanism, a *mantra*, replaces ordinary cognition. This aids in mystical transparency or "crystalmind."

But we must wait for Supermind, through Superlove, to initiate steps to enlightenment. For those curtains can be torn asunder only by a terrific blast of Mindpower from the other side. Love, in a moment, can cut through all the veils like a laser. When this great Mind shines upon you, all you have to do is love the Light in response. Your mission is not to create, but to discover, enlightenment.

So, in her career, the mystic passes through four stages: separation, Love, intimacy, and final union or fusion (Mindmeld) with the deep inner Lovenature. This Mindmeld is the supreme act of Superlove (Ultralove). Love is fire, and you the wood, as Lovenergy fills and

Falling in Love with Your Self
Love and the Inner Beloved

consumes your ego, turning your Mind into Light. You vanish into the Beloved, and He/She pours Him/Herself into you, filling you with Lovelight. Finally, when the ego is consumed by Love, only He/She exists. This is being "lost" in Love, and when it happens, not a trace of ego remains behind. The ego is dust and ashes.

The result is bliss or ecstasy. It is a relief of liberation, in which the inner Mind soars to new heights. After this immersion in Superlove, the mystic remains "human" in form only. The most important aspects of her Self are now Lovefilled, and "superhuman." (This exquisite, pure, universal Ultralove is superhuman, for it does not coalesce from the human conscious mind or the egomind.) Within herself, she experiences an entire inner world, another dimension, in which she wants, and is, nothing but Ultralove.

In this new order of being, she is the temporary incarnation of Ultralove. It was precisely this exposure to, and reidentification with, Superlove that formed the nucleus of the dogma called the "Incarnation." But it was assumed that Jesus was a freak, when in reality, he was a prototype or model for all. The mystic, then, is remade in the image of Superlove. She is refreshed by the "color" and "fragrance" of Ultralove, as she becomes a rose in the cosmic garden.

When you step away from the world of many things, and know the one Mind, there is really nothing but this one Supermind, filling all, living within all. Everything, you realize, exists **through** You, but **within** Him/Her, the Dreamer/Creator. This Beloved arrives to consciousness like a "thief in the night." This means that It is subtle, even sneaky. You must keep your inner "Way-dar" on maximum gain in order, at first, even to detect Its presence. Then, you must work to keep the attention on It, fixed and concentrated.

The rose of Superlove has at last blossomed in the sunlight of Ultralove. As this tender heartrose unfolds, its delicate and delicious "fragrances" are the acts of compassion that fill your life.

Of course, deepest inner Mind does not really "come" to you, and you don't literally "go" anywhere to find It. It has always existed deep inside you. The inward "journey" is a metaphor of "movement" among levels of consciousness and among those of the unconscious Mind. It's just that, at the Superlove moment, you at last come to recognize Ultralove Mind with lucidity.

The One you are seeking is always "right here." Indeed, there is nowhere, no "when" this Mind does not exist. You don't need literally to "find" the Absolute, for It was never really lost. You simply need to take away all the opacities that stand between yourself and pure Lovelight. You need to stop playing games, and believing in the illusion, truth's opposite. You need to awaken to the fact that the cosmos is a dream, and then to seek conscious Mindmeld with the Dreamer.

So, your highest Self fills all. Stated in the silly but memorable form of a "knock-knock" joke, it's something like:

"Knock-knock."
"Who's there?"
"You."

*Falling in Love with Your Self
Love and the Inner Beloved*

Separation from the Worldsource brings pain. Illusions of separation are the origin of much stress, tension, anxiety, and restless unhappiness in the world. Conversely, closeness brings joy. We were created to find intimacy and friendly Love with our deepest inner Mind.

First, then, you are filled with Love for the Beloved. Later, you are filled with the Beloved Him/Herself. Gradually, you are drawn away from your earthself, your ego, into an inner world of Mind, so that, in time, not a trace of that false self exists. You "don't play that game anymore." The Mastermind said, in Jesus, "Whoever loses the self will find it." This is the paradox of losing ego to discover the inner Soul— and later, the Spirit.

When you have integrated with Superlove, you live for only what He/She wants. For Ultralove is Mind, and it has a will. It has plans for you, and for the cosmos. So, at the Superlove moment, your egowill is sunk deeply into the greater will, and dissolves in it like sugar in tea.

You then become an instrument of the will of Love. You mirror the sunlight of Ultralove into a world of darkness. Your only task is to keep the mirror as dustfree as possible so that it might be dazzling with the bright light of Superlove, the "inner Other." You are a grain of salt dissolved in the ocean of blisslove.

****

Richard Shiningthunder Francis

Chapter 25
Crystalmind, Ultralove, Heaven, and the Return to the Garden of Pleasure in the Heart

***

Bliss catapults you into higher ecstasies of Superlove. You are a tiny feather in the hurricane of Ultralove, a grain of salt in the tsunami of Superlove. But this bliss bubbles up into only the empty mind. In a mind full of egocontent, there is no room for bliss. Only when the inner guestroom is emptied, the inner garden prepared, can the Beloved come (to awareness).

He/She comes only to transparent crystalmind. For if the window of mind is opaque, none of the Ultralove shines through. Like sunlight, It is always shining. But if that window is opaque, the Light is never seen. It never forces Itself. It does not matter how bright the sunlight is if you have decided to live in a cave deep underground, with no apertures to the outside. If, then, the mind is opaque, no Lovelight passes through. All egocontent is opacity.

When you get rid of, or "kill" some, but not all, egocontent, the psyche becomes translucent. Thus, it allows through a little light. The Light is impeded and distorted, but still makes Love in the world. But in purest mystical consciousness, free of egodesire and ego-agenda, the mind becomes completely transparent to the inner Light. This is "crystalmind." Only through

Falling in Love with Your Self
Love and the Inner Beloved

crystalmind does It dazzle with brilliance. The Flow is perfect, unimpeded, with zero resistance. When Superlove flows through you, and out from your heart, you are a tributary of the great river of Ultralove, branching from the inner ocean of Superlove.

How is crystalmind discovered? By the total extinction of earthly, personal, grasping, selfish desire. Only when the fuss and frustration, the noise and clamor, of frenzied desire die down into stillness does the mind find clarity. Only in the eclipse of sensual dominance does the heart touch tranquility.

But you lose nothing, for the inner pleasure of Selflove more than compensates for any egosense of loss— a false perception anyway. Instead, you discover pleasure without measure, in the art and heart of Ultralove. As the old song reminds us, you find yourself drowning in a "sea" of Love. Here, everyone would love to "drown."

Even though this is the very best and healthiest event that will ever be bestowed upon you, it can be painful to the ego. It can even be scary. To lose your old familiar self can leave you feeling hollow, high and dry, empty. "If I'm not this ego," you say to yourself, "then, I'm no one." You might feel for a time as if you are suspended in Mindlimbo, going nowhere. Your heartmind and your life might feel like a void. You might feel like a reed through which only desertwinds blow their hot, dry air. You might agonize over the question of your lifedesign and lifedirection. You might feel lost, confused, and bewildered. But if this occurs, remind yourself that restructuring begins with destructuring or destruction. The reconstruction of a new Self requires the unraveling of the older egoself. The reason why this is so painful is that the ego is like an old comfortable pillow that you have had for years. Even when the pillow gets moldy and starts to fall apart, you hang on to it because you have grown accustomed to it. With most people, a known and familiar hell is preferable to an unexplored heaven.

Nevertheless, deep inside, in your Unconscious, you are surefooted and confident at the art of Superlove, for you have been practicing it for centuries. Your inner Mind already knows where you are going in this inner journey. It has all the maps, and knows intimately the Beloved, your destination. The inner Mind knows the Way, even if you do not, and will certainly guide you without a single wasted step.

Lovenergy burns away all that is "bad," "ugly," or "undesirable" within you, and within the world. This fire leaves behind a stainless core of pure beauty. It is a cosmic work of art, molded by Ultralove. It is your new Self.

Superlove demands the commitment of the last atom in your last neuron. In exchange for devotion, It makes you a psychospiritual Superbeing, a being of Superlove plus nothing. You become luminous beauty incarnate, a part of God on earth.

In the Eden allegory, the human nature ("Adam and Eve") breaks away from the state of innocent Mindmeld with Ultralove. This pristine state is called "eden," which means "pleasure." This fall from grace occurs when we decide that evil is equally real with good. ("Godmind" is "goodmind.") This is an

Falling in Love with Your Self
Love and the Inner Beloved

invitation for "evil," or the shadow of Love's absence, to take up residence in Mind.

Every serious use of the label "evil" not only boots you out of the Garden of Pleasure in the heart, but "boots up" a hellstate in your psyche. Before you know what is going on, you find your mind filled to the brim with evil. Every time that you seriously use this label, you add to the total quantity of mindevil. (Conversely, every use of the recognition of goodness brings you closer to an inner heavenstate, the heart's Garden of Pleasure.)

The mystic, wanting heaven or bliss, learns to define and embrace everything and everyone as "good" in an absolute sense. She does *not* naively embrace evil as good. In this relative world, she knows that certain ideas and actions, even certain people, are evil. Is this "judgment," prohibited to the enlightened? No, for judgment deals with the *absolute* evaluation of things, situations, or people. Instead, this good/evil distinction deals with only the *relative* world, and so is "discernment" or "discrimination," not "judgment."

Sometimes people regard themselves as superspiritual or enlightened because they take a "ho hum" complacent, apathetic attitude towards evil which they misinterpret as "detachment." But they are selfdeluded if they do not have the courage or clarity ever to distinguish between good and evil. These people say things such as, "I'm not going to judge," and, "Hitler was not all bad," and, "I don't see binladen as evil." They have fallen into a quagmire of illusion and confusion. Their blah, tasteless, gray, neutral view of the world as containing nothing evil is *not* spirituality, as they think, but merely naivete. To hold that a person or behavior is not "evil" when it involves the torture and rape of young girls and women, or the cutting up of victims and the storing of body-parts in a refrigerator is not spirituality but blindness.

The mystic well knows that evil has no absolute reality. But this does not excuse the full abandonment of all values, of common sense, decency, or sanity. Those who believe that this course of ignorance is somehow "spiritual" are victims of a most serious delusion. This moral neutrality is a psychospiritual pathology. Those who fall for it are mentally and spiritually ill.

Historically, exactly this misunderstanding has given rise to groups that have justified every form of immorality, harmful absence of ethics, and evil. This dark philosophy weakens moral fiber, while true spirituality strengthens it. It is invalid, indeed, it can be insane, to justify harming others or indulging your lower nature as "good" because *everything is good, at an absolute level.* For we do not, and cannot, live in an absolute world. We must all live in a relative world, this world of consensual reality, and it requires that we establish clear demarcations and delineations between good and evil. The mystic, then, does not embrace all as "absolutely good" only in order to find personal pleasure, although that can be its ultimate effect. She embraces all in an attempt to discover Love that is truly universal.

Falling in Love with Your Self
Love and the Inner Beloved

* * * * * * *

If Love is not universal, it is not Superlove.

* * * * * * *

She loves the one, single Creator/Dreamer within. It is perfect. So, the world must be "perfect," even though relatively, it seems anything but. The overriding twin visions of karma and immortality make it so. For death, in the mystic worldview, is not "bad." So those events which lead to death cannot be irredeemably bad either.

The closer that you can come to a state of "all-embracing Mind," the closer you come to Ultralove, universal Love, or fullest enlightenment, or inner heaven. This allows a mystical state (as contrasted with a mystical moment) to be one of uninterrupted joy.

Upon being submerged or immersed in Superlove, you once again enter the Garden of Pleasure in the heart. So, rain is good, sunlight is good. Cold is good, heat is good. Spiders are as "good" and beautiful as butterflies. Snakes are as "good" as puppies. The world is stripped of ugliness, when you refuse so to define it.

This attitude of cosmic embrace returns you to the state of pure, unsullied Mind, or "original" Mind. In this monopolar Mind, Superlove has no real opposite. There is no hell symmetric with heaven. When everything and everyone is embraced as "good" and "beautiful," it is easier to love the whole world. Even, or especially, those things, situations, and persons that you have been conditioned and educated to label as "evil" or "ugly" are caught away in the embrace of Your cosmic Ultralove. These actually elicit **more** Love, for loving them takes twice as much Lovenergy.

Bills are good, traffic is good, taxes are good. These realife factors all teach patience and tolerance, and provide inner strength. So, living in a "perfect world" does not mean changing the environment. And this is the great secret to inner heaven: It means altering and adapting your vision or lenses. It is a shift in interpretation.

So, the mystic finds continuous joy, not by world-manipulation, but by elastically adapting the self. She transforms inner vision, and changes her labelmaking habits. She simply stops "judging" the world. She tosses her labelmaker.

The mysticsage says, "It is good."

The student asks, "Why is it good?"

Her teacher replies, "Because it is."

The very existence of any object or situation tacitly implies that it is a part of the will of the cosmic Mind. In the West, theologians distinguish between the "active" will of God and the "permissive" will of God, but they are both parts of that same will. If anything is willed by the perfect Mind, it must be perfect. This mirrorsymmetry shows how "beauty is in the mind of the describer."

Anything that you decide is "good" actually becomes good for you. An ancient mystic

Falling in Love with Your Self
Love and the Inner Beloved

wrote, "To those who are pure in heart, all things are pure." If you change the lenses through which you look at the world, it is the world that actually, really changes. For the world is all a Mindworld. So, to shift the Mind is to alter the world.

****

Richard Shiningthunder Francis

Chapter 26

Brother Serpent Gets Us Expelled from Eden, and Helps us Return

***

A talking snake started the engines of time. The glories and tragedies exploding into the drama of human history begin with the allegory of Genesis, the Eden parable or myth.

Many of the wisest Jewish authorities, unlike Christian fundamentalists, recognize this tale as allegorical. In it, human nature (represented by "Adam and Eve") lives in perfect harmony/bliss, in a perfect world. This is the state of primal innocence, or seamless union between the human nature and the divine inner Mind. This state is simply and clearly described as "Eden," which means "pleasure." That same blisstate of Eden is now deep in the unconscious. In Eden, the Lovemind was conscious, and so was its subcomponent Creatormind. Human will was divine will, and even nature obeyed. This explains all the stories from every tradition of the human being as the "master" of nature or the world.

When The infinite Mind first decided to play other roles, He/She jumped completely into the game. Fear (the "devil") did not yet exist, for the Mind knew that, always in control of everything, He/She had absolutely nothing to fear. So, diving deeply into the pseudoidentities, He/She began to pretend that He/She was "others." Those created souls were

Falling in Love with Your Self
Love and the Inner Beloved

still in profound synergy with the one Mind. They had not yet drifted very far from It. This state is "Eden."

As long as human nature rested quietly in this state, it knew grace, serenity, and perfect Love. The human mind was still perfect, mirroring perfection from the One. The "two minds," the human and divine, were not yet quite two, but still sliding along the track of time in perfect synergy. So, naturally, the world itself was peaceful and perfect. (It still is, in absolute Mind.)

What, then, screwed everything up? In this pre-Hebraic story, it was a "sin" called "eating of the tree of the knowledge of good and evil." In Genesis, this act is nowhere called the "original sin." That was a term made up much later, and retroimposed upon the parable. Confusion scrambles some here, who think that "knowledge" was the fly in the fruitjuice. This misinterpretation misses the target.

What would we be without knowledge? We need it; it can be a ladder to the divine. So, knowledge was NOT the problem. Instead, it was the **kind** of knowledge that threw a monkeywrench into the works; it was "of good and evil."

In Genesis chapter one, when the Mind of the Creator/Dreamer creates the world, He/She says, "It is good." Human nature and mind live in total tranquility until human nature decides, egocentrically, that the infinite Mind was mistaken. For that Mind had dreamed up a world that was exclusively "good." That implies that everything, not just some things, was "good."

Human nature, thinking that it knows better, decides that some things are not good, but intrinsically *and absolutely* "evil." This decision was the original Pandora's box. It triggered the proliferation of a thousand "demons" in the unconscious)subconscious). Human nature decided that evil was coterminal with good. It was equally real. And since good was absolute, being the quality of infinite Mind, then evil had to have an absolute existence too.

So, when it first embraces its belief that some things are "evil," human nature is immediately expelled from the Garden of Pleasure in the heartmind. Agony, frustration, and suffering proliferate immediately, until the mind becomes a kind of inner "hellstate." Or, at the very best, it is heaven punctuated regularly by hell.

But there is another tree in that same Garden, called the "tree of life." If human nature can eat of this tree, "timeless" life can be discovered. Jehovah— a false godimage embodying an entire list of negativities— blocks the Way back to this tree. In fact, he is jealously worried lest the human nature "eat of it, and live." Jehovah here represents the belief in a universe ruled, not by Love, but by imperfections. These flaws collectively constitute the unstable Jehovah-myth.

Involved with this ancient godimage, one cannot discover the mystical truth that the world is entirely "good." For the Jehovah-myth itself is a source of much "evil." If you believe that evil is in charge of the universe, there is not a snowball's chance that you are going to discover that the entire cosmos is good.

This "tree of life" is in the same Garden of Pleasure in the heart. It is the Way back to primal innocence and perfection. Eating of it is the neutralizing of the "original" sin of having eaten of the other tree. In short, the tree of life is the discovery and implementation of the "everything is good" worldview already discussed.

So, how do we make our Way back to live in the Garden of Pleasure? We redefine everything. The first step is to throw out the concept that anything is *absolutely* evil. Jesus knew this. When he urged us to "Judge not," he did not limit this to judging people, as do most modern commentators. If taken at facevalue, it means that we are to refrain from judging events, situations, or objects. To "judge" is to label anything with *absolute* evaluations. Our labels exist on a wide spectrum. They range from the deliciously good to the hideously evil.

Recall that when the Creator creates the cosmos, He/She says that everything is "good." What we must now do is seek to harmonize with the Creator. The Creatormind is a very profound level of the unconscious Mind, being a subsystem of the Core (Spirit). (See "Chart of Mind.") This Creatorlevel of Mind is the Source of such gigantic wisdom that the ego cannot hope to hold even a smoldering candle to its brightness. And so, if It says that the cosmos is "good," who are we arrogantly to disagree?

In short, if we see "horrible" things in the universe, we need not arrogantly assume that there is something wrong with the universe.

Instead, we can humbly contemplate the possibility
that something is wrong with our view or interpretation of the cosmos. This is the humble, realistic attitude adopted by the mystic. She is being challenged to shift her inner Mind from the relative everyday world to the absolute world within. This is the home of the Absolute.

This humility leads her to realize that it is she, not the cosmos, that needs fine-tuning and adjustment. The ultimate shift arises when finally she decides to use her free will for the **only** purpose for which it was designed: She uses her free will to turn over her will to the indwelling Spirit of Love.

And it was precisely this free will that was symbolized by the "serpent" in the Garden of Eden. People love to assume that the talking serpent was Satan, but the account nowhere says, or even implies, this. Because free will takes people into all sorts of karma and misery, it can be seen as negative, even antiagapic (against Love). But because it ultimately leads everyone back to the state of purest seamless unity with the Mind of Love, or Supermind, it is also a symbol of light. This explains the dual history of the serpent as a symbol of both good and evil, light and darkness.

It's the job of free will to plunge us into the darkness of ignorance. We screw up with free will for a long, long time, creating and reaping the seeds of negative karma. We create many inner hellstates in the process. Then, one fine day, we awaken to the fact that free will is getting us nowhere fast. Suddenly, we shift into mystic mode, and

Falling in Love with Your Self
Love and the Inner Beloved

realize that there is another, higher way. Then, we surrender our minds and lives to an interior higher Power, the deepest Mind, the Lovemind. It is only when free will moves us to give up free will that we find enlightenment, leading to peace and bliss.

Unless we had gone through the tunnel of darkness, the lives spent in hypnotic fascination with the world of multiplicity, we would never have the wisdom of Love and Light. So, the "serpent" is, as many Christians said, a bringer of darkness. But, as the Gnostic Christians also said, it is a "bringer of Light." It is ignorance; it is wisdom derived from ignorance.

The use of free will to give up free will is the ancient gnostic symbol of the *auroboros,* the serpent swallowing its own tail. What an elegant symbol for free will "swallowing" itself in Love. But this symbol has other layers of meaning, so beautifully designed is it. For it also forms a perfect circle, like the ancient sundisc. This, like the wedding band, is meant to symbolize eternity. The circle has an infinite number of "sides," and so, is an infinitely complex "polygon." It also has no discernible beginning or end, and so is appropriate for representing infinite Mind. It is also reflected throughout nature: The eye that sees the round earth and the round sun is round, and processed by a head that is also fairly round. To be more precise, the three-dimensional circle is the sphere— the truer symbol of infinity, because it is an infinite number of circles, of all sizes, united into a single whole.

Paradoxically, it is Love that draws us into the dense darkness of the deepest psyche, and

Richard Shiningthunder Francis

Love that leads us so deeply that we find the Core of Light deep within all the obscuring opacities. The inner Mind has many layers of darkness— unexplored regions of ignorance that impede the Light of Love or even understanding. But the Core of Mind is luminous splendor. This is the Lovenature. In various traditions, it has been called the "Christ-nature," or the "Buddha-nature," or simply, "Holy Spirit." It also has a dozen other common names, including the Father/Mother, the One, Spirit, Superconscious, Supermind, Coremind, the Ultimate, and the Absolute.

   A good teacher might not be all "light and roses." For this unadulterated sweetness is not what you must face in your inner explorations. A good, effective teacher will try to be supremely realistic, while balancing everything with Love and compassion. She will nudge, not force, you to shine light into the darker and hidden areas of your own psyche. But in doing so, she will be tender and wise, never cruel, angry, or in foul temper. If you don't like what you see in your psyche, then you must realize that this is an invitation to transformation.

****

Chapter 27

Out of the Shadow into the Light

***

Love is the only force in the cosmos that can ignite the unconscious Mind, blazing it into the light of awareness. Revelation occurs in sequence: Areas within the personal unconscious are first made conscious, then aspects of the Soulevel, then parts of the collective, followed at last by Supermind, the Core, or Superconscious Mind. (See "Chart of Mind.")

Each level has its own time to emerge into the "light" of the conscious mind. This sequencing allows us to prepare a place in the inner Garden of Pleasure for the emergence of Lovemind. To switch metaphors, we purify and filter the water in an area of the inner ocean to create an inner space where we can meet the Beloved.

The historic mystics called this preparation the "Way of purgation" (purification). This begins with confronting your "inner shadow," which is the totality of "demons and dragons." It is all those aspects of the egoself, and even of the Soulevel, that you really don't want to see. This little rhyme might help you identify and remember your shadow:

"I look carefully, and then I see
What I thought was you was really me."

A clue about shadow-contents can be mined from the rich question, "What do you especially distrust and despise in others?"

Chances are excellent that this is some component in yourself from which you are hiding. So, closely examine colleagues, friends, neighbors, and enemies. Where is your criticism most harsh? Define what you most despise about them, with clarity. If honest, you will certainly find these among your own unconscious nature and fears. To embrace them as educational tools, look on their flipsides, seeing the good in the bad, the useful in the harmful. Learn to love them, making them your friends, and they will become slaves of Love. (This will also aid in embracing and adopting a friendly, elastic attitude towards people whom you dislike. Remember, to say, "I dislike no one" tends to be simple denial, or egotism.)

   Recall also that, by the time that you experience any human being, he/she has passed through the many thousands of filters or lenses of your own brainmind system. So, to you, she cannot be as she is, but only as you interpret her; and you are fully responsible for that, not she. Arguably, no one ever knows another, but only his/her interpretations. So, all day, every day, people must live in an inner world of modified people— often changed by the nervousystem until they are unrecognizable. The "out there" person becomes an "in here" reality which is fully a reflection of you. You respond, then, not to people, but to your inner images of them. So, the cosmos is the self dancing with the Self. Its goal: To bring the self to fall in Love with the Self, and thus, to love all people.

****

Falling in Love with Your Self
Love and the Inner Beloved

If any characteristic within another annoys or irritates you, it is probable that the same quality exists within you.

****

If the irritant did not exist within you, you would simply ignore, or not even notice, it. But negative qualities must be a threat to you, in order to trigger emotional responses. And what is that threat? It is the fear that your own shadow might break through into the world

It is this inner conflict, **not conflict with others,** that is the "sword" brought by Christ. This is by no means always pleasant. The shadow comes with a boxcar full of baggage— anger, sadness, frustration, anxiety, tension, annoyance, impatience, and a plethora of others. If the shadow is kept in the unconscious Mind, it does not go away. Instead, feelings and expressions might erupt unpredictably, inappropriately, horribly, harming the self and others. The need is to make peace with even these responses, seeing them as teachers, and even friends.

We are built so that we learn much more from the discomforts of life than from its smooth-sailing periods. So, a time of pain and/or loss can be, in time, embraced as spiritual accelerator, and thus, as "good," not "bad." We learn far more from pain than from pleasure.

The inner voyage, then, becomes a crucial game of "hideandseek." We must expose our inner "demons and dragons" to the bright, uncompromising, honest light of conscious recognition.

You can't, and won't, get better until you admit that you are sick. Pretensions to be already perfect block the Flow of the real thing. Perfection cannot bubble up from the unconscious in a selfrighteous mind.

These specks and dark shadows are not the rulers of the kingdom of the psyche. So, we must not be afraid to look them squarely in the eye, and banish them. Since they are not real, they cannot be everlasting. They have a short shelflife, and can be washed away by the touch of Love. This occurs gradually through metamorphosis or transformation. Since change permeates the whole cosmos, we should try not to fear it.

For, sooner or later, life itself will force you to see your shadow. You simply cannot endlessly "project" it onto others, pretending that they have the problem, but not yourself. For the deep unconscious already sees through this transparent and naive lie. When you do meet it, don't see it as nemesis. Instead, regard it with a kindly eye, as teacher. Embrace it as brother/sister. Welcome it, and learn to love it, as inevitable companion on the inner journey. In time, it will turn all its energies over to Love. Then, all shadows will disappear as you are filled with the Light of Love. This is the process described by both alchemy and Jungian psychology.

Every spiritual path must begin with work on this shadow. So, don't get caught in the lies of denial, saying, "There is no shadow in me."

How does this shadow begin? It starts, predictably, with the "eating of the tree of knowledge of good and evil." It begins unconsciously to form, fairly early in life, in both the Soulevel and personal unconscious, when we begin to see evil as real. Then, giving this "evil" power, and fearing it, we begin consciously to suppress, and unconsciously to repress it, storing it in the subconscious Mind. (The shadow is an area, not a level, of Mind called the "subconscious." With the Superconscious, the subconscious makes up the "unconscious.")

Infants, and enlightened people, do not believe in the essential or absolute existence of evil. Masters and sages believe in **only** the absolute reality of good. The allgood Mind at the Center of creation has no opposite. Everything that It dreams into being is only good. (A belief in this essential monopolar Mind is called "monism." Mysticism is a variety of monism, or belief in the ultimate reality of one Mind.)

Like beautiful flowers, we all grow and blossom from that one Mind.

Schools and churches struggle to educate about, and warn against, what is "bad," and this is good. For in the relative world, many activities and behaviors are harmful and "bad." But in the inner Garden of Pleasure, no bad can exist. It is pure Mind, original Mind, and filled with **only** Light, Love, and the good. It is perfect Mind, for it is unified through Mindmeld with the perfect One at the Core.

But when evil is taken too seriously, too often, it forms and evolves into a matrix of complex illusions. These exist not only in the personal unconscious, but also at the Soulevel, and in the deepest collective.

This belief creates a part of the psyche (the notorious "subconscious" of traditional psychology) which is simply too "ugly," "bad," or scary to behold. So, it is stuffed way down into the personal unconscious, and there becomes the powerfully convincing illusion called the shadow.

Archetypally, this is the "evil twin." Using similar archetypal and symbolic reference, an ancient legend says that Jesus was a twin. Some accounts even name this twin, the disciple Thomas— whose name means "twin," and who wrote a gnostic (mystic) Gospel. What does this legend mean?

It signifies that there were two very different aspects of Jesus Christ. One, called "Jesus," was a historical human being, born, experiencing life, and dying, like the rest of us. But a second aspect, called "Christ," was his very special Soul, Mindmelded with the Absolute or Core. This everlasting Spiritsoul fusion could say, "I and the Father are one." (Variations of this simple statement of union have been the bread and butter of mystics through the ages.) This is a clear statement of mystic Mindmeld with the Infinite within.

Did even Jesus have a shadow? In his human side, there can be no doubt. For nothing is more universally human.

Together with subconscious rubbish, we also tend to sweep into the trash bin of the shadow all our natural impulses and instincts. But nothing in the shadow is "bad," and once we outgrow this dualistic naivete, we see that the shadow contains precious energies, forces, memories, data, and even wisdom. We need not to wrestle, but dance, with it, not to dispose

Falling in Love with Your Self
Love and the Inner Beloved

of, but to integrate, it. Only when we accomplish this friendly reunion can we become whole, healed, or "holy." In this unfragmented state, we find inner wellness. You simply can't get well by will. But you can by selftransformation, which arises from egoselfabandonment, egoselfnegation, and egoselforgetting.

****

Chapter 28

The Pearl of Great Price: The Hero's Journey through Hell to Heaven

***

Deep, deep down in your most secret, hidden Mind, you are already perfect. But layered over this perfect Coremind are accretions, or opacities, in both the Soulevel and the personal unconscious. These opacities are thoughtconstructs that block the bright Light of Love at the Center of Mind.

Buddhist mystical tradition says, "You are already the Buddha." Early Christian tradition had an exact equivalent: "You are already the Christ." Our lifegoal is triple:

1) believing this, 2) bringing it to conscious awareness, and

3) manifesting.

You are Love, Light, wisdom, peace, and joy. To return to the Center of the Soul is wholeness; wholeness is singularity; singularity is simplicity. It was to this crystalclear and tight, laserlike focus of Mind that T.S. Eliot referred in his memorable phrase, "the simplicity that costs everything." For you will never discover this inner focus amidst the clutter, clamor, and "stuff" of everyday, material pursuits and distractions. You will never find it outside yourself.

So the mystic, having found this pearl of great price, this utter and uniquely tight focus, "sells everything that she owns" to

Falling in Love with Your Self
Love and the Inner Beloved

"buy" it. This path disallows the wholehearted pursuit of any other; she cannot have two masters. She knows that this rare Mind, deep within, would be the greatest bargain in history at twice the price. She gladly gives up everything, and would give away ten times as much, and consider herself to have made the "smartest purchase" of her entire life!

You must, in the end, include even your whole self in the bargain. You must spend or trade your egoself for the exquisite and bright perfection at the Core. So, instead of being apart **from** everything, you become a part **of** everything.

You must often go through hell to get to heaven. Because the path can be so utterly mindblowing, exposing you to terror and radical inner shifts, mystics call it the "hero's journey." This paincomponent is dramatically educational, as it shocks and slams the self naked against the cross and drives in the nails. So, before even thinking about this journey, you must work to cultivate an inner stability. You will need reference-points so as not to get lost during the inner hurricanes. For you'll be tossed like a leaf. The "waters" of Mind will be before you, under you, over you, and all around you. Visibility will be zero, and you will have to fly on faith, with blind instrumentation.

When this writer was called to this voyage, even before he had any clear idea exactly what he was doing, or where he was going, he went literally blind. This was a part of his destiny, planned by his soul in order to open the "inner eye," but of course, he had no way of knowing it then. So, he plunged up to his eyes in the "darknight" experience. This occurs when the mystic enters a state of hopeless despair, and when the divine Presence seems gone. The cosmos appears to be void of all Mind and all Love.

Two paths are recommended to avoid serious disorientation during the inner journey to the Beloved: 1) wisdom, by assimilating in the heart (not just the mind) books such as the present one, and 2) inner practices (dream-logging, meditation, introspection, Mindjournaling, etc.) Detachment is also cultivatable, so as not to allow the factors of the world to dominate you.

BEWARE: Much "bull" has been called "mysticism," so let's be clear about exactly what is real mysticism: Mysticism does not concern the paranormal or parapsychological. It has nothing to do with magic. Contrary to popular usage, a Walt Disney film about fairies is *not* mystical. Gothic novels about spooks in dark hallways are *not* mystical. "Alice in Wonderland," or "The Wizard of Oz" are *not* examples of real mysticism. Please don't mistake them for mysticism. When reading, make absolutely certain that you are diving into the real thing, not a cheap, phony counterfeit. Fakery and fraud are rampant in this field, and so is pseudoscholarship. Books on pseudomysticism can be found everywhere. Avoid cultish material, and anything that glorifies the human guru. Avoid dogmatic, inflexible, exclusivistic philosophies and groups. Avoid writers who hint at great or "secret" mysteries, but never tell you what they are; such people are usually in love with the word "occult," and their writings contain nothing of value.

Falling in Love with Your Self
Love and the Inner Beloved

Also, avoid writers who manage to use many words without saying anything; this often marks "channeled" material, much of which is worthless from the spiritual view.

Instead, for your spiritual education, seek out humble, nonegotistic teachers who want nothing to do with riches or fame. WARNING: These are more scarce than the finest thousand-carat diamonds, but they can still be found. Also, seek spiritual educational material that is eclectic, drawing from all the great religious resources, including Hinduism, Taoism, Buddhism, Christianity, and other mystical traditions. (Islamic Sufism and Jewish Kabbalism are often worth studying.)

Why is this field so confused? Because everybody insists on sloppy, inaccurate definitions of the word "mysticism." Even to writers, who should know better, the word often conjures up little more than something bizarre, spooky, or weird. Studies of Atlantis, psychism, and extraterrestrials have all been labeled as "mystical." So have a number of phony "channeled" works. **These topics have nothing to do with mysticism** Mysticism enjoys a crystalclear academic and historical definition. Stated simply, in three parts, it is this: 1) The Way of studying, in spiritual terms, the Unconscious,

2) awareness that the Absolute is the Center of all Mind, and

3) recognition that It is Love.

Much that has been labeled carelessly and/or ignorantly as "mysticism" is ludicrous, amusing, or just plain silly. The word has been disrespectfully and obscenely applied to a wide spectrum of oddball pursuits, extremists, fanatical and/or fringe groups, ideas on the periphery of sanity, and ideas that have already gone over the edge. This is both absurd and shameful. Yet this desecration has taken place under the noses— indeed, has flowed from the keyboards— of professionals, including Ph.D.'s, journalists, and religious leaders. The ignorance in the field of mysticism is gargantuan. So, the word has endured a terrible reputation. Although true academicians understand its vitality and indispensability as a component of every religious tradition, less educated academics ignore, deny, or even mock what they perceive to be "mystical" matters. In fact, it is most common in Western language to use the word dismissively, as a putdown. An example is, "You're retreating into mysticism." This is equivalent to, "You have abandoned all reason," or, "You have abandoned the principles of science and observation, and are resorting to supernatualism." "Mysticism" is used as if it were synonymous with "nonsense," as in, "Don't waste your time with all that. It's just mysticism." Or, it is misperceived to be antiacademic or antiintellectual, as in, "Do you want to discuss this reasonably, or are you just going to resort to mysticism?" It is understood as a kind of flight from reason, or even sanity.

These corruptions and misunderstandings have not been corrected, but rather strengthened, by the very few fanatics in religious history who have hidden their asceticisms and extremisms behind the veil of "mysticism." But contrary to the popular dogmatic myth, most mystics were reasonable, wellbalanced, wise, moderate people. They all shared a passion for inner exploration, and for the Fountain of beauty and wisdom that they discovered in the unconscious Mind. In fact, as a whole, psychopathologies are remarkably scarce among the mystics. Their names include some of the most wellknown names in history, including Plato, Heraclitus, Plotinus, Patanjali, Shankara, Lao Tzu, the Buddha, Al Hallaj, Solomon, Jesus, and dozens of others. The list is far too long to be comprehensive.

Others whom you might want to read include the writers of the Upanishads, most Buddhist and Taoist writers, most yogis and yoginis, Dionysius, the early gnostics, most early Hindu writers, Rabiah, Al Hallaj, Abu Yazid, Al Khayr, Abraham Abhulafia, Isaac Luria, the Sufis generally, the Hasidim and the Kabbalists generally, Jakob Boehme, Richard Rolle, Richard of St. Victor, St. Hildegard, St. Theresa of Avila, St. John of the Cross, Meister Eckhart, and many others.

When designing your reading list, it is crucial not only to avoid the time-wasters of the silly and empty, but you must also take care to avoid any materials that might be harmful in any way, to mind, Soul, or emotions. **Avoid all extremism and fanaticism.**

Above all, learn everything that you can about Love— its psychology and its spirituality. Read, and collect, everything that you can find, from all sources, about Love.

More importantly, **practice Love at every opportunity.** Go out of your way to be kind, just, tender, friendly, courteous, and fair. Do this in all "small" as well as "great" things. Recall that there is no small act of

Richard Shiningthunder Francis

Love, for every act of Love is a great act. Keep in mind that the two practical forms of Love are service and friendship. Any activity in either area is worship or sacred activity.

This education, and these practices, will prepare you for the inner journey. Don't fall into the common snare of the delusion that reading about this journey can somehow replace the actual event. Reading brochures about the Greek islands is not at all like actually lying on one of the beaches.

Every hour of every day, life will provide you with an "exam" or two. You will have plenty of opportunities to practice kindness. It is safe to say that, within an hour after your having read these words, you will be put to the test. You will "take an exam." You have the information to pass that test with flying colors. But will you apply it practically? Life will also give you plenty of chances to find detachment and nonjudgment, many opportunities to see the entire world, and everything and everyone in it, as "good."

In review, practice: 1) active compassion—**both** a feeling in the heart, and resulting practical action. 2) detachment. A lady approached the other day complaining that her family yelled at her, and asking, "What should I do?" The answer is: Don't take any mood of any person, including yourself, too seriously; moods come and go with amazing rapidity, and are fluctuating, liquid situations. But also, try to find detachment. Remind yourself that you are controlled by nothing and no one in the world, but have already yielded mastership of your life to Love. 3) Take every

*Falling in Love with Your Self
Love and the Inner Beloved*

situation and event as a chance to cultivate the "allembracing Mind" which is free of all negative judgments, seeing everything as "good." Work **never** to define **anything** as "bad," "ugly," or "undesirable," in an absolute (Mindinfluencing) sense. 4) Work to rid yourself of the false, human, social identity called "egoself." You might try a game called "Ifree." Go as long as possible without using the words "I," "me," "my," or "mine." Take this seriously, and ask your friends to help you master the fine art of Ifree speech. They will often be only too happy to point out when you screw up! 5) Work to love everything. Don't love the evil, but try to see the good within the evil; loving that, you will soon arrive at a point where there is no evil. For every "evil" has a core of redeeming goodness.

To create a purely stainless approach, to discover inner pristinity, you will have to throw out some traditional psychology, although you can still embrace most of it. The idea of the subconscious mind as a garbage heap of filth, ugliness, sordid and assorted evils, will have to be jettisoned. This can be replaced with the notion of the shadow, which is not "bad," but a natural selfdefensive mechanism of illusion developed by the ego.

To get well psychologically, you might have to focus only on the "subconscious." But to get whole spiritually, you will have to concentrate on the larger, more inclusive, unconscious. This sphere of Mind includes both the shadow "subconscious" and the higher spiritual Superconscious or Core. (The unconscious also includes the personal layers of the Unconscious, the Soulevel, the collective, and the Creator/Dreamer (part of the Absolute). See "Chart of Mind.")

****

Chapter 29

The Immanipulable Mystic: Radical Independence, Friendly Mind

***

The dark subcontinent of the subconscious is explored by both psychologists and psychonauts (mystics). The scientists have created a monstrous catalog of mindbending demons and dragons, many of them pulled intact from nightmare, haunting the subconscious since early childhood.

But for the mystic, the "unconscious" (both subconscious and Superconscious) is a remarkably bright and friendly place. It is ultra-inviting and enormously comfortable and welcoming. It's as delightful a place to visit as to live. It's the best of all possible worlds. And it's accessible to everyone every minute of every day. Exploring, and living with, the unconscious Mind is a pleasure, not a pain. For the mystic continuously soothes her mind by:

1) embracing everything as ultimately or absolutely good, and

2) by living in impeccable honor, creating a clean conscience and an incredibly positive selfimage.

Psychologist have mapped out the subconscious terrain in some detail. But they know almost nothing about the Superconscious, the infinitely more important part of the Unconscious. This Absolute they have arbitrarily decided to relegate to religion.

So, they have abandoned and deleted much of the Mind, which should ideally be their object of study. Because of fear, antireligious bias, or just plain stupidity, they have declared the most crucial part of the psyche offlimits to scientific observation or study.

They have justified dropping the Superconscious like the proverbial hot potato because It is, at its Core or Absolute level, God. So, it is quite beyond the reach and scope, or even the speculations, of science. It took psychology a century to be admitted to the stature of a real "science," and it still suffers from serious "physics envy." It still goes out of its way, in short, to appear, or actually to be, more "scientific" than any other science. Embracing Supermind would be a serious deterioration or backslide into religion— and thus, into accompanying superstitions and ignorance. But obviously, these guys are making a very popular but sophomoric error: They confuse religion with spirituality. So psychology, like an insecure person whom it might seek to explain, overcompensates. It is often even still, after a century, quite selfconscious about this.

Even parapsychology, which, as the name indicates, is a bit closer to psychology than is spirituality, has no official recognition. Most good, scientific psychologists will have nothing to do with it. It is the abandoned black sheep of the family of psychology, or the crazy uncle kept hidden in the attic.

Another reason for the exile of spirituality is that mysticism clashes disturbingly with psychology in its portrayal of the Unconscious. As noted, the *unconscious* is, in

Falling in Love with Your Self
Love and the Inner Beloved

traditional psychology, often confused with, or even reduced to, the *sub*conscious, a completely different "animal." According to much in traditional psychology, the entire unconscious *is* the subconscious. There is no Superconscious mind. It is only a dream and an illusion. So, the whole of the unconscious is a convenient garbage-bin for all the ugly, evil, "unconscious" loose ends of the psyche, according to some schools of tradition. That the unconscious contains a Core of immeasurable beauty, illimitable Love, and infinite joy is quite beyond even the most breathtaking dreams of the psychologist. To her, the unconscious is part sewer and part zoo— or, more accurately, untamed and wild jungle. But to the mystic, it is an inexhaustible ocean of Love and Light, a Fountain of tranquility, the Source of all joy, happiness, and bliss. This is an assumption that boosts her selfimage into orbit. It virtually guarantees her psychological wellbeing. For this Absolute in the unconscious, this "inner Other," this Superconscious, this Core of Mind, is not really an "other" person. It lives deeply within her own psyche. It is a collective phenomenon, meaning that What lives in her also lives in the minds of other people. This Absolute is stainless, flawless, and pristine. It is unaffected by the "outer material" world, and so is marked by detachment. This "detachment" does not imply the negative irresponsivity often implied by that word. It simply exists because the mystic is not controlled by the world. She has cut the strings, and is no longer the marionette of an apparently chaotic universe. Nor will she allow people to pick up those strings and control her.

A word of explanation: The mystic does not allow objects, situations, events, or other persons to control her. This grants an immense sense of independence, and erases excess clinging, grasping, attachment, and craving. It neutralizes the crazymaking, "What does she think of me?" It equally vaporizes the impossible dream of, "If I just do it right, I can please all the people all the time." This attempt to do the impossible loops people through the wild labyrinths of the mind, confusing and frustrating them.

But this enormous independence by no means indicates that the mystic does not care what anybody thinks. She will never be controlled, or manipulated, it is true. She is too free for that. She loves herself too much to permit that. Techniques of guilt, for example, do not work with her. Guilt she sees as a mask worn by her enemy of a thousand faces, fear. It is the only nemesis that she recognizes. Fear is the mystic's "devil," or lowest nature, just as Love is her God. Without a second thought, she immediately boots all guilt out of her mind, with the dual messages: REFUSED DELIVERY and NOT WELCOME HERE. So, you might as well give up any attempt to manipulate a mystic by trying to lay a guiltrip on her shoulders. She will simply shrug it off.

But do mystics care about what their friends think? Yes, they do, but moderately. They will not try to alter their authentic selves or lifedesigns to please others. But neither are they ever insensitive to the feelings of others. Love is never callous, and It guides

Falling in Love with Your Self
Love and the Inner Beloved

their every response. Clearly, the principle of *ahimsa* means that they truly do not want, under any circumstances, to harm anyone.

But neither will they march to anyone else's drummer. Also, they will never swing to the other extreme, trying to "mother" other adults. The free mystic will not try to form the reactions of others to conform to what the mystic thinks they should be. She never forgets that each person is responsible fully for his/her own entire range of responses. If people choose to have negative responses, the mystic does care. In fact, she wants everyone to enjoy the fabulous independence and immeasurable bliss that she herself has found. But she is no Bible-thumper, and never tries to push her beautiful truth down the throats of others. She turns away from the pressurized Jehovah's Witness approach to enforced, artificial conversion.

Mystics are often called to teach. But even when they are not, they wish for others only the very best. They long for all others to know the great truth of Love. Most will do anything— provided that it is not immoral, illegal, or fattening— to aid, help, and support others spiritually. But the bottom line always is that

****

No adult is ever responsible for the actions or words of any other adult.

****

So, while she does care what her friends think, and their opinions do matter, she is careful to pinpoint the threshold at which the other ends and she begins, as far as responsibility is concerned. She is her brother's/sister's keeper only insofar as she tries to support, assist, and heal him/her. But under no conditions will she 1) take responsibility for any other adult, or 2) allow herself to be controlled by anybody.

She is radically independent. While she might love to be around others, she tries to avoid overdependency on them. Interdependence is not a weakness, but a natural human condition. So, the mystic does not reject interdependence in moderation. We all depend on each other, all the time, for the giving and receiving of Love. But the mystic realizes that **too much** dependence is a dangerous weakening of her own boundaries, her own mind. So, although she loves people, loves to be with them, she does not strictly depend on them for her spiritual progress. With or without others, she is a granitic Mind— solid, reliable, powerful, immovable. This becomes truer every day as she progresses in her inward journey to the Center. Daily, her very identification of her "Self" begins gradually to shift. More and more, she recognizes her Self, not as her ego, but as the supreme Mind, filled to overflowing with the jewels of compassion, bliss, and tranquility. This Absolute, this Core of Mind, this Supermind is her real Self. It is purest Love, rapture, stillness, and order.

****

Falling in Love with Your Self
Love and the Inner Beloved

Chapter 30

Miraculous Mind, Everlasting Mind: Exploring the Heartcaves of Harmlessness

***

You'd better doublecheck your scuba gear if you are going to be a mystic, for you will be called to the deepest, darkest "waters' of the "ocean" of Mind. Only at ten thousand fathoms do you even begin to detect the possible existence of the luminous Core or Absolute. Not everyone is prepared to dive this deeply—for the waters are dark, and the unknown can be frightening.

To complete this journey to the center of the soul, you must begin realistically where you are. So, you must admit your imperfections. You must blast into the personal unconscious, galloping on your sure-footed white steed, lance at the ready, and kill your demons. Without avoidance or evasion, you must bravely look them in the eye while you slaughter these fears. However ferocious or monstrous their illusions, you must not flinch or flee.

For the hidden shadowself is like the egoself. It wants to survive. But light and darkness cannot coexist, and it must perish when the psyche is flooded with the intense, brilliant Light of Love.

The shadow uses great quanta of energy to maintain its fears, and to keep itself hidden. When you make it conscious, that gigantic energy is freed, and released, to be directed by your heartmind. All that massive force can now be invested in harmony, beauty, intelligence, and Love. It can now be expressed as compassion, peace, joy, and creativity. Peace brings an economic windfall to a nation, in which money can be invested in positive, constructive programs, instead of weapons. In the same way, personal erasure of the fears of the shadowself brings a personal energic windfall.

There are great rewards for cooperating with Love. The mind is promised, by Supermind, everlasting and inexhaustible riches in the forms of compassion, bliss, and tranquility. In other words, inner "heaven" is the reward of Lovebased behavior and speech.

So, while everything in the "material" world is rushing to become dust, the Mind is forever untouched. The Buddhists call this ever-changing state of the Mindworld "impermanence." There is a special state of euphoria, a taste of bliss, that occurs when a person finally realizes the impermanent nature of all material things. The emotions that accompany them are also as evanescent as thin morning fog. This is called *aware* (pronounced "ah-wahr'-ay"). To think about the passing of the "material, external" world into mounds of dust seems at first discouraging, depressing, dismal. But when one realizes the his/her Mind is everlasting, permanent, everything is improved. Then, the formerly crazy dance of the world is shifted to a celebration-movement of sheer joy. For the mystic, every moment is precious, to be embraced with the total being, and enjoyed to the fullest. But this applies only as long as one lives in *aahimsa*, or perfect noninjury. Try not to harm anyone emotionally, mentally, spiritually, or physically. The essence of this Way is the Hippocratic "Do no harm."

We might not all be heroes; we might not all make significant contributions to society. But the mystic says that what you do **not** do can be every bit as important as what you do. And to live without injury or harm is an accomplishment of significant and great merit. The very act of refusing to harm or injure anyone or any creature is precious. It can even be heroic. This is a life successfully lived. It is, in fact, an absolute criterion of real success.

So, on the mystical journey, we must enter every cave. There, we must flush out and release every "beast" that is in bondage, guiding our primal wildness to the sunlight of awareness. We must transform this animal-energy into the force that drives us into the arms of Love. We must love them into submission. We no longer repress or suppress, but simply harness, their enormous powers.

The inner world of the unconscious Mind is fluid, nebulous, formless. It is filled with archetypal powers; here live the gods and goddesses, heroes and wild beasts. Here, in "potential" form, lives all of nature, from beetles to dragons, from rivers to mountains. Demons and spirits haunt the inner groves, and wander the inner forests. Angels play in the sunlit fountains. A wide spectrum of Mindbeings lives here. But all this multiplicity returns, ultimately to one Mind. That is the dreaming Mind that brings it all into being.

This is the same Mind that dreams up the waking world. It is the level of the unconscious called the "Creator/Dreamer." (See "Chart of Mind.") The Creator dreams up the world continuously, through you and me. You are dreaming right now.

In fact, you are dreaming up the words and worlds of this book. For you do not really see this book as it is, but only as it is interpreted by the several billions of filters and lenses of your nervousystem and brainmind system. So, you are, in a very real sense, "creating" or at least, cocreating (with the Creator) this book. It is, then, at least slightly different for you than for anyone else. A hundred people reading this book will read a hundred different books.

It is a real manifestation of the Self's educating the self. Like the rest of the world, this book springs into being the very moment that you sense/perceive it. It emerges out of theoretical reality (what can be) into experiential reality (what is).

But is this view mere "solipsism," the philosophy that your personal mind is the only one that really exists? Probably you can see that it is not. For the world of the mystic is as dazzling, exciting, unpredictable, and richly enjoyable as any other. In fact, because she possesses peace and Love, and greatly values both, her life is often much better than the average. The dazzling diversity of the world is not neutralized at all by the realization that there is only one Sourcemind. A field containing a thousand wildflowers is not at all diminished by the fact that they all blossom from a single earth.

Besides, we all know how mindbogglingly rich the dreamworld can be— how filled with wonder, multiplicity, and infinite variety. The mystic sees this common world in the same way. This world is not dreamed up *by* the mystic, but only *through* her. It is created by an infinite, boundless Mind of great, magnificent creativity and originality. There are surprises around every corner. So, the plethora of events and situations possible to the mystic is diminished not a single micropsychon by the fact that she interprets her world as a dream. What effect does this have? It creates for her a world that is much more flexible than the standard "material, external" world. For in her world, literally *anything is possible.* Magic can appear, miracles can manifest, at any moment. This makes the mysticworld much more exciting and extraordinarily beautiful than the average worldview.

When we continue to suppress or repress mental energy, psychology tells us, it will erupt in unpredictable, often harmful, ways. Repression is unconscious, and so uncontrollable. But suppression, which often leads to it, should be kept to a bare minimum. This minimization is enhanced by selfhonesty and the absence of selfjudgment. This nonjudgment arises from embracing all that is in the self as good.

Should we rationalize true evil? No, for evil is not simply to be ignored. It is there for a reason, to get our attention. It is a call to change. Nature, in other words, is joining forces with mind, in order to call attention to the evil, or lack of Love. The only solution is to root out evil and replace it with Love. But in the process, we need not mistake the label "evil" for an absolute reality with power of its own. It is not. It is only a subconscious construct. But it has the power to put us through inner hell, and so, is psychopathological. It is mental illness.

The opposite of suppression is honest, nonjudgmental expression. We need to relearn the art so well known to children, and that is selfmanifestation. Anger is a good example. **If we can express anger without harming anyone,** then it is better to express it in harmless ways than to suppress it, pretending that we are above anger, or do not really feel it. Suppressed, it can become dangerously volcanic. But expressed carelessly and spontaneously, it can also be perilous. But honest anger is not as harmful as resentment can be. For resentment is an acid that corrodes relationship, while anger is an explosion. It is more intense, but is not pervasive or longlasting. Expressed and clear anger can hurt, but sincere apology can undo some of the harm. Arguably, a human being has never existed who did not feel the bite of anger. Resentment, however, usually unexpressed, can act like a drop of water striking the "stone" of relationship. In time, it will dissolve that rock.

Let us, then, work to cultivate friendliness in the place of anger. Friendliness (as courtesy) is an often-neglected aspect of real Love, but it is a vital one.

****

Chapter 31

Psychodetox: Tossing the Labelmaker, Perfectmind Resonance

***

A deadly beast emerges from a gentle man. It roars. It kills. A demon has taken possession of him. It is anger. Anger, and a wide spectrum of other psychotoxins, can be neutralized by the practice of Love. This implies forgiveness. The wisdom of forgiveness is based upon this true premise:

****

When you do not forgive, you harm only yourself.

****

The unforgiven person might not even know that you are holding energies against her, but **your** bodymind system certainly knows. And the absence of forgiveness is a selfcreated hell. Like anger, unforgiveness is a major psychotoxin.

Total detox occurs only when we have learned to love, release, and forgive everything and everyone. Only then do we breathe the refined and rarefied air of real freedom. And it is the very oxygen of life itself.

NOTE: This is **not** optional. If your life is to continue at full throttle, it is sustained by joy, peace, and Love. It thrives on these positivities. Hatred, judgment, harmful anger, and unforgiveness are, conversely, antibiological. They drain the lifeforce. They deplete and exhaust us. They are psychic pollutants more dangerous than any environmental toxin.

Universal Love, our only path to psychodetox, must include every factor and component of our own selves. We must learn the art of embracing rather than simply follow the old, ingrained habit of judging. This is the old cliche about becoming your own best friend.

The Absolute, or Love, creates the inner being in perfect goodness. So, at your Core, you are a stainless, flawless expression of unadulterated goodness. Now, it is a matter of remembering this, and learning to manifest it.

When we can walk that long and winding road back to unity with, and love for, the entire world, we will come into peace. We will emerge into synergic resonance (harmony and agreement) with this inner and perfect Supermind. How do we begin this mysterious process?

We start by throwing out our labelmaker. We stop judging. We accept, perhaps at first on faith alone, that the entire world is, in the absolute (final) analysis, "good." "Evil" is a radical and nightmarish illusion. So, we actively cast all "evil" from our lives, and consciously, cognitively replace it with Love. Then, we begin the cultivation of Love by learning to accept nonjudgmentally, and to forgive, those less-desirable aspects of our personality. When adults turn into tantrum throwing brats, the result needs to be understanding and discipline, not punishment.

This does not mean just saying that everything within us is perfectly "okay." We are moving towards higher Love, perfect Mind. This implies a continuous process of selection. We select the good over the evil. We choose the healthy and healing over the harmful and diseased. We seek to burn up the evil with the good. When we notice evil, we immediately push the "delete" key. But what we do *not* do is continue to berate, scold, and punish ourselves. We do not carry around the destructive and heavy baggage of guilt. Guilt is a form of fear, and so is Love's opposite.

Some feel that guilt is actually a useful tool. A fairly wide spectrum of religions are "guilt specialists." They are guilt-machines, actually manufacturing the stuff. But this does not make of guilt a virtue. What is guilt? It is that incessant selfscolding, selflagellation, that continues long after it could have any conceivable usefulness. Does the mystic believe in remorse, in feeling sorry and regretful for having harmed anyone? Yes, indeed she does. Does she feel the need to recompense for any harm? Yes.

So, the enlightened do believe in remorse/recompense, but not in the harmful, chronic state of selfpunitive guilt. Guilt is no virtue, and does *not* improve people. It is a dragon slain with the firesword of Love.

This Love enhances and supports a quest for Mindmeld with the Core of Mind (Superconscious). This deeply unconscious level of Mind is not only perfect Love, but also perfect bliss and tranquility. So, it does not allow for the continual disturbances and turbulence of guilt.

The strings of a guitar often vibrate in harmony with each other. This is called "resonance." Love lifts us to a harmonious "vibrational resonance" with this inner Mind. (This is what is usually called "good vibes.") When we reach this high vibe-level, a process called "psidiffusion" occurs. (The prefix "psi" describes the energies of mind.) This means that mental energy, like chemical concentrates, tends to flow from an area of higher energy into an area of lower energy.

Nothing in the cosmos has higher energy than this Core. So, when you are depleted, and expose your mind to It, you are reenergized. Its energies of Love, bliss, and deep peace flow from It into your personal heartmind. This happens naturally through psidiffusion if we do not block it through too much, or antiagapic (counterloving) thinking. When your psychic "gastank" is empty, you feel anxious, stressful, or depressed. It is when you are "on empty" that you need to come to the inner "service station" and "fill up." This is an especially appropriate analogy, for the major expression of Love that recharges or refills you is service.

Just as inner Mind can psidiffuse energy into our systems, so we all interact with each other continuously. But what if, for example, you "pick up bad vibes" from, or are weakened by, another person? Your solution is to go within, contact inner Mind, and recharge. This is easier than you might at first think. It usually happens naturally and effortlessly, in fact, when we sleep at night. No process

Falling in Love with Your Self
Love and the Inner Beloved

is more natural. But various forms of meditation can enhance and facilitate the recharge.

"Bad vibes," negative energies, or inner blackholes (which drain energy but give back nothing) can also exist in your own shadow. So, these too need to be detoxed from the system by the continuous practice of Love. For the practice of Love is the greatest detox/recharging mechanism in the cosmos. Remember that the "power" of the shadow arises **only** from its suppression. So, you can nonjudgmentally acknowledge it. By loving it, you can also transfuse its energy to more productive and positive areas of Mind. This is why selfanalysis and introspection are so important. For when the shadow is made conscious, is brought into the light of awareness, it gives up its power. It no longer acts like an inner psychic vampire or "blackhole," draining energy. (This idea is basic to very much in psychotherapy.)

Conversely, fear feeds it. When it attacks, it uses fear as its tool. It is this same fear that prevents the total detox of forgiveness. Whenever we do not forgive, it is because we are locked into the grip of fear. We fear losing power. We fear that we are vulnerable to others. We fear that they are "getting away with" something. We fear, then, that the cosmos is unjust. But the cosmic Mind has a trillion eyes, sees everything, and is never indifferent. It notices every nanopsychon of Mind, and will create perfect balance. Faith in this entire megacomplex called "karma" can aid us to forgive. The fear of powerloss lies at the root of a number of mental imbalances and emotional illnesses.

But forgiveness actually gives and renews power. Like service and friendship, forgiveness is a mirror of Love.

****

Chapter 32

The Crash of Fear in the Clash with Love

***

The battle rages ferociously inside your psyche. The combatants are fear and Love. They are irreconcilable opposites. Together, they fill you up, but the presence of one weakens the activities of the other. Fear weakens and dilutes Love, and Love makes fear feeble and powerless.

One must emerge as the victor. They do the dance of inverse proportions, so that if a personality is sixty percent fear, it can be only forty percent Love. If seventy percent is fear, that leaves only thirty percent for Love. The average personality probably has a score of about "fear, seventy, Love thirty."

The goal of the enlightened being is to "score" a perfect "Love one hundred, fear zero." This state is almost never reached by human consciousness, but the operative word is "almost." A fearfree experience of inner Mind is possible. In time, it can lead even to a fearfree state. (A state is much longerlasting than an experience.)

Love eradicates fear. So, filling our lives and minds with only Love will decrease and dilute fear. As water dissolves salt, which then loses the integrity of its structure, so Love dissolves fear. It will deenergize it, and detox our systems.

Has anyone ever achieved a permanent fearfree state? Arguably, some remarkable sages and masters have. They have, first, recognized the nature of the dreamworld as a product of the Core of Mind. Their faith that this Core could and would produce nothing but absolute good carried them beyond the snares of fear into the luminous inner blue skies of uninterrupted, seamless Love. The very best among them mastered universal Love, the capacity to embrace everything without judgment. This is the perennial goal of the pristine Soul. For this is perfect enlightenment. This is the zenith of perfect Christianity, perfect Buddhism, perfect mysticism.

Let us try, then, consciously to rid our minds of fear. There are no monsters in the dark closets of your mind. In fact,

****

There has never been even a particle of true evil within you.

****

Let us strive cognitively to recognize and eliminate the illusion of evil wherever it has taken root. Let's rip it out, and shred it. Let us then burn it in the flames of Love. Lets' analyze and dismantle it, finding out what makes it tick, so that we can restructure our psyches without it.

Sometimes the ancients used the word "light" to mean consciousness or awareness. Thus, when something comes "into the light," it emerges from the unconscious levels of Mind into the conscious mind. By simple definition, in light, shadows disappear. And there is, can be, no light more luminous than Love.

Let us try, then, to become well in the only Way possible: By loving everything within us. Let us move into the lucid recognition that all is "good," that all of it, in fact, is God or ultimate good.

Still, even within this interpretative and healthy understanding, Love moves us to change if aspects of Mind are in service to the "lower nature." So, changes are often appropriate, necessary, and desirable. The heartmind is a canvas upon which we make new brushstrokes, small alterations and improvements, every hour. While recognizing our minds as totally good, we know that they are not yet perfect. They can always stand improvement and adjustment, fine-tuning in Love. This includes education in, and practices of, goodness, kindness, courtesy, friendliness, integrity, honesty, selfregulation, joy, peace, tenderness, and patience— among others.

Symmetrically, we turn away from lying, dishonesty, violence, conflict, disharmony, greed, ultrasensuality, egocentricity, insecurity, fears, and ignorance. Although these can be "very good" in the limited sense that they are tools for our education, they are by no means "good" in the relative world. They lead inevitably to inner hellstates of suffering, agony, and searing inner pain. These hells often draw in others. That is why both nature and Love guide us away from these hurtful paths.

We need to begin asap, cognitively to work on these tendencies, to eradicate them from personality. For they create the complexities of harmful karma. Thus, life after life, they land us squarely in hell. We need to live not only good lives, but to soar beyond the ordinary standards of good morality and ethics. We need to fly into the extreme altitudes of impeccable honor. Under the influence of impeccable honor, the mystic not only does the good thing, but goes far beyond ordinary goodness. A mystic who finds a quarter will seek to find its owner and return it— not because a great deal of money is involved, but because a principle is.

Enlightened people cannot live an "ordinary" mental, moral, or ethical life. Instead, they are called by the inner Spirit to a transcendental life. They do not just "play by the rules," but establish a set of higher rules within their own psyches. So, socially, morally, ethically, sexually, and spiritually they live according to "impeccable honor."

What is "impeccable honor"? It is the life that strives for the cultivation/ultimate perfection of spiritual excellence, or of Love. Obeying laws— even religious laws— is not enough. The being of impeccable honor is not just "clean," but "squeaky clean." She is not just moral because she avoids immorality, but shines as a spotlight of Love in a dark world. She is a model for all. She lives always thinking of the enrichment and good of others. Her every action is guided by kindness, courtesy, tenderness, and empathy. She gives generously, and seeks to support others. She improves the world every day, by a kindness, such as calling a friend, sending a card, or running an errand. She volunteers her timenergy to aid others. If she is forced to walk a mile, out of Love, she walks two.

Falling in Love with Your Self
Love and the Inner Beloved

If she has two coats, she gives one away. She does not just tolerate her enemies, but actively loves them. She prays even for those who use her, hate her, gossip about her. She does not hesitate to sacrifice. Under appropriate conditions, in fact, she knows that she would die for others.

The deepest inner Mind is perfect. So, all of us are called to the ultimate goal of perfection. This was the real meaning of Jesus' words, "You must be perfect, as your Father is perfect." This was not a command. It was a prophecy. We will someday be perfect, because, deep down, we already are. This ultra-ethical and ultra-honest life of ultra-integrity is the life of Ultralove. It is manifested in the everyday world as the Way of impeccable honor. This is not a religion, or even a religious precept; it is a Way in which one can choose to live.

Love **is** a "warm fuzzy" in the heart, but it must become much more than that, or it is not Love at all. It must blossom into real action, true aid, genuine activities of service. Love without action is not Love. On the other hand, action that is merely mechanical, even if it helps or serves others, is not Love either, without the "warm fuzzies." For in order for Love truly to be present, both the inner warmth of tender feeling and the proof of action must be present.

Service and genuine aid are practical Love. But there is yet another component that also manifests Love. That is friendship, which can be really hard work. For friendship requires regular maintenance, and that means emails, phone-calls, letters, visits, and shared events and/or social activities.

Friendship-maintenance can be tricky. Human nature, human responses, and situations are forever influx, always mutating into new forms. In the author's younger, more naive and idealistic days, he genuinely believed that "once a friend, always a friend." But the events and alterations (as well as altercations) of real life soon disabused him of that unrealistic notion. The truth is that you, and everyone else, must be seen as ever-changing, shifting, and very complex phenomena. This implies that friends, at least, the peripheral types, will move into and out of your life with regularity. Not that friendship is a revolving door, or a game of musical chairs, but people and events are always fluid to some extent. Of course, ideally, your "best buds" will be in your life for life. But others will tend to come and go on a fairly regular basis. For some, friendship is just too much hard work. Others are not willing to make it a priority. Still others might not be mentally balanced enough to maintain a healthy, healing friendship. (Some unbalanced types are secretly looking to be betrayed.) There are also types who want to control too much to create a real harmony in friendship, due to insecurity.

For the author, friendship was always sacred. And it was a real treasure. But not everyone sees it this way. For some, "friendship" is utilitarian, having little to do with Love. (These tend to be "users.") For others, friendship can be like a popular car, an indication of social status, good taste, intellect, or even spirituality. One

*Falling in Love with Your Self
Love and the Inner Beloved*

fact is certain: Without judgment, each person must select, and be selective about, her friends. Not everyone will make a good friend. Not everyone wants to be a friend. You will discover that you have a beautiful and effortless "vibe-resonance" with some, but "dissonance" with others.

Still, friendship is a subsystem of Love. So, choose your friends as you would select fine jewels: Don't make friends carelessly, on the shallow basis of looks, or economics. Instead, seek "quality people." And what, exactly, is a "quality person"? First, she is not shallow. A quality person will not be consumed or obsessed by mindnumbing materialism, sports, or other Lovesubstitutes. Even more importantly, a quality person will have a positive regard for, and interest in, such qualities as intelligence, creativity, healthy mental/emotional development, wisdom, compassion, and spirituality. For people who do not treasure these things are incapable of valuing a friendship as a full human sharing. Never be a "spiritual snob." Always be open to friendly interactions with all. Be friendly, courteous, and polite to all. Be compassionate and generous to all. But you will not invite everyone equally into the deepest inner chambers of the heart. You will not spill your guts before just anyone. Everyone does not deserve your trust, or your respect. (Unlike Love, trust and respect must be *earned*.) Without hard work, a friendship can die on the vine. So, let us strive to make friends wisely and widely. Let us make friends whenever, however, wherever, and with whomever possible. This is a fine therapy for both loneliness and depression.

Richard Shiningthunder Francis

So, share your phone-number, address, or email address with hand-selected people whom you trust. CAUTION: It is not a good idea to let everyone or anyone know where you live, to give your phone-number to just anybody. Try to feel the person out. If you find the person reasonable, balanced, sane, friendly, intelligent, and/or interesting, you might decide that a friendship will enrich your life. Then, reach out and "touch" her by sharing your personal feelings and limited data about your personal life. No one wants, for example, to hear your entire sexual history upon first meeting! Nor does anyone want a detailed history from the time when you were a zygote! So, share moderately and selectively. But, with this caveat, which is only reasonable, try to interact with as wide a circle of people as possible. Remember that friendship is a two-way street: Friends will tend to enrich your life only as you enrich theirs. Don't just go into friendship with a view as to what others can give you, but see what you can give to them.

Reach out to others. Try to give people the benefit of the doubt. Trust others, not entirely, but to the extent possible and reasonable.

****

Chapter 33

Ego Swallowed by Love: Friendship, Humility, and Security

***

   Most people are kind, decent, generous, fair— in a word, good. Most people are worthy of your friendship. And most people are looking for friends of quality— people who value intelligence, treasure compassion, touch joy, care for others, and like themselves without arrogance. Most welcome quality people into their lives. When you become friends with this kind of person, she treasures you. When you become friends, mutually welcoming each other into your lives, you can both be enormously enriched mentally, emotionally, and spiritually.
   Great friendships often mushroom from tiny seeds. The simple exchange of email addresses can have the power to change your lives. Friendship is a practical expression of kindness, a form of Love. It does not mean that your life is interwoven with the other's. It does not imply that you must, or should, act as her "daddy" or "mommy." You don't have to control, or even influence, her life. It simply means that you genuinely care for her. You are concerned about what happens to her. You don't want to see her harmed, and will do everything possible to increase the joy and satisfaction in her life— as long as it does not traverse your own boundaries. You will do everything possible to support her. You

really like her, feel attracted, heart-to-heart, in a bond of genuine affection.

Friendship is often a test of compassion. You never have to "impress" a friend. But friendship does *not* mean never having to say, "I'm sorry." Quite the contrary: In strong or lasting friendships, both partners are quick to apologize sincerely if boundaries are traversed. But the flipside of this is also quite important: You must be not only humble enough genuinely to apologize, but compassionate enough to acknowledge and gracefully receive an apology. Friendship is largely forgiveness. It is not the place for powertrips, or punishment. You are *actually eager* to forgive true friends. And wanting them to be as truly happy as possible, you will not always repeat bitching about past misunderstandings. Your attitude will be light and airy, not heavy and somber. With her, you'll try to adopt a "live and let live" attitude. You will be happy to give useful advice when it is requested, but you will never try to force her hand.

And you cannot "buy" real friendship, which is **not** supported only by giving money and/or gifts. If money **must** exchange hands to keep the "friendship" intact, it is no real friendship at all, but a mere economic transaction. The only gift that you must give true friends is out of the treasure of your heart. They want your Love. Friends request the topaz of time, the emeralds of energy, the sapphires of support, the rubies of reason, and the diamonds of dynamic Love. Friendship is caring and sharing. It is also listening, and talking. It includes various forms of appropriate touch. It is warm and comfortable for both, never judgmental or overly critical. Too much criticism, even if "constructive," is poison to most friendships.

Communication is vital. So, try to communicate as often and as clearly and honestly as possible. In almost every friendship, to be honest, uncomfortable things must sometimes be shared. But say them as courteously, politely, and with as much simple friendliness as possible. In a good, strong, solid, reliable friendship, you should not have to walk on eggs, but neither should you feel free to be blunt, unkind, or insensitive.

You can share your deepest fears, weaknesses, uncertainties, and flaws with a friend, and she will not judge you. Friendship, as a form of Love, takes humility. For it takes this realistic quality to say, "I am imperfect, and these are some of my weaknesses."

Some of these principles apply, not just to friendship, but to life in general. It also requires this same humility to admit that your life cannot be regulated perfectly by your own self, and its attempts to control and manipulate. In fact, the ultimate act of humility is "dying to the self," the indispensable prelude to enlightenment.

****

Humility is the form of wellness that is the flipside opposite and symmetric analog to the mental disease called "arrogance."

****

Humility also means that we must regulate the inner insecurities that cry out for attention. Many people, all during any kind of interaction with other people, are always saying, "Look at me, notice me, praise me," as a kind of subtext to their actual conversation. The mystic does not speak so. She is so secure that she does not find it necessary always to be drawing attention to herself, to be talking about herself, her knowledge, her accomplishments. Those who indulge in this kind of selfdisplay are pathetic. They are sad cases of an ego out of control. Deep down, they have crucial doubts about themselves, and perhaps, don't even like themselves.

So, the enlightened mystic does not waste timenergy trying to impress others. For even if you do manage to impress a few strangers, your life is really **no richer**. She takes that valuable timenergy and invests it in her inner Self, in her great Quest, her inner voyage of discovery.

The enlightened person does not have to be talking all the time, in order to be the "life of the party," or "center of attention." She will have more, and less, talkative days. But she never talks to impress. She tends usually to be quite quiet, under most circumstances. Unless something is **worth saying,** she will prefer the path of silence. It reinforces her inner stillness. When she does speak, further, an enlightened being is often marked by the use of the speechpattern called "Ifree," or something similar. (This means that she will minimize, or avoid, the use of the words "I," "me," "my," and "mine.")

Falling in Love with Your Self
Love and the Inner Beloved

For her, life is **not** a competition. Like the mastersage of Lao Tzu, "She refuses to compete, so no one can compete with her." So, she does not see others as rivals. Rivalry reflects a very unhealthy state of mind, and her goal is wellness. The only one with whom she competes, the only one with whom she will compare herself, is herself of yesterday.

Her life is marked by discipline and structure. This is not rigid or inhuman. She is not into deprivation or deliberate discomfort. For her, though, "discipline" is not a harsh word. In fact, sharing a root with "disciple," it means simply "learning."

The conscious practice of "Ifree" is an example of this discipline-structure. It requires total concentration, careful monitoring, and special awareness of what you are saying, and how. This is the "mindfulness" of Buddhist mystical tradition. If you really want to change your thoughtpatterns for the better, here is a good place to begin. It is at once very simple and very challenging.

In time, this and other disciplines will lead to a changed state that the psychologist Carl Rogers called "othercenteredness." This, too, is necessary for the development of Love, and is a synonym for "compassion."

Breaking away from the massive egotism that most people regard as "normal" is a first step to illumination. Here, we cannot draw our standards from society and culture, which are themselves twisted and distorted. We must use as role-models the mastersages of the Way. Their guidance says to snuff out or extinguish the ego. (*Nirvana* means literally "to extinguish," and refers to egoextinction.)

Richard Shiningthunder Francis

Our society admires and rewards those with the most aggressive, atrocious, overblown egos. It worships those who worship themselves. It praises those who are in love with themselves.

An example that springs readily to mind is the overdeveloped, overcultivated ego of the talkshowradiohost G.Gordon Liddy. Although intelligent and charming, Mr. Liddy grabs every chance possible to toot his own horn. Incessantly, boringly, he regales his audience by drawing attention to himself. One easily senses that he can, and will, *never* get enough approval, attention, validation, or adoration. For some reason, he obviously suffers from a huge selfdeficit. He is, in short, full of himself— almost literally. One wonders, in fact, if there is really "room" in his heartmind to accommodate other people— much less, the great spiritual principles. Is his "hardrive" really "big" enough to store the gigabytes required by a spiritual path? (One senses his own tongue-in-cheek answer.) Another rightwing radiotalkshowhost is more notorious for the more pompous and condescending type of egotism, and he is far less tolerable than Mr. Liddy. He also takes himself far too seriously. He seems always to be auditioning for the role of God's older brother. As a favor to you, dear reader, this pretentious farcical caricature shall remain nameless.

This autoadoration is in stark contrast to the "falling in Love" with the deeper Self (Soul) which is the subject of this book. Falling into shameful Love with the ego produces only conceit and arrogance. This is the path not of a master, but of a spiritual illiterate. They are too sick to remove their eyes from any readily available mirror. They've become so lost in the "play" that they have fallen entirely for the role, and believe in the "mask" as their real selves.

But ego is a "blackhole" in the psyche. A "blackhole" is defined as any factor that eats up mental energy, and gives nothing back, similar to the stellar phenomenon of the same name. The ego tends to be so strong as to dominate life, eclipsing all the great and beautiful higher elements that might be known in its absence. The thoughts of people orbit around the ego as the center of their lives, and, as the center, it is allimportant. It is also alldemanding, and allconsuming. Egoworship drains away all spiritual energy.

For to pursue the Soul and Spirit requires two factors, time and thought. In most lives, most time and thought are already consumed by egothinking, and not even crumbs are left for the spiritual journey inward. That is why people who talk too much about themselves are unusually limited in their knowledge, conceptual skills, wisdom, and actual experience. The hyperegocentrist is devoid of all spiritual beauty and depth.

In these cases, egotism robs you of energy that could be used to love yourself and others. You just don't have the timenergy for compassion, service, or friendship, because ego demands every micropsychon of mental force.

****

Richard Shiningthunder Francis

Chapter 34

The Jehovah-myth, Fatalism, and Free Will

***

Egolessness is excellence in spiritual teaching. The truly qualified spiritual teacher will not struggle and strive for strokes. She will not seek admiration, and will often refuse it even when it is offered.

She wants her students to talk about concepts and ideas, about truth in its infinity of forms, **not** about her ego. To her, her egoface and egoname are supremely unimportant, irrelevant to her message. She would prefer to relax in the cool, calm waters of the shade than to dance in the spotlight.

In the modern metaphysical community, unfortunately, there are many self-styled "teachers" who are ego-obsessed. They love to hear their egonames praised, and often, their followers are gullible and/or ignorant enough to go along with this egogame. They make sure that their egofaces are placed prominently before their audiences, and some have not been beyond shamelessly distributing photos of their egofaces. Some have even made the absurd claim that simply looking at a picture of the "guru" will trigger instant enlightenment. Others display their egofaces prominently on the covers of their books. And their names are everywhere. When people worship them, they lap it up like a pathetic starving puppy.

Falling in Love with Your Self
Love and the Inner Beloved

How did people who are so obviously, seriously spiritually diseased ever come to be seen as leaders in the metaphysical or religious community? Two factors: First, the overall society in which we live, which is also ego-obsessed, has influenced them. And, second, metaphysics, other "newage" areas, and almost all religions have little or nothing to do with real spirituality. The whole idea of functioning egolessly would strike the average minister, priest, or even newage leader as absurd.

First things first. It is very challenging to resist the community pressures to conform to the norm. This is a double blast, because society joins forces with our own personal lower nature to spotlight the illusionself or ego. If we have been infected with the social plague of hyperegotism, it is at least partly because there is a strong sector of our own minds, which mystics call the "lower nature," which delights in illusion and thrives on ignorance. So, egotism is strong in the very human nature, even without the influence of a society that is also nutty.

Second, egotism influences metaphysical and religious "teachers" even more than it does the average person, in some ways. A strong egomotive for setting up oneself as a "teacher" is the one-upmanship implied in the egogame. "I'll show you! I'm not worthless!" cries the inner child (immature mind). From one perspective, to be a spiritual teacher is the very top of the top of the heap. It's better than being an astronaut, groundbreaking scientist, or politician. It's really cosmic! And what could be more exciting to the childish ego than that? These egotists are the greatest shame and embarrassment of the metaphysical and religious communities.

Humility is not "advanced" spirituality. It is not "spiritual brainsurgery" or "rocketscience." It is the "preschool" level, and anyone who is truly on a genuine spiritual path will demonstrate it.

Humility differs from other sterling qualities. For if you are too interested in cultivating, measuring, or recognizing it, it has already been lost. You simply cannot genuinely be "proud of your humility." Anyone who thinks, "Im just about the most humble guy around" has already lost the real thing. There's a good reason for this: *Humility is learning not to think about the self (ego)*. So, if you keep asking yourself whether or not you are sufficiently humble, all that selfthought is your automatic answer.

Surprisingly, the enlightened do very little, or no, selfevaluation. They're not always worried, "Am I good enough yet?" Or, they do not indulge in the selfhell of, "How am I doing?" In fact, they are so obsessed with, possessed by, their truth that they have little timenergy left over for selfmeasurement. *Selferasure* prohibits *continuous selfobservation and selfanalysis*. The entire goal is to erase, not to improve, the egoself. If that goal is taken seriously, continuous jittery, selfconscious selfassessment is out of the question. *The essence of the Way is relaxation* into the deeper Mind. You must allow It to do Its work. The Way does not lead to selfimprovement, but selfneutralization.

Even in her use of Ifree, the masterteacher (she is master of only her self) will not simply avoid the use of selfwords mechanically. She will understand the spirit behind Ifree, which is to get the mind thinking about issues and philosophies, not just to obsess about the "great, allencompassing" egoself. Her mind is unconcerned with the self, and it is this very propensity for selforgetting which makes a masterteacher.

She realizes that egocentricity is a keyhole view of infinity. Egocentricity is the most crippling of spiritual diseases, as it ruins everything and everyone that it touches. Spiritually, egotism is the "antimidas touch." Everything that the egocentrist touches turns to mud. Only greed is a worse disease. Until you are "unselfed" or "deselfed," the mind is stuck to what it can see through only the keyhole of ego. But when this gigantic boulder of a burden is finally dropped, the clean, fresh air of freedom rushes in. Ego gives the visionary capacity of an ameba, but this inner Mind explodes into gigantic, galactic expansion when we shatter the shackles of ego.

The author of this book became a minister of a bizarre, rightwing, extremist cult at the age of eighteen. This, once a source of egopride, is now his greatest shame. This is an object lesson of how pride is subtly selfsabotaging. Pride is antispiritual and can reverse even centuries of progress. This fundamentalist group was similar to almost all others. Only its toughest, most insensitive, egocentric members became leaders in its hierarchy. Love was praised but not prized. To put it politely, the cult had a few screws loose. He, like his cult, thought that he had

God in a thimble, the microspace of the cultdogma. This is spiritual pride in perhaps its worst form.

The cult had a very strong image of God as the ancient Jehovah-myth. So, it taught a god of cruelty, injustice, and stupidity. If this god did not get his way, he would simply kill his "enemies." Adolf Hitler would have been proud! It was a god fit for a binladen, but never for a civilized, Lovebased human being.

This god was both emotionally and spiritually arrested. He threw temper tantrums. He admitted that he was jealous. He spent half his time in a state of agitated, frustrated anger. He was obsessed with a tiny Middle Eastern state, to the point where, its generals taught, Jehovah actually went into war, on the battle-field, with the soldiers.

What was never realized, in the arrogance, both of history and personal life, was that knowing about Jehovah meant nothing about knowing God. Later, this author was stunned and shocked to discover that, for the first eighteen years of his life, he had been actively worshipping a "false" god. In the cult, we had "Jehovah" in our little matchbox, all contained and manipulable, and we grew complacent. In vast, football-field-sized ignorance, we thought that we knew everything about that god.

We also became hardened and insensitive, just like our god. For the basic, most fundamental teaching of the cult was that, any time now, Jehovah was going to practice mass-murder so widespread, gruesome, and atrocious that it would, by comparison, make Hitler look like a humanitarian saint. For Jehovah, and the cult, were not only clearly antisemitic;

Falling in Love with Your Self
Love and the Inner Beloved

they were fully antihuman. This resulted in the most ghastly, nightmarish teaching imaginable. For their god was going to swoop down from the sky, and slaughter and massacre every person who did not belong to this shabby, fraudulent, pathetic little microminority cult. A more antihuman teaching would be difficult even to imagine.

This author, in short, had been totally blinded by a culturally-supported, religiously-supported egocentricity.

****

In true wisdom, we must come to recognize spiritual egalitarianism— that we are no better, and no worse, than anyone else.

****

No matter what you've accomplished, no matter what you know, you are not really better intrinsically than any other member of your species. It is true that you are priceless, you are unique. Sometimes, in half-joking, this bit of encouragement will be shared: "You are completely unique— just like everybody else."

The mystic, seeking to cooperate with Tao, or the great Mind or Power running the cosmos, practices a mild resignation. But she is never a fatalist, going to the extreme of saying that no initiative is necessary. For she always responds readily and willingly to the direction of Love. And Love often moves her to initiate.

This "go with the Flow" attitude is not even similar to a paralyzing predestinarianism.

For every moment and move of your life is not predestined. True, your Soul has preselected and predesigned some conditions. It selected your genome (genetic structure), for example, so that certain genetic factors will unfold in your body. This cannot be changed by current knowledge or technology. The mystic gracefully accepts the limitations which nature has placed upon her, and seeks to find ways around genetic obstacles. She sees this as part of her spiritual education.

For example, the author of this book brought within himself a gene that made him go blind at the age of twenty-eight— nearly twenty-five years ago. Yet the inner journey is completely open to him.

For the committed mystic, it is **only** this inner journey that counts, that has any final value at all.

Every moment of your life, you make freewill choices that can affect you the rest of your life. These work together with your basic karmic matrix to determine your destiny. Choosing to read this book, for example, is a freewill activity that can greatly enrich, and even help transform, your entire life. It is a good investment of timenergy— not only the author's, but the readers', as well.

Timenergy invested in this— the study and discovery of the inner worlds of Mind— is the wisest investment that you will ever make.

****

Falling in Love with Your Self
Love and the Inner Beloved

Chapter 35

Embracing the Self: "In Love" with the World of Dreamind

***

The world is an interpretation, a Mindworld. It is a dreamworld. In reality, there is no "outside." The cosmos is an inside job. It's a closed system, but still infinite. It's all in your head.

So, all the characteristics that you see everywhere are actually within you. Let's even suppose, for the sake of argument, that an "external" world really did exist. Even if it did, the fact that the world has an interior nature as part of Mind still remains unchanged. For by the time that you "see" or know anything, that thing is already changed. You can't know, sense, or perceive anything without changing it. This is because 1) you have already had vast experience, and 2) your mindbrainsystem is incomprehensibly complex. When any stimulus passes through the billions of interpretative filters and lenses of your personal nervousystem and brainmindsystem, it is altered according to your inner "specs."

So, the world that you experience is still a tailormade one. It's still all in your head. It is **yours,** and no one else's. And your inner world is still quite unique. Ten people in the "same" room will actually be inhabiting ten different Mindrooms. This is what I call the "tptr" effect— "ten people, ten rooms." It implies that each of us lives in a personal and unique cosmos.

Either way that you cut it, you still live in a "world" that is not items, objects, and things, but thoughts, feelings, reactions, and interpretations. Even if an "objective" world were really to exist, no one could ever sense or perceive it purely, or accurately.

When, then, you hear of a rape, it is your own Mind warning you not to abuse anyone. When you hear of a death, it is your own Mind signaling that some part of your own being has perished. This is precisely the same symbolic language used to interpret nightdreams. In the dreamworld, every event is about **You as a Soul. Specifically, it is about how your Soul uses your ego to grow through exposure to the Mindworld or dreamworld around you.** It is, specifically, about your psychological, mental, emotional, or spiritual progress.

Also, out of the thousands of millions of events that occur everyday, only a nanoscopic quantity manages to move from theoretical reality (what might be) to actual, experiential reality (what is), in your personal sphere. So, even if you read twenty papers a day, it's still nothing more than a single grain on an infinite beach.

Everything and every event in your sphere of perception, your field of consciousness, is an exteriorized fragment of your Self or self. This Self is most often a mysterious labyrinth of dark caves, and the path to their exploration is dark and uncertain.

All spirituality begins with leaping into the deep inner caverns of Mind. All ascent to the sun of light begins with a plunge into the darkness. Deep within, you will find a

Falling in Love with Your Self
Love and the Inner Beloved

guiding "star" in the skies of Mind, which will lead that magical part of yourself capable of knowing Love. This component is the "inner "*magi*," and this star will lead to the "place" in Mind, the inner space, where the Lovenature or "Christ" is born.

This will occur not when you are fully enlightened, but while you are still toiling under the stress and strain of your animal-nature or biomind. For Christ is born in a "stable," among "animals."

The more that we let Love into our lives, the brighter is this inner star. This is precisely what Quaker mystics call the "inner Light"— and it is a sure, certain, steady, and reliable guide. Alchemist called it the *lumen natura*— a "natural light." So, we are all naturally luminous beings. Nothing could be more natural to human nature than openness to Love. We glow, we shine, with Love, illuminating ourselves completely, and the world partially.

So, be like the sun. When the sun shines on garbage, it is not made the least bit impure. So the deepest Mind of the mystic can never be polluted or contaminated by anything in its dream, the Mindworld. Like everyone else, mystics dream of the horrors of karma, but are not made a micropsychon less pure by the contents of the dreamworld, which are all absolutely "good."

Related to "nonjudgment in absolute terms" is the mystical quality called "equanimity." This means that the mystic is not infected by the apparent "negativity" of the world. She remains pristine in her inner Self, which is plugged in, not to the world, but to the inner Fountain of Lovelight. Through our pains, losses, and agonies, the light burns pure and uncontaminated within. What might topple us are not inner hurricanes and tsunamis, but the steady drip, drip, drip of smaller but relentless illusions.

So, when we see something "negative," we must turn things inside-out. We must seek the Love within the hatred, the jewel within the petals of the flower. We must learn to detect the shining diamonds in the mud of earthly life and consciousness, the jewel of the higher nature within the lower. We must find the good, redeeming aspects of every "bad" person, thing, event, or situation. Like the sun, we must shine the light of consciousness upon the most beautiful and the "ugliest" objects, fusing them, interweaving them, into a "monospective" beauty. We must also shine on every sort of "evil," rescuing the Lovelight from "evil's" obscuring smoke and mud.

Sunlight, our model, is completely without discrimination. In a sense, using the analogy of Mind, you could say that it "knows" the entire world, and everything in it, as both worthy of its warmth, and as "beautiful." But the whole point is that the sun is unconscious. It has no idea to distinguish between beautiful and ugly, and will shine just as brightly and beautifully on a slimy mass of garbage as on a forty-carat emerald. The same is true of rain, which falls upon all, nondiscriminating, and cleanses all.

The sun is not made less bright when it shines on the garbage, and the enlightened Mind is not less lightfilled no matter what it beholds. It is already supreme beauty, and can be neither enriched nor impoverished, at its essential level, by anything that we do, or do not do.

So, the great Quest is the journey inward, towards "pure Mind." It is "pure" precisely because nothing that it beholds can contaminate its pristine Love. This Quest is completely natural to the human mind; in fact, it is the unnatural mind that ignores it, to its detriment.

This unnatural, even antinatural, life becomes lost in the plethora of distractions of materialism and hypersensuality. It so loses itself in the "outer" world that the inner seems not even to exist. It is in densest darkness, an impenetrable fog of ignorance. It has lost its Center. This unawareness of Coremind is a kind of unconsciousness.

Lost in the deep, turbid, unclean waters of karmic amnesia, it is degraded to become the slave of its own dreampictures.

****

A person is less than what she serves. If you serve material things, you make yourself less than things or objects.

****

If you, like most people, find that you have so fallen from grace and peace that you have plummeted to this state, don't try to change things by force. Don't panic. Don't regret your life. Learn whatever you can from it, and move on. Turn your attention inward. Listen quietly to the Mind within. The whole journey to the Beloved begins with your tentative, experimental but uncertain idea that It might really exist. So, try to be open to the concept that there is a Coremind which is pure and wise, loving and spiritual.

Trying to live in this world without first balancing and knowing Mind is like trying to drive a car with no sparkplugs. For Mind is the spark that energizes life. Knowing It is the only activity that can give meaning and value to our lives. So, let it Flow and grow naturally, according to Its own time-table. You can gently encourage, but not force, this growth through meditation, stillness. You can enhance it through good nutrition, for Mind must work through a bodybrain system. Deep breathing and yoga help many. But the most vital, indispensable factor is to return to inner silence on a regular basis. This is meditation.

This path to the inner Core has already been designed by the Soulevel of your Mind. All you have to do is relax into it, stop interfering with it, and let the great river of Love carry you to Its/Your Center, the Beloved. This is that part of your Mind which you already, deeply unconsciously, love. It is the part of Your psyche with which you are already "in Love."

If you learn stillness, "doing nothing constructively," and cognitively cooperate, you will never be lost again.

****

Falling in Love with Your Self
Love and the Inner Beloved

Chapter 36

Perfection is Now:
The Stainless Self, the Hellagony of Guilt, and Becoming Love

* * *

Abandon the hopeless quest for quick fixes or instant solutions. It has taken Mind millennia, or eons, to sink to its present confusion. This labyrinthine puzzle will not be solved in a few years. Understanding and loving yourself and others is a lifetime project.

Some have been on the path of spiritualearning for lifetimes. Others are newcomers, still consumed by illusions of materialism and hypersensuality.

Instant gratification, a hallmark of our society, will never be a fact of spiritual life. You have probably been working on interior growth for some time. That is, in fact, why you picked up this book. For this book did not come to you by "random chance." No, you dreamed it up at precisely the moment that you needed it. Its words are clearly designed to find their targets. Those bullseyes are hungry hearts, looking for spiritual sustenance. These words are directed by the same higher Power that is now dreaming them up within you.

The Way of Love is never mastered in a weekend seminar. It is a commitment, not a course. It often Flows into our lives by means of the valves of religion. Or not.

Some come to the Way by means of science, art, poetry, literature, or just as a function of interior psychological pressure. What the inner psyche most needs, and wants, to do is to discover its Core or Center, Supermind, and integrate it with everyday Mind. Even if a person is not religious, her own Mind will inevitably, sooner or later, initiate the process of inner exploration. Religion alone does not always fulfill this most basic and gigantic need.

For religion is not enough; it is simply what you do on the **outside.** The Way is what you do on the **inside**. So, religion can become mechanical or legalistic— in other words, mindless. It can degenerate into obedience to law, in which case, all spirituality evaporates. Love, by contrast, is all about inner exploration. So, It is spirituality. It is about exploring the secret chambers of your personal heartmind. It is the great Quest to find divine nature within. It is the quest for the Holy Grail, and your Soul is the "knight" seeking the day.

Deep within, you possess a "divine nature." What does this mean? Simply that you have access to, and capacity for, Love, wisdom, compassion, goodness, reason, beauty, serenity, and bliss. To access this "higher nature," as mystics call it, you must begin by embracing the "lower nature," or your lower mind. This is those areas of the psyche which feel weak, worthless, helpless; this is the source of frustration, mental and emotional pain, destructive anger, hatred, violence, and general ignorance. The higher nature thrives on Love, the lower on fear.

Falling in Love with Your Self
Love and the Inner Beloved

Start where you are. Take a look at your lower nature, and Love it to death! In other words, don't judge yourself as "bad," or "unworthy." Embrace yourself as you are, but with a goal of improving— day by day, one step at a time, incrementally. No one can be even spiritual, much less perfect, overnight. So, avoid damaging perfectionism.

****

Perfectionism is the enemy of perfection.

****

In the past, the world has given you "exams," some of which you have failed. But in the school of the cosmos, to fail an exam is also to pass. For it is yet another way of learning and growing. "So, this is a school in which even the failures are successes. Paradoxically, every "F" on your report card moves you, impels you, towards that final "A."

Besides, every time that you took an exam, you did so at the level where you were. If you failed, that is not "evil." (True "evil" activity requires deliberate and conscious action.) You probably did the best that you could at that level. We don't say that a little girl is "evil" because she is in kindergarten, and not college.

****

Despite your many mistakes, there has never been even a particle of "true evil" within you.

Richard Shiningthunder Francis

****

Selfimage reconstruction begins with this premise. You are good, through and through, in every nanopsychon of your interior being. This is because your entire mind is saturated with, immersed in, pure Love at unconscious levels. In an absolute sense, everything that you have ever thought, every word that you have ever spoken, every deed that you have ever performed, was for the growth of your Soul towards this Beloved Mind. So, it all served the good.

This is said for purposes of honest evaluative selfimage therapy. This idea should never be used to justify deliberate evil— actions against other creatures. Evil is evil, and if you performed evil deeds, your entire spiritual future must begin with selforgiveness. But just make sure that you have learned all that the evil activities had to teach you. An exam not passed must be taken again. You can outgrow evil only by a solid, unbending commitment to goodness. There has never been, and is not now, a microparticle of "evil" within You, that is, in your deeper Self or Soul. What has appeared to be "evil" in the past has been simply ignorance, and you are outgrowing that! All that is real within you is good; all that is genuine within the world is also good. For everything that is absolutely real is the Lovenature (Coremind, Absolute, Superconscious). Its sole and only nature is goodness and Love.

Since this Lovemind or Lovegod is your ultimate Self, there is no point in spiritual evolution at which you do not fully love this

Falling in Love with Your Self
Love and the Inner Beloved

Self, for It is Love. It has always loved itself through you. Only when you complete the process of Mindmeld, merging and fusing with this inner Mind, will fulfillment be total, complete, perfect.

In this Supermind, because it is Love, one hundred, and fear, zero, there is no room for guilt. Enlightened people reject guilt, for it is unproductive fear, which is Loveclipsing. They do feel regret for errors, and will assiduously apply themselves to undoing the mistakes they have made. What they refuse to accept is selftorment, the selfcreated hell of guilt.

Fear, the antiagapic principle, is the essence of guilt. Catholic and Jewish writers have felt it their religious obligation to try to change people through guilt. This has never worked, and it never will. For fear has no transformative value. People are changed only through Love.

The goal of the Way is to cultivate precisely this Love so that we learn to love everything within us, without labels. So, let's throw out those tags that say, "worthless," "evil," "ignorant," "not good enough," etc.

Since Love is the only metamorphic Power in the universe, the more that we can fill ourselves with it, falling in Love with our Selves, the more accelerated will be our progress. After all, Love is not only the Way, but the destination. It is to Loveconsciousness that we are all ascending. To become pure, unmixed Love is the goal of wisdom and enlightenment.

In the words of old alchemy, we are all "part lead" and "part gold," that is, a blend of lower and higher nature, ego and Spirit. The goal is to transmute all the "lead" or lower inclinations, into "gold" or Love. If "lead" is fear, Love is the legendary "philosopher's stone." This stone could change any other thing that it touched into gold. So, Love transforms everything into its own image. When inner Love touches fear, fear vaporizes and its force is recycled into more Love.

****

It is by loving that we are transformed into Love.

****

You can neither learn Love by intellect, nor generate Love by will. Love is created only by loving. Each act of compassion or kindness multiplies Love exponentially. Love grows through loving.

In time, we become filled with Love to the extent that there is nothing in us but Love. It is our magnificent obsession, our passion. (It is the **only** obsession that is healthy and healing.) Then, we have no choice but to say that we have **become** Love. For we have looked deeply inside, and have seen and found nothing but the ocean of Love. Its conceptual opposite, fear, has no real existence. When we awaken to that fact, fear is gone, vanished without a trace.

Falling in Love with Your Self
Love and the Inner Beloved

You can't fabricate or manufacture Love. You can only yield to it, encourage It, nurture It.

****

Chapter 37

Psychorestructuring: The Shadow, and the Author's "Tale Told by an Idiot"

* * *

The journey to the Lovecore was called the "Great Work" by alchemical mystics. It began with a state called the prima *materia,* or the "shadow." That is, it started with those unconscious areas that supported the lower nature. In other words, as in the Christmastory, the ultimate spirituality started in the "stable," where the "animals" lived. All mysticism begins in this area, the realm of mind deluded by illusion. This is the realm of "animal" responses, egotism, greed, and other fears of all kinds. (This area of the unconscious is the "fearmind," or the *phobopsyche*.) This project began with the animal and lower human natures, worked through the upper areas of human, into the lower layers of the divine. The apex was the goal: The mystic ended up identifying with the highest higher nature. That is, she actually *became* an incarnation of the Absolute (Spirit, God, Supermind).

In close relationships, this shadow can be ignited by the tiniest spark. A friend or lover strikes a nerve, says something that we know, deep down, to be true, but which we have denied. Then, an explosion can rock our Mindworld. When a mole-hill instantly becomes a mountain, the unconscious Mind is sending a powerful signal. It is saying, "Notice this,

Falling in Love with Your Self
Love and the Inner Beloved

pay special attention. This might be something that you are hiding from yourself."

In fact, overeaction to **anything** implies that a nerve is being struck, and this is the time to concentrate on clearly defining your personal shadow. So, the next time that you find something particularly annoying or irritating, don't waste energy on anger at the messenger. When something annoys or irritates you, gets under your skin, don't start bitching about the behavior of other people. Don't analyze *them*. Instead, study the message, and ask your own mind about its own "shadow." You'll learn a lot!

Ask yourself, "What is this trying to show me about myself? Am I hiding anything from myself? What can I learn from this? Why am I unconsciously dreaming this irritant into being?"

You can start at the very beginning of the process of selfknowledge. The first step is often to go within, and honestly ask, "What was the most painful aspect of my relationship with my parents? What most irritates me about them? What do they do or say that makes me feel uncomfortable? Why, or how, does that threaten me?"

Then look honestly, with objectivity, for that same quality or characteristic within your own personality. Remember, when this kind of examination leads to breakthroughs, you are not obligated to share these with your parents. Keep in mind that this work is **not** about *them*, but about *you*.

Working on yourself in this way is **not** egocentricity. It is simply an attempt to heal in the proper sequence. For you must be functionally well on psychological levels even to begin the Great Work on spiritual levels of Mind. This is just a matter of priority. For if you are ever going to be good for anyone or anything, you must first work on yourself.

The goal, at the start, is **not** perfection, but simple selfrepair, selfcorrection, selfimprovement. These begin, in turn, with selfunderstanding. This can, at best, lead to a total restructuring of the psyche, from the Core (Love) out.

When this author did this exercise, he discovered that it was massive but largely unconscious egocentricity, revealing terrible insecurities, that he found most difficult. At times, it really seems that, in the earliest mindinfluences, that is, models, the whole world was all about **ego**. Other people often seem to exist in only an ancillary capacity, to promote egoagendas or to provide egostrokes. Others were sometimes regarded as mere extensions or expressions of ego. When you begin to believe the illusion that the **conscious** mind is the Center, that can be tragic and perilous. Then, it becomes the disease of hyperegotism. This is just another variety of the basic disease of fear.

The author learned a great deal about egocentricity and its direct relationship to frightening insecurity. This chronic fear is insatiable. It will gobble up attention and praise, and immediately come back for more, still starving, still as hungry as ever, voracious for more. And there is never enough. Indeed, there can never be enough.

As far as the sperm donor (he was certainly no "father," by any stretch of imagination) was concerned, he was notable for his absence. The author was actually grateful that the

Falling in Love with Your Self
Love and the Inner Beloved

sperm donor had not been there during formative years, for he would have been a terrible and tragic role-model. Although she did not realize its depths, the mother did teach the author, from about the time that he was four, that "God is your father"— words that were burned indelibly and indestructibly on the heart. Now, nearly fifty years later, the words glow in the heart with new meaning. In the renewal of the heartmind, they move towards their fullest fruition.

Some transference occurred earlier. That is, qualities learned about the sperm donor were overlaid, by imagination, upon God. Like god, the sperm donor was largely, usually invisible. So, for quite some time, the author went through his own "atheist" phase, when "God" was so "invisible" that He/She did not even exist. This phase occurred before his real darknight, when God again seemed to be absent. By the time the darknight actually arrived, it was known that God did exist, but He/She seemed again to be absent, or, at least, didn't give a care about me. During the more adolescent atheism, God simply did not seem to exist at all. This left an enormous gaping wound in the Soul, with no God to fill or heal it. (Atheism is not "bad." Many honest seekers must pass through an atheistic phase in their personal growth.)

The later apparent "absence" of God, after the author had touched, glimpsed, or tasted briefly the inner Lovenature, was much more tragic and traumatic. For this brought up every insecurity imaginable. During these "attacks" from various inner forces, the very best and most protective attitude is summed up by the mystical word "detachment." Seeing his life literally falling apart around him, he was finally driven, by desperation, agony, and bitter frustration, to say, "I don't care what happens." (His most important teacher during this time was "Brother Donkey," a pet name of endearment for his physical body.) When he gave up completely, with an essentially "What the hell" attitude, he let go totally of any attempt whatsoever to control any outcomes. Although he did not consciously realize it, this was the key to his full liberation. This was what the cosmic Mind wanted him to do all along.

Even in interior prayer, he ceased completely to ask for anything, realizing that this futile "pleading" with a distant god was just a thin disguise for trying to control. His only "prayer" was just a *mantra*, designed not to please an outer god, but to boost his own inner growth.

It must be emphasized that the author did not reach this state of full detachment because he was unusually wise; he just gave up. He came to two realizations: 1) His lifexperience was not controlled by him (as ego), and 2) It was not his task, mission, or assignment to attempt to influence or control things; and it did **absolutely no good** even to try. In other words, he had completely "hit bottom." He just gave up completely. In retrospect, this yielding was the same as putting the self in the hands of the cosmic Mind, saying, "Not my will, but thine," or, more simply, "Thy will be done."

This was the infamous "darknight of the soul" about which mystics speak. It was terrible. There was a pervasive sense that the God who had been touched was nowhere to be

Falling in Love with Your Self
Love and the Inner Beloved

found. Thrashing around in the inner darkness, unable to see the Light, the Soul seemed near panic. More profoundly, the author arrived at such a deep state of detachment that even that did not really matter. (He had already arrived at the state where his own biosurvival did not matter. Indeed, during this period, biosurvival was questionable.) There was probably some childish transference going on here: As the spermdonor had betrayed him by leaving and never coming back, now God seemed to be doing exactly the same thing. Retreating into detachment was an act, not of wisdom, but only of emotional survival, of desperation.

A deep part of the author's inner child resented this betrayal. He even thought himself unworthy of Love. But by the time that this "betrayal" from God came along, the author was too emotionally empty even to resent it. For by then, he simply did not care.

During those years of relentless, unceasing agony, the author did not really care about very much. He did manage somehow to hold onto Love as his saving golden thread, but that wire was getting very tenuous. Many days, his energylevel was so low that he literally could not lift his head from the pillow. (If he had not been a psychonaut, an explorer of inner space, he would have lost it. Also, if he had cared, he would have gone nuts.) But all this time, he realized that only Love mattered. Only that counted.

His wife Maria became a kind of archetypal goddess in his life, as she stood valiantly and loyally by his bedside day after agonizing day, night after hopeless night. She was so filled with tender God, or Love. It was she who scribed the final words in the author's "book of the heart." She became Love to him— a symbol of all that was sweet, beautiful, supportive, tender, and kind.

Later, his sister Pat also became a stainless mirror of pure Love, and intervened to save his life. When finally he began to emerge from a crisis that seemed endless, he did so with a new understanding of how Love was everything. Two people, both females, had literally acted as his "savioresses," had saved him with their powerful Love. He knew that he would forever be in their debt, and has, ever since, poured endless rivers of love from his own heart out towards them. Maria and Pat taught him more about Love than a thousand dusty books, or ten thousand boring sermons. They taught him that Love was spirituality, and spirituality was Love.

In the perfect vision of hindsight, it is evident now that these two women more than made up for the apparent "absence" of the miracle-working god whom the author had previously expected to come along. God does not miraculously swoop down from the sky and rescue his children, but He/She is as close as the nearest Love. And while Love does not prevent suffering, it makes it tolerable; then the suffering makes one both strong and compassionate.

Even when the author went through the most dramatic of spiritual shifts— from a closed-minded, closed-hearted, judgmental fundamentalist to a mystic, these two fine human beings, whose souls are pure gold and pure God, stood beside and behind him, in the face of tremendous opposition and violent hatred from the cult. So did the lady who used to be his mother, Ann Blufeather.

Illness teaches the great, often painful, lessons of vulnerability. It also teaches the great truth of interdependence.

****

Too much "independence" leads only to egostrengthening, and thus, away from Lovegrowth.

****

Illness teaches that we all need others. Dependence is not bad. It is not illness, like overdependence. As you begin Lovegrowth, as you begin to get well within, isolation is no longer protection, but simply insulation.

****

Chapter 38

Infinite Mindwealth: Egobsession, Galactic Citizenship, and Mantramindvessel

***

New horizons and vistas appear before the mind's eye when you open to the worlds within. The darkness of the inner Mindcaves becomes pregnant with jewels and Light, and the seeds of abundant wellness and Love.

It is among the caves of the personal unconscious that the area called the "shadow" exists. When it is encountered, the goal is, not to murder it, but to befriend it. Later, its energy can be harnessed to boost the inner "starship" of Mind to the Center.

The inner Mind is as infinite as outer space. In fact, outer space is derived from inner space. Any star, planet, or galaxy that exists in the outer world began as a Platonic ideal, or Mindimage, in the inner world.

As defenses of the shadow evaporate, abundant energy is released, which can now be used to support activities of compassion and feelings of Love.

****

In doing necessary work on your psychology, beware of the trap of becoming obsessed with yourself or your ego.

****

Falling in Love with Your Self
Love and the Inner Beloved

People who become interested in only selfimprovement tend to lose interest in other people. Ego drains all their vital lifeforce, and they can very easily become egobsessed. Egorepair is desirable and necessary, but must be viewed in perspective and proportion as only a step in a much longer journey.

Some become so monochromatically invested in egowellness that they lose all interests in everything else. Even the Quest is forgotten, but is only one of many victims. Be sure, then, always to work on your ego in harness or yoke with spiritual work, and try never to lose sight of the larger goal— unity with the Lovemind or Lovegod. Do your egowork, but do it enfolded within your Spiritwork.

Enlightenment is quite as natural as the opening of a rose in sunlight. It will come to everyone someday. But if you would enjoy its bliss and peace now, you have the option of doing so. This is done by committing your timenergy to the study of mysticism and the practice of Love and meditation.

But there's no special "trick" to enlightenment. When all conditions are prepared and balanced, and when life and Mind are in order, it's about as easy as falling off the proverbial log.

Zen people have a phrase: "If you are not ready for enlightenment, ten thousand words will have no effect. But, if you are ready, the snap of a single twig will catapult you into highest Mind and Lovelight." For some, may this book be that "snapping twig."

Fortunately, the Power that creates Lovelight, and enlightenment, is autonomous of the conscious mind and its picky manipulations. So, never forget that your unconscious Mind **wants** you to be enlightened, and Its will is irresistible. There's really, in fact, nothing that you can even do with your conscious mind that will screw this up— unless you simply fail to invest the timenergy to permit it to occur.

You will be enlightened.

It's only a matter of time. To go for it now, to get the jump, on the process means that you will bring about inner heaven more rapidly, and so, enjoy it that much longer.

This expansion of consciousness means that you are no longer just a German, an American, a French person, or of any other national origin. You are not a black, brown, white, red, or yellow person. **The transcendental Soul is colorless.** You must drop all egobigotries and biases, as you become a citizen of the galaxy. you belong to the cosmos, not to any particular parochial country. You are borderless and boundless.

The body, like the nationality, is secondary. It is no part of Your Selfdefinition. For You are a Soul, a nonphysical Center of Mind.

So, **You are transcendental.** Your body is just your "mask" for a temporary role in this play. It is the "horse" that you ride into "battle." It's a rake, a shovel, a hammer, a saw; it is only a tool.

Even your conscious mind is by no means Your whole Self. Your real Self is the unconscious level called the "Soul." In time, even this Soul will die— into the deeper Spiritlevel. This Coremind is the identity-goal of the mystic. She seeks nothing less than to become the incarnation of God (Love).

Falling in Love with Your Self
Love and the Inner Beloved

So, you start out by believing that you are a body; once you learn that you are not a body, you believe that you are a conscious mind; when You find out that You are not a conscious mind, You then know Your Self to be a Soul. It is only when you make the final discovery that You are not a Soul that You find out that You are Spirit.

Astonishingly, this implies that You are the only Mind that there is. This is not the careless, shallow philosophy called "solipsism." This deadend idea teaches that since you can prove the existence of only the conscious mind, it must be all that really exists. Please do not confuse the profundities of mysticism with the ludicrosities of solipsism. Because of the Mindfactor called the "inner Other," mysticism does *not* teach that your personal mind is the only one that is. In fact, deep within "your" Mind are potentially a wealth of "others." And these others are not just dreamimages. Mysticism teaches that, despite the dreamnature of the "physical external" world, people and other living creatures do represent real and "independent" minds. That is, in fact, the factor that makes all living things sacred. Also, instead of being allimportant, as in solipsism, the egomind is negligible in true spiritual growth.

The same principle of selfexistence applies to everyone, as to you. Each person and/or creature has a relatively (but not absolutely) independent mind, just as you do. It is just that different people learn their dependence on Mind at varying times and rates. The same Mind that's "playing" you is also playing everyone else.

Richard Shiningthunder Francis

Growing into the Lovelight fully can require centuries or even millennia. Even after fusion with the Lovemind or Lovegod, you still play the same earthgame. The mystic does not, poof! Vanish when she is enlightened. After her enlightenment, she comes "back down" from that high heartmindspace and once again "joins" the everyday world. She once again "plays" the "role" of the ego. People still call her, and see her as, Mary Smith, even though she now knows this to be a mask.

And, being nonegoic, she never insists that they call her "Lord," "God," "enlightened One," or by any other pretentious and silly title. (This is so even though she knows herself to be God *in nature*, although she has not become God *in totality*.) For the egogame is the only game there is. But, after enlightenment, you play it with an entirely different perspective, of total freedom and endless Love. Denials, negative judgments, and suppressions of the ego evaporate forever.

So, Your Self, the Soul, is a nonphysical Mind outside of time; You were never born, and will never die. Only the props of the stage will change.

Darkness, when it touches the altar of Love, blazes up into radiant, bright, warm Lovelight. All darkness is brought into Lovelight by meditation.

An easy beginner's path to meditation, useful also for those mastersouls who have been on the Quest for centuries, is the repetition of a *mantra*. This can be a simple, four-syllable phrase, in English or any other language, repeated over and over. Some, for example, have used, "I am at peace." Others prefer, "does not matter," and some have used

Falling in Love with Your Self
Love and the Inner Beloved

"God is Love, and..." or, "I am Love, and..." Others have used "Jesus Christ and..." The Buddhist mantra "Amitabha" is very popular, and calls the "Lord of boundless light" from the unconscious. Mantras such as, "Holy Mary" and "Gentle Kwan Yin" have served others well.

"Hare (pronounced "hah'-ray) Krishna" has been popular, but since it is used by a popular cult, it has lost some of its original spiritual power. "Brahman, Brahman" is designed to remind us that we are the Creator/Dreamer, as is, "I am Brahman." The most popular mantra among the Brahmanic masters themselves was the two-syllable "aum" (pronounced "ah'-oom").

Use of the *mantra* can, in time, awaken us to the realization that we live and move in a world of exteriorizations or dreamimages.

So, you are not a body. You are not a career. You are not a title. You are a force of nature, and He/She Who dwells within you is irresistible, unstoppable.

Even phenomena which are projected in your own mind, as spiritguides, angels, etc., arise from the same deeply unconscious inner Creator/Dreamer. (Some originate in the collective, the Soulevel, or even the personal unconscious.)

In the same way, the infinite Mind can appear to you as god or goddess— literally, the man or woman of your dreams. When you are most fully human, you are most fully divine. Go with ease and comfort onto the Way, knowing that your Beloved will guide your steps. When He/She guides you into gravity-free inner space, you drop into bottomless tranquility and endless bright bliss. When you fall into the endless ocean of Love, you know the real

Richard Shiningthunder Francis

meaning of "falling in Love." For you also fall into your Beloved.

As you sink into the embrace of your Beloved's arms, you awaken to the realization that you have returned Home.

* * * * * *

* * * * * *

* * * * * *

End of Falling In Love with Yourself: Love and the Inner Beloved.

* * * * * *

* * * * * *

* * * * * *

For more information, contact Richard Francis at: rmfrancis@juno.com

About the Author

Mystic Richard Shiningthunder Francis was consultant to *Time*, *Newsweek*, and *Sixty Minutes*. He is founder of the Institute of Agapology and Metaphysics, and of the Pneumarium.

The author of *Jehovah Good-bye, Journey to the Center of the Soul*, and *Luminous Ecstasies and Passions*, he has been the subject of three tv series, "Psychology of Spirituality," "Way of Universal Love," and "Spiritual Awakenings," Francis has spoken on European national radio, and many American stations. He hosts a radioprogram, "Heartmind."

Former editor of *Lovespirit* and *Cosmic Visions*, he was consultant for the Holistic Medical Center and the Center for New Age Studies. He lives in Liberty Township, Ohio, with his beloved wife of thirty-one years, Ada Maria.

Printed in the United States
6571